Creating Regenerative Cities

Prof. Herbert Girardet is a prolific author, conference speaker and international consultant in the field of cultural and urban ecology. He is a recipient of a UN 'Global 500 Award for Outstanding Environmental Achievements', a member of the Club of Rome and the World Academy of Art and Science, and an Honorary Fellow of the Royal Institute of British Architects. He is a former chairman of the Schumacher Society, UK, and a trustee of the charity Artists Project Earth. In 2003 he was inaugural 'Thinker in Residence' in Adelaide, developing regenerative development strategies for South Australia which have been largely implemented. He is a co-founder, former programme director and honorary member of the World Future Council. Most recently he has been working extensively in the Middle East and also in Bristol.

Creating Regenerative Cities

Herbert Girardet

First published 2015
by Routledge
2 Park Square, Milton Park, Abingdon, Oxon OX14 4RN

and by Routledge
711 Third Avenue, New York, NY 10017

Routledge is an imprint of the Taylor & Francis Group, an informa business

Publisher's Note
This book has been prepared from camera-ready copy provided by the author.

British Library Cataloguing-in-Publication Data
A catalogue record for this book is available from the British Library

Library of Congress Cataloging-in-Publication Data
Girardet, Herbert.
Creating regenerative cities / Herbert Girardet.
pages cm
Includes bibliographical references and index.
ISBN 978-0-415-72446-3 (paperback) -- ISBN 978-1-315-76437-5 (ebook) 1. Urban ecology (Sociology) 2. Sustainable urban development. 3. City planning--Environmental aspects. 4. Sustainable architecture. 5. Urban renewal. I. Title.
HT241.G537 2014
307.1'216--dc23
2014003163

ISBN: 978-0-415-72446-3
ISBN: 978-1-315-76437-5

Typeset in Open Sans
by Rick Lawrence

Printed in Great Britain by
Bell & Bain Ltd, Glasgow

Contents

Foreword	vi
Chapter 1 - **Introduction**	1
Chapter 2 - **Agropolis, the city in its local landscape**	15
Chapter 3 - **Living in Petropolis**	25
Chapter 4 - **Petropolis goes global**	45
Chapter 5 - **The urban metabolism**	67
Chapter 6 - **Ecopolis, the regenerative city**	95
Chapter 7 - **Case studies, part 1**	133
Chapter 8 - **Case studies, part 2**	163
Bibliography	195
Index	202

Foreword

First of all I would like to say that I could not have written 'Creating Regenerative Cities' without substantial financial support from Hans and Ann Zulliger and their Third Millennium Foundation in Zurich, and from Mr. Azad Shivdasani. I am profoundly grateful for this. I would also like to thank the World Future Council for supporting the writing of this book.

The book emerged out of 30 years of work concerned with the environmental implications of an urbanising world. I have done much writing and consultancy work, and have spoken at hundreds of conferences on urban futures which have fed into its content.

Making documentaries about environmental issues across the world over 15 years has given me the opportunity to see firsthand the impacts of the resource use of cities on distant ecosystems, such as the Amazon rainforest in Brazil and the forests of Siberia, as well as on farmland in the United States and parts of China. These experiences encouraged me to think about the global ecological footprints of an urbanising world.

I would like to mention a few organisations that I have been particularly close to: in 1995 a friend of mine, John Jopling, and I created the Sustainable London Trust. We tried to fathom what sustainable development might mean for a large city such as London. Subsequently, we came to work closely with the Greater London Authority, which was much more interested in long-term perspectives than previous London administrations had been. I then made a documentary on London's metabolism for Channel 4 TV called 'Metropolis' which raised many questions about the challenges of future-proofing London.

For two years I worked as a consultant to UN-Habitat in the run-up to the UN City Summit in Istanbul in 1996, when humanity was at the verge of becoming a predominantly urban species. In the years that followed I was involved in many conferences on the Urban Agenda 21, aiming to formulate steps towards integrating the environmental and social challenges facing cities. My book 'Cities, People, Planet' emerged out of this work.

In 2003 I was the inaugural 'Thinker in Residence' in Adelaide, with the job of developing strategies for greening Metropolitan Adelaide on behalf of the government of South Australia. I wish to thank former Premier Mike Rann for this very interesting opportunity. The results are summarised in Chapter 7 of this book.

At the World Future Council (WFC), which I co-founded in 2006, I have worked closely with Stefan Schurig on a commission on 'Cities and Climate Change', which brings together 20 eminent thinkers and practitioners concerned with the consumption patterns of cities, and their impacts on the world's environment. In 2009 I wrote the report 'Regenerative Cities', which was the seed grain for the current book. I wish to thank Stefan and other WFC staff members for our interesting work together.

In the last few years I have spent much time in the Middle East, and particularly Saudi Arabia, working as a consultant to the 'Saudi Sustainability Initiative', which is trying to get to grips with the huge challenges of creating a resilient urban civilisation in a desert environment. Some of the text in Chapter 6 draws on this work.

I want to thank Alex Hollingsworth for commissioning 'Creating Regenerative Cities' and for a very constructive working relationship. Completing the book took a little longer than originally envisaged, but here it is. My special thanks to Hannah Champney at Routledge for editing the text in a calm and competent manner.

A very big thanks goes to Rick Lawrence for taking such great care in designing this book, for placing the images, and for the diagrams which he developed and refined from our discussions.

I am also grateful to the many organisations and individuals who allowed me to use their photographs and diagrams, which have become an integral part of this book.

A brief word about the references at the end of each chapter: a book on a very topical subject such as urbanisation and its environmental impacts will inevitably make use of websites on related topics. I am aware that websites are 'less permanent' than printed books or reports. I have carefully rechecked the web references at the end of July 2014. They were all current at that time.

My wife Barbara was very supportive indeed of my work on this book, but she also had to cope with my silences and mental absences at our dining table. It is great to be able to get back to a less stressful and more active life together. Barbara, thanks very much for all your great kindness and loving support!

Herbert Girardet, May 2014

For my grandsons Harper and Sawyer:
I have tried my very best on your behalf.

Chapter 1

Introduction

If we do not do the impossible,
we shall be faced with
the unthinkable.

Murray Bookchin

Introduction

In confusing and stressful times, some people anticipate disaster and even collapse while others try to make plausible proposals for a safer world. This book belongs to the latter category, though recognising the urgent need for new approaches to dealing with the systemic environmental, economic and social challenges facing an urbanising world.

This book is about developing and implementing the concept of *regenerative urban development*, first outlined in my 2010 World Future Council report 'Regenerative Cities'.[i] It proposes that in a world in which the majority of people live in cities, we need to find ways of initiating:

- **an environmentally enhancing, restorative relationship between cities and the natural systems they depend on;**
- **the mainstreaming of efficient, renewable energy systems for human settlements across the world; and**
- **new lifestyle choices and economic opportunities which will encourage people to participate in this transformation process.**

We all rely on a steady supply of natural resources from across the planet and are often oblivious of the environmental consequences. Yet there is growing evidence that our resource use is gravely damaging the life support systems on whose integrity our cities ultimately depend.[ii]

In an urbanising world we must learn to take pleasure in protecting the integrity of nature. The term 'regenerative' encapsulates the actions that can help to continuously renew and restore the ecosystems that underpin the existence of our urban systems.

The central contradiction we currently face is this: humanity is building an urban future, yet urbanisation in its current form is threatening the very future of humanity and the natural world. With ever larger numbers of people living in ever more resource-hungry cities, we are risking the long-term chances of human well-being and even survival. What positive initiatives can we take to address such fundamental systemic problems?

The concept of regenerative urbanisation is intended to find answers to this question. It is not just about greening the urban environment and protecting nature from physical urban expansion – however important such initiatives are – but about city people taking positive steps to create regenerative urban systems of production, consumption, transportation and construction.

Across the world, a wide range of technical, management and policy solutions towards this end are already available, aiming to generate tangible environmental, social and economic benefits.

Cities are both living organisms and technical systems. As *living organisms*, or even *superorganisms*, they are the buzzing hubs of human reproduction and creativity. They are the stage for intense human interaction with the Earth's living systems. They grow and transform over decades and centuries, reflecting the cultural choices adopted by each successive generation.

As *technical systems* they are the largest and most complex structures ever created by humanity. Their buildings and infrastructure systems are unprecedented. They develop according to capital investment priorities, technology options and as centres of economic innovation.

Villages become towns, and towns turn into cities, and sometimes, megacities. Compact towns built of brick and stone grow into sprawling cities made of tarmac, concrete, steel and glass.

Since the 1950s, in many parts of the world new cities of unprecedented size have sprung up on the locations of villages and small towns, yet few questions are being raised about whether this is inevitable and how it affects both the inhabitants and the global environment. Can a predominantly urban world be a pleasant, resilient home for humanity? Can we curtail our appetite for resources to create urban systems that are compatible with the living planet?

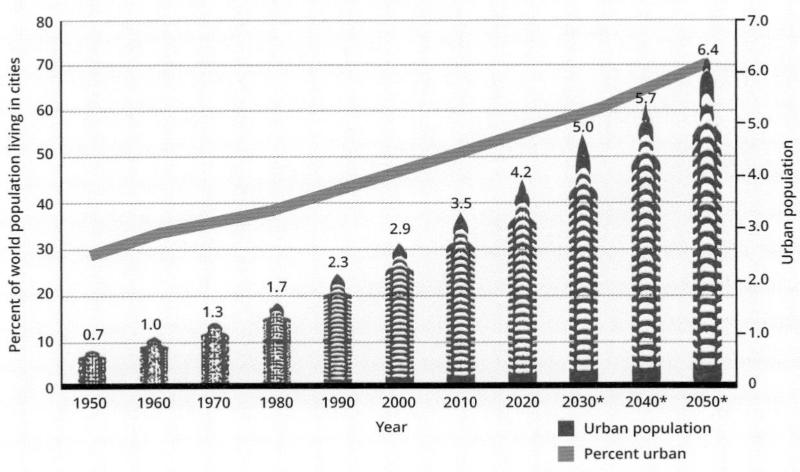

Figure 1.1: *The making of the urban age. Under current trends, urban populations will grow nearly tenfold in a hundred years, making up two thirds to three quarters of the human population.* ***Source:*** *UN Department of Economic & Social Affairs, Population Division.*

Modern cities of millions of people are an astonishing human achievement. As centres of innovation they are humanity's cultural playgrounds. Their communication and transport systems have developed a global reach. They are attractive to investors because they can offer a vast variety of services at comparatively low per-capita costs.

But the aggregated environmental impacts of an urbanising humanity are a great cause for concern. Our demands now substantially exceed the Earth's capacity to sustain us. In 2012, we used more natural resources in eight months than the Earth can produce in a year. For the remaining four months we lived not by drawing on nature's income but by running down its stocks of capital.[iii] Under current trends we will need two Earths to supply us with biological resources by 2030.[iv]

Resource use in an urbanising world

We live in astonishing times. From 1900 to 2013, the global human population increased 4.5-fold, from 1.5 to 7 billion. During that time the global *urban* population expanded 16-fold, from 225 million to 3.6 billion, or to about 52 per cent of the world population. In 2011 the more developed nations were about 78 per cent urbanised, while the figure for developing countries was about 47 per cent. By 2030, 60 per cent of the world population, or 4.9 billion people, are expected to live in urban areas, over three times more than the world's entire population in 1900. Nearly all the world's population growth is occurring in cities, and mostly in developing countries.[v]

But regarding human impacts, other figures could be even more important. The twentieth century was the age of the 'great acceleration' – of ever increasing resource use on a finite planet: world economic output grew 40 times, fossil fuel use 16-fold, fish catches grew by a factor of 35, and human water use nine-fold.[vi]

In this age of the *anthropocene*, planet Earth is being transformed by the presence, the technologies and the actions of humanity. This is also the age of the city: urban areas are the world's economic powerhouses, in which 80 per cent of global GDP is being produced.[vii] Urban resource demands and waste outputs define human impacts on our home planet more than any other factor.[viii] Global urbanisation is thus a primary manifestation of the *anthropocene*.

Urban growth is a seemingly unstoppable worldwide process. In recent years much has been written about this historic trend and how it could further accelerate in the coming decades. A fossil fuel-powered urban revolution, amplified by neo-liberal globalisation, is sweeping the planet and is transforming the lives and behaviour patterns of billions of people.[ix] In developing countries, cities offer easier access to resources and job opportunities than rural areas, as well as cultural, education and health benefits. As centres of economic power and social interaction, and of both production and consumption, they have a magnetic attraction.

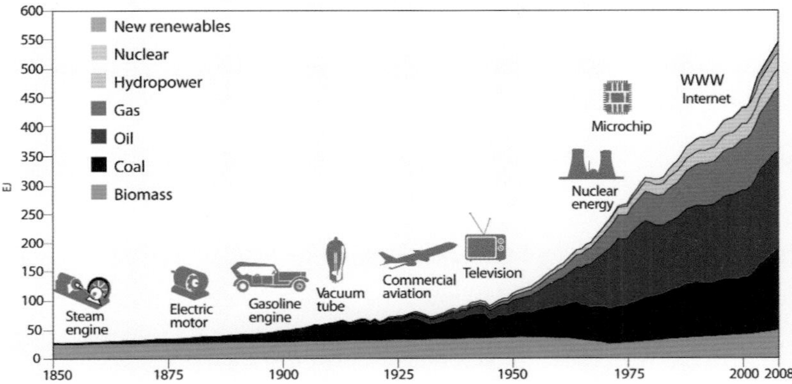

Figure 1.2: *Energy and technology from 1950 to 2000. Fossil fuels have been the energy source of the modern world. Will renewable energy transform the picture? Reproduced with permission from the International Institute for Applied Systems Analysis (IIASA).*

In the rich countries, the consumption patterns of urban and rural people of comparable levels of affluence appear to be very similar. In fact, rural living in these countries is often less resource efficient than urban living: in particular, people use more energy in transport, and in heating or cooling detached houses. Concentration of people in cities is therefore sometimes claimed to be more sustainable than rural living. One author, David Dodman, suggests that 'well-designed and well-governed cities can combine high living standards with much lower greenhouse gas emissions'. Public transport and denser housing help urbanites to have lower carbon footprints, though the design of cities significantly affects their residents' emissions.[x] Similar points are also made by Edward Glaeser in his 2010 book, *The Triumph of the City*.[xi]

But what about rapidly urbanising developing countries? Studies from China and India have shown that people moving from a village to a city will, typically, increase their resource consumption four-fold.[xii] The reason is quite evident: traditional rural living there relied mainly on locally available renewable resources. The large, new cities in developing countries, in contrast, offer people much easier access to fossil fuels and a huge array of other resources and products, and allow them to adopt consumer lifestyles that were not available to them as villagers, farmers or nomadic herdsmen. Country people moving to the city will inevitably adopt lifestyles dependent on mineral resources as well as long-distance food and timber supplies. Urban growth in developing countries is therefore a major factor in humanity's ever growing global environmental impacts. As hundreds of millions of Asians, Africans and Middle Easterners become urban consumers, in some instances escaping grinding poverty, the consequences for the future of the region and the world as a whole are huge.

Large modern cities are dependent systems. Much information now exists about the vast amounts of energy, water, food, timber and the many other raw materials they require. However, so far little is being done to ensure the long-term availability of these existential supplies. Can modern cities scale down their demands on the world's living resources? Can they help to replenish them? Could they exist and even thrive with a much higher degree of regional self-reliance than today?

Many people celebrate the 'triumph' of the city and, yet, it could also be a tragedy in the making. Whilst cities are built on only 3 to 4 per cent of the world's land surface, their ecological footprints cover much of the productive land areas of the globe. In an urbanising world, urban populations collectively use the bulk of the world's resources and are prime contributors to pollution, environmental damage, biodiversity loss and climate change.

What goes in must come out again. Where do the vast quantities of solid, liquid and gaseous wastes end up? We all have a vague idea that the solid waste we throw away is buried in landfills in the urban vicinity or may be trucked away to distant locations. But few of us know what is contained in the waste we discharge from our homes and what ultimately happens to it.

One dramatic example of this is the vast off-shore sewage plumes around coastal cities. Flying over Rio de Janeiro, one can see a vast sewage plume oozing out into the sea. It is a grey-brown lagoon of many thousands of hectares, clouding any vegetation in the waters below and letting no light through. This one-way traffic of plant nutrients – from farmland, via cities, into the sea – is causing havoc to life in coastal waters across the planet. In addition to the nitrogen, potash and phosphate contained in the food consumed in cities, artificial fertilisers leeching from local farms and industrial poisons are also part of the mix. If we are to create regenerative cities, we need to clean up urban sewage, and return plant nutrients back to the farmland feeding cities.

Figure 1.3: The sewage plume of coastal cities such as Rio de Janeiro. The triple problem is clouding of coral reefs and sea grass meadows, chemical pollution of sea water, as well as the one-way transfer of plant nutrients from the land to the sea. ***Source:*** *H. Girardet.*

Urban systems theory for the 21st century

These are matters that should be central to discussions about the future of cities. But the position of urbanists today is similar to that of astronomers before Galileo: cities are regarded as the centre of the universe, and the world's ecosystems are seen as somehow revolving around them. And yet cities are only appendages of living systems. The Earth's climate and its soils, rivers, lakes and oceans are their life support systems. The Earth is a vast web of life of which urban life has to be a beneficial part or not at all.

Instead of scarcity, nature's economy is defined by abundance. Ecosystems are all about connectedness and sustained interaction; their vast variety of organisms is engaged in a never-ending give and take. Nutrients and energy circulate within fluid boundaries, powered by solar energy. To live in unison with the living Earth is becoming a central task for an urbanising humanity.

Cities, as centres of production and consumption, use the bulk of the world's resources and produce most of its waste. Despite the many changes to the global environment that have occurred, life on Earth is quite robust and, left to its own devices, has the capacity to regenerate. But our actions are increasingly turning inherently renewable systems – soils, forest ecosystems, coral reefs – into non-renewable systems. By eroding life on Earth, rather than living off its regenerative income, we are increasingly foreclosing options for future generations.

The collective consumerism of city people has become the main interface between humans and nature. These impacts of an urbanising humanity on planet Earth need to be vigorously and positively addressed. Cities everywhere are discovering that they have a quantifiable *metabolism:* energy and materials – carbon, nitrogen, phosphorus, metals, water, industrial products – enter the city from the biosphere and the global economy, and percolate through urban systems before returning to the biosphere in a degraded form.

Today we face the key challenge of selecting approaches to urban design and materials and production methods that comply with natural ecosystem laws. The urban metabolism, which currently operates as an inefficient and wasteful linear input–output system, needs to be transformed into a resource-efficient and regenerative *circular system*, as outlined in Chapter 5 of this book.[xiii]

A new integrated science of urban planning and management is needed. Yet recent books on creating a new science of cities are generally concerned with ordering and structuring cities themselves rather than about developing an understanding of the relationship between cities and the living world beyond. [xiv]

On a finite planet there are inevitably limits to economic and urban growth. The only way to overcome notions of ever greater scarcity is for cities to continually regenerate the living systems on which they rely for their sustenance. To this end, we need to evaluate the metabolism of individual cities by smart data collection. Dissemination of resource flow data can empower urban decision makers and citizens to actively and creatively engage in the necessary transformation processes.

If cities are to be our primary home we needs to learn to comply with the laws of ecology – the science of 'home making'. The planning of new towns and cities, as well as the retrofit of existing ones, needs to undergo a profound paradigm shift, as implied by criteria developed by Barry Commoner:

The four laws of ecology

1 **Everything is connected to everything else. There is one ecosphere for all living organisms and what affects one affects all.**

2 **Everything must go somewhere. There is no 'waste' in nature and there is no 'away' to which it can be thrown.**

3 **Nature knows best. The absence of a particular substance from nature is often a sign that it is incompatible with the chemistry of life.**

4 **Nothing comes from nothing. Exploitation of nature always carries ecological costs and these costs are significant**

(Adapted from Barry Commoner, ***The Closing Circle****, 1971)*

It is in cities where human creativity is most vibrant, where new ideas are often generated, and where most political, financial and economic decisions are taken, where NGOs are concentrated. They are the places where solutions to the world's environmental and climate problems can be most easily implemented, because by living closely together we can make efficient use of resources. But are we prepared to look beyond our local concerns and minimise the global impacts of our cities?

The age of the city

From 1900 to 2012 human numbers increased 4.5-fold – from 1.5 to 7 billion.

The global urban population has grown 16-fold to over 50 per cent of the world population.

By 2030, 60 per cent of the world population, or 4.9 billion people, are expected to live in urban areas, three times more than the world's entire population in 1900.

In developing countries, as villagers move to the city, per capita resource consumption typically increases four-fold.

Cities, located on 3–4 per cent of the world's land surface, use 80 per cent of its resources, and discharge most solid, liquid and gaseous waste.

Redefining urban ecology

Urban ecology is the study of living organisms and their relationship to each other and their surroundings in an urban context. Urban ecologists have documented the rich variety of living organisms and how they interact within cities. Urban gardens, waterways, wasteland and even the cracks in pavements can harbour a great variety of life. Urban ecology has also started to focus on the impacts of urban resource use on regional ecosystems. Some urban 'restoration ecologists' are working to return degraded land and water bodies to more natural, pre-urban conditions.

An important finding of urban ecology research has been that cities can harbour a much greater variety of living organisms than farmland in the surrounding countryside which often grows monocultures of just a single crop to the exclusion of wildlife and species variety. A garden can contain thousands of worms, spiders and hundreds of different plants. Small city gardens can be just as good at attracting wildlife as larger ones. And these are wonderful spaces for city people to enjoy.

But in a world defined by urbanisation, the study of urban ecology needs to expand its remit. It also needs to address the ever further reaching impacts of cities on biodiversity, biochemical cycles, hydrology and climate. Beyond its local horizon, the science of urban ecology needs to expand its tasks to include all the territories involved in sustaining urban systems. By including the ecological footprints and climate impacts of cities, urban ecologists can help clarify how regenerative urban development can be conceptualised and implemented in practical terms.[xv]

Figure 1.4: *Burning Amazon Forest. Fires, set deliberately, have been consuming vast areas of rainforest – in the Amazon, as well as in Malaysia and Indonesia. Rainforest converted to cattle ranches, soybean fields and palm oil plantations has become part of the global hinterland of cities across the world.* ***Source:*** *H. Girardet*

Urban regeneration or regenerative cities?

In recent years there have been a great many *urban regeneration* projects in run-down cities of industrialised countries. These have greatly benefitted those immediately affected. But the concept of *regenerative cities* goes further: it focuses on the linkages between city people and nature, between urban systems and ecosystems. To find solutions to the damage we have done to the world's ecosystems, we need to start thinking about *regenerative* rather than just sustainable urban development.

Regenerative development is about *giving back* as well as taking – maintaining a proactive relationship between humanity and the world's ecosystems, and nurturing nature's dynamism and abundance whilst drawing on its income. We need to help regenerate the soils, forests and watercourses that our cities depend on, rather than just accepting that they are 'sustained' in a degraded condition.

This book, then, is about dealing with existential challenges for an urbanising world: finding positive ways of minimising reliance on fossil fuels; restoring biodiversity, ecosystem resilience and healthy soils; countering soil erosion; reforesting watersheds and mangroves; restoring water tables and addressing water pollution; moving towards zero-waste cities; countering climate change.

The book argues that these issues need to be addressed vigorously by suitable policy measures, by technical means and with active public participation. We can no longer ignore the *externalities* that affect the long-term viability of both cities and life on earth. We need to address the welfare of future generations with a new sense of urgency. Thus, *regenerative urban development* is about a fairer, restorative relationship between cities, the natural world and future life. By the use of appropriate technologies and business practices, we can address these issues and build vibrant new local green economies.

Across the world, different cities are at very different stages of development, and invariably they face different challenges. In Europe, North America and Australia, urban growth is very limited and the primary task is to undertake 'ecological retrofits' of urban systems. In rapidly urbanising countries in Asia, Africa and South America, urban development needs to be 'smart from the start': defined by high standards of resource efficiency, with renewable energy as a key component.

In poor cities the 'brown agenda' is the primary issue, and environmental problems are seen primarily as local, immediate and health-threatening. In middle-income cities they are often regarded as regional, delayed and threatening to people's health as well as to the wider environment. In affluent cities these impacts are increasingly seen as global and inter-generational.[xvi]

This book sets out to define measures that are *necessary* in an urbanising world, and then explore how we could expand the scope of what is politically *possible*. The case studies in Chapters 7 and 8 are examples of regenerative city innovations that are being implemented across the world.

The book acknowledges that the concept of regenerative development is a new challenge for most policymakers, urban planners and the general public. It argues that a major redesign of urban systems is a win-win scenario with great environmental, social and economic benefits.

This book is about:

- **the historical evolution of human settlements;**
- **key challenges facing an urbanising world;**
- **reconciling modern cities and the world's ecosystems; and**
- **building new, green urban economies.**

Sections of the book are concerned with rapid changes that are currently underway. These have to be seen as snapshots in time that may be overtaken by events sometime soon. Since this book deals with processes of change, some of its content may soon be overtaken by events that have not, as yet, taken place.

History tells us that cities are rather resilient places that reinvent themselves again and again. But across the world there are also examples of cities that have failed and ended up as heaps of rubble, because of the loss of their sources of sustenance or as victims of war. Today, in a global age of the city, strategies that enable an urbanising world to coexist harmoniously with the natural systems on which their long-term well-being depends seem more necessary than ever before.

Understanding the environmental implications of an urbanising world is a new challenge for humanity and this requires the evolution of a new consciousness, linking the wellbeing of individual urban citizens with humanity's collective interest in the health of our home planet. Only by relying on *regenerative* energy resources and by *continuously regenerating* ecosystems and the soils from which they draw their sustenance can cities be a viable long-term home for humanity. By proposing the progression from Agropolis, to Petropolis and towards Ecopolis, as presented in this book, it is aiming to contribute to the ever intensifying debate about how to future-proof an urbanising world.

> ***People believe environmental 'bads' are the price we must pay for economic 'goods.'***
> ***However, we cannot, and need not, continue to act as if this trade-off is inevitable.***
> ***(Achim Steiner, Executive Director, UNEP)***

Notes

i www.futurepolicy.org/fileadmin/user_upload/papers/WFC_Regenerative_Cities_web_final.pdf.

ii WWF, Panda News, http://wwf.panda.org/wwf_news/?204732.

iii The Encyclopaedia of the Earth, *Net Primary Production*, www.eoearth.org/view/article/153031/.

iv WWF *Living Planet Report*, wwf.panda.org/about_our_earth/all_publications/living_planet_report/.

v United Nations (2011) *World Urbanization Prospects*, UN, New York.

vi European Environment Commissioner Janez Potočnik (13 April 2013), http://ec.europa.eu/ireland/newsletter/2013/apr_jun/newsletter_4_april_2013_en.htm.

vii Steiner, A. (2011) Foreword, *UNEP Global Decoupling Report*, www.unep.org/resourcepanel/publications/decoupling/tabid/56048/default.aspx.

viii Wikipedia, *The Anthropocene*, http://en.wikipedia.org/wiki/Anthropocene.

ix Brugmann, J. (2009) *Welcome to the Urban Revolution*, Penguin Books, London and New York.

x Dodman, D. (2009) Blaming Cities for Climate Change, *Environment and Urbanization*, 21, pp. 185–202.

xi Glaeser, E. (2010) *The Triumph of the City*, Penguin Books, London and New York.

xii Sankhe, S., Vittal, I., Dobbs, R., Mohan, A., Gulati, A., Ablett, J., Gupta, S., Kim, A., Paul, S., Sanghvi, A. and Sethy, G. (2010) *India's Urban Awakening*, McKinsey, Boston and Bangalore.

xiii Girardet, H. (1992 and 1996) *The Gaia Atlas of Cities*, Gaia Books, London; Girardet, H. (1999) *Creating Sustainable Cities, Schumacher Briefing 2*, Green Books, Dartington.

xiv Batty, M. (2013) *The New Science of Cities*, MIT Press, Cambridge, MA.

xv Wikipedia, *Urban Ecology*, http://en.wikipedia.org/wiki/Urban_ecology.

xvi McGranahan, G., Songsore, J. and Kjellen, M. (1999) Sustainability, Poverty and Urban Environmental Transitions, in Satterthwaite, D., ed., *Sustainable Cities*, Earthscan Publications, London.

Chapter 2

Agropolis

The city in its local landscape

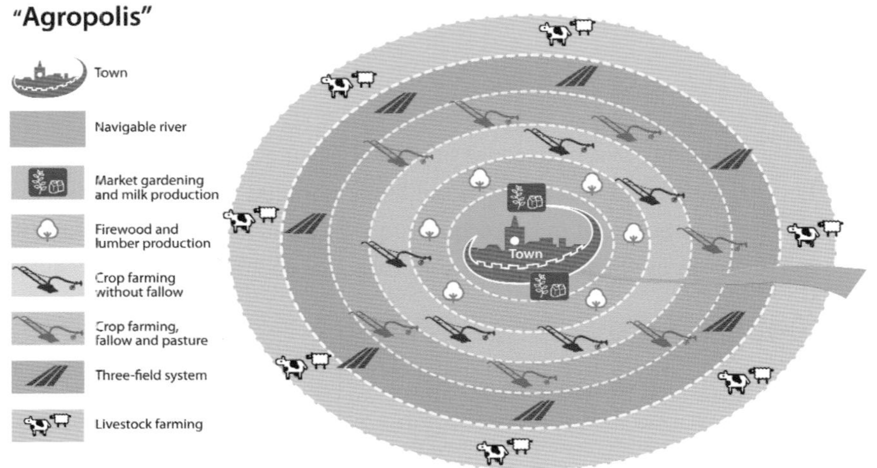

Figure 2.1 Agropolis: *The 'isolated' traditional town with minimal transport connections to the outside world,, self-reliant in food and forest resources from its local hinterland.* ***Source:*** *J.H. von Thünen, H. Girardet and R. Lawrence*

To get to grips with the give and take between human settlements and the natural resources they depend on it may be useful to look back at traditional land use practices.

In his book *The Isolated State*, published in 1826, the pioneering German geographer and economist Johann Heinrich von Thünen developed the theory that there is an inherent logic in the relationship between farmland, forests and isolated human settlements. He described how villages and towns, in the absence of major transport connections to the outside world, were systemically embedded in their local landscape, employing specific modes of cultivation according to a spatial logic. Land around towns and cities was cultivated according to three interconnected variables – the cost of growing crops, of transporting them to market, and the land rent a farmer could thus afford to pay to a landlord.[i]

Von Thünen described how isolated communities were surrounded by concentric rings of varying land uses. Market gardens and milk production were in the first ring, located closest to the town since perishable vegetables, fruit and dairy products must get to market quickly. Timber and firewood, which are heavy to transport but essential for urban living, would be produced in the second ring, the town forest, which was also had a recreational function for local people. The third, fourth and fifth rings consisted of land used for producing grain and other field crops which could be stored for longer. Ranching was located in the sixth ring because animals could be raised further away from the town due to being 'self-transporting' on their own legs. Beyond these zones lay uncultivated 'wilderness' of less economic relevance to urban sustenance. These complex land use arrangements helped to ensure food security for local urban populations on the basis of sound ecological practices.

In the late 1980s, I saw how the medieval town of Dinkelsbühl in southern Germany was still surrounded by market gardens and fields used to grow crops for local supply. Intriguingly, a herd of cows was being stabled within the largely intact town walls. The cows were herded out to graze on local pastures in the morning and herded back again in the evening to be milked in a cowshed inside the town. The cow manure was collected from the stables, composted and spread on the farmland as part of a regenerative urban cultivation system. The oldest streets of Dinkelsbühl, like those of many other towns surviving from the middle ages, were named after traditional professions – farmers street, fishermens street, carpenters lane, stone cutters lane, millers street, priests lane, leather workers street, smiths and shepherds street. All streets, of course, led to the marketplace at the heart of the town.

Figure 2.2: A traditional walled town in Germany (Aachen) surrounded by a concentrically arranged landscape of gardens, fields and grazing land. ***Source:*** *Braun and Hogenberg, 1560s*

In many parts of the world, traditional settlements had similar systemic relationships to the landscapes from which they emerged, depending on nearby market gardens, orchards, forests, arable and grazing land and local water supplies for their sustenance. F. H. King, in his book *Farmers of Forty Centuries*, published in 1911, describes how at that time many villages and towns across Asia were still largely self-sufficient in food and fuel as well as fertiliser, returning human and animal wastes to local farms to sustain the natural productivity of their soil. The only energy sources used were firewood, muscle power and, perhaps, small amounts of wind- and water-power.[ii]

Similar arrangements are also described by Robin Jenkins in his book *The Road to Alto*, an account of life in an isolated village in southern Portugal, where people were entirely reliant for their survival on hundreds of irrigated terraces cultivated by intricate farming practices developed over centuries, carefully utilising manures and crop rotations to maintain the fertility of the land. The life of the villagers was determined by 'perpetual reproduction of a simple mode of production'. Everything changed when a road was built in 1950 which connected Alto to the wider European economy for the first time. Imported fertilisers soon replaced manures, and cash crops could now be exchanged for consumer goods. Ecology was converted into economy, and the local world changed forever.[iii]

Before the Industrial Revolution, settlements tended to emerge in places of natural abundance. Only villages and towns located close to navigable rivers, roads or the sea could supply resources from further afield and meet essential needs by way of trading relationships. For isolated communities, muscle-, water- and wind-power, firewood and charcoal were their only energy sources. The bulk of their food and energy supplies had to be obtained from their own immediate hinterland, whose productivity had to be maintained by crop rotations, and by returning appropriate amounts of manures and compost to it.

This traditional settlement type could be called 'Agropolis'. The arrangements for utilising local land and resources practiced across the world were the basis for resilient urban communities. Significantly, traditional land use planning was not only concerned with the land surfaces on which cities were built, but also with the land required for assuring urban sustenance.

Figure 2.3: In and around Chinese cities urban agriculture is common practice to this very day. Beijing still administers large areas of peri-urban land for local food production. ***Source:*** *H. Girardet*

Cities and local food

As the Industrial Revolution progressed, and as vast areas of farmland and forest were gobbled up by Europe's burgeoning cities, lack of access to local food supplies and to recreational areas became a major concern. The emergence of industrial cities, with often appalling living conditions for the urban poor, led reformers to initiate schemes for making land in and around cities available for food growing, enabling people, young and old, to improve their diet and to experience nature.

Similar schemes were initiated in many European countries. In Germany they were called Schrebergärten, after Dr. Moritz Schreber, a prominent physician working in Leipzig in the mid-19th century, who linked the occurrence of ill health in people to urban pollution, to inadequate diets and to lack of access and exposure to the living world. He was particularly concerned with improving children's health. Today, Schrebergärten can still be found in every German city.

In Britain in the 19th century, land for growing food was made available to the urban poor, many of whom had only recently left rural areas, in many cities. In 1908 such initiatives were backed by government policy. The Small Holdings and Allotments Act placed a duty on local authorities to provide sufficient allotments, according to popular demand. After the end of the First World War the Land Settlement Act made allotments available to all returning service men. Further legislation was passed in 1922 and 1925.

During World War II 'dig for victory' campaigns were initiated by countries on both sides of the conflict. In towns and cities across Europe formal gardens, lawns and even sports pitches were transformed into allotments, and millions of people were encouraged to become vegetable growers.

In addition to land for growing food, the provision of green spaces in and around densely built-up cities became a major concern from the 19th century onwards. Health and well-being of city people was increasingly linked to popular access to parks and gardens. In Britain, the first ever publicly funded civic green space was the Birkenhead Park on the Wirral Peninsula near Liverpool. It was designed by Joseph Paxton and it was opened in 1847 and extended to 125 acres. Many other public parks followed in cities across the country.

In the United States, Frederick Law Olmsted drew on the Birkenhead Park for his design of New York's Central Park, opened in 1857. Like Paxton, he believed that common green spaces must be accessible to all citizens. Subsequently he drew up plans for many other urban parks. In 1898 he was one of the founders of the American Society of Landscape Architects. He played a leading role in protecting wilderness areas and creating landscape parks across the United States.[iv]

Back in Britain, enabling people to live away from the grime of industrial cities and close to nature became a concern for some 'enlightend' entrepreneurs. The Quaker entrepreneurs George and Richard Cadbury decided to build a model village for their chocolate factory workers. Bourneville, near Birmingham, was built in 1863 to 'alleviate the evils of modern cramped urban living conditions'.

Ebenezer Howard (1850–1928) took up this theme in his visionary book *Garden Cities of Tomorrow*, published in 1898. He proposed relocating millions of people from ugly and unhealthy urban environments to new garden cities on green field sites with the aim of combining the advantages of town and country living, whilst avoiding the disadvantages of both. At the same time the old cities could be opened up by partial demolition of overcrowded terraces to create new green urban spaces and allotment sites. Howard wrote: 'Town and city must be married and out of this joyous union will spring new hope, a new life, a new civilization.'[v]

Howard proposed establishing his first garden city for 32,000 inhabitants on some 6,000 acres, of which only 1,000 were to be built on. The surrounding agricultural estate, owned by the city, would make it into a resilient, largely self-contained 'agropolis-style' settlement.

Howard had very clear ideas about land use as well as land ownership. He stipulated that all land was to be owned by the whole community. Increases in land value would be ploughed back into municipal improvements. When a garden city had reached its optimal population of 32,000, another one would be built within its own zone of land.

Howard and his colleagues were able to implement two garden city projects in Hertfordshire, Letchworth in 1903 and Welwyn Garden City in 1920. Both continue to be the hugely influential icons of the garden city movement and continuously receive visitors from around the world.[vi] But today neither retains its own agricultural estates.

In Germany the landscape planner Leberecht Migge (1881–1935) became an important voice in urban planning 'with nature in mind', and with food growing as an important part of urban life. Migge was strongly influenced by Howard's book, as well H. F. King's *Farmers of Forty Centuries* and Peter Kropotkin's book *Fields, Factories and Workshops*, which advocated self-sufficient cooperative settlements. Migge was able to implement several significant projects in German cities. He has recently been brought to prominence in the English-speaking world by David Haney's book *When Green was Modern.*[vii]

In Britain, after some 500,000 homes had been destroyed in the Second World War, Howard's idea of enabling people to move out of overcrowded cities into New Towns, loosely modeled on the garden city concept, was taken up. Between 1955 and 1975, three million people moved from Britain's old cities to New Towns, most of which were built in clearly defined spaces surrounded by greenbelts. By 1990, 28 new towns and cities had been built, the best known being Basildon, Harlow, Milton Keynes, Skelmersdale, Stevenage and Telford.

But unfortunately most did not live up to expectations, due to lack of job opportunities as well as the indifferent quality of design and building materials. Few have been able to regenerate from their own resources because in the 1980s their development corporations were dissolved by government decree, and their assets were privatised. An opportunity to create and maintain financially self-sustaining garden cities had been tragically lost.

In the United States, it was Frank Lloyd Wright who put much of his creative energy and imagination into a proposal closely related to Howard's garden city ideas. He called his utopia Broadacre City, and his motivation was clear: "The Broadacre City, where every family will have at least an acre of land, is the inevitable municipality of the future... We live now in cities of the past, slaves of the machine and of traditional building. We cannot solve our living and transportation problems by burrowing under or climbing over, and why should we? We will spread out, and in so doing will transform our human habitation sites into those allowing beauty of design and landscaping, sanitation and fresh air, privacy and playgrounds, and a plot whereon to raise things."

Figure 2.4: *Frank Lloyd Wright's Broadacre City. This model, exhibited at New York's Guggenheim Museum, shows Wright's 1930s proposal for the creation of self-reliant, low-density settlements incorporating vegetable gardens, housing, businesses and farmland. Each US family would be given a one-acre plot of land for cultivating crops as well as for leisure use. Wright pursued this agenda for much of his working life.* ***Source:*** *H. Girardet*

Frank Lloyd Wright never got an opportunity to implement his Broadacre City proposals. Instead, low-density sterile suburbs as appendices of large nearby cities became the norm in the US and elsewhere.

As the next chapter argues, Agropolis – the traditional town embedded in a local landscape – has been replaced by a new concept of urbanism, Petropolis, across the world. But further on the book proposes that a new model of regenerative urbanism, Ecopolis, will be required to address the troubled relationship between cities and the natural world in the twenty-first century.

Notes

[i] von Thünen, J. H. (1826) *Der Isolirte Staat*, Pertes Verlag, Hamburg.

[ii] King, F. H. (1911) *Farmers of Forty Centuries: Organic Farming in China, Korea, and Japan*, Courier Dover Publications.

[iii] Jenkins, R. (1979) *The Road to Alto*, Pluto Press, London.

[iv] Olmstead, F.L. (1910) *Basic Principles of City Planning*, American City Magazine.

[v] Howard, E. (1902) *Garden Cities of Tomorrow*, Faber & Faber, London.

[vi] Hetherington, P. (21 July 2003) *Rebirth for Decaying 1950s New Towns*, The Guardian.

[vii] Haney, D. H. (2010) *When Green was Modern*, Routledge, London and New York.

Chapter 3

Living in Petropolis

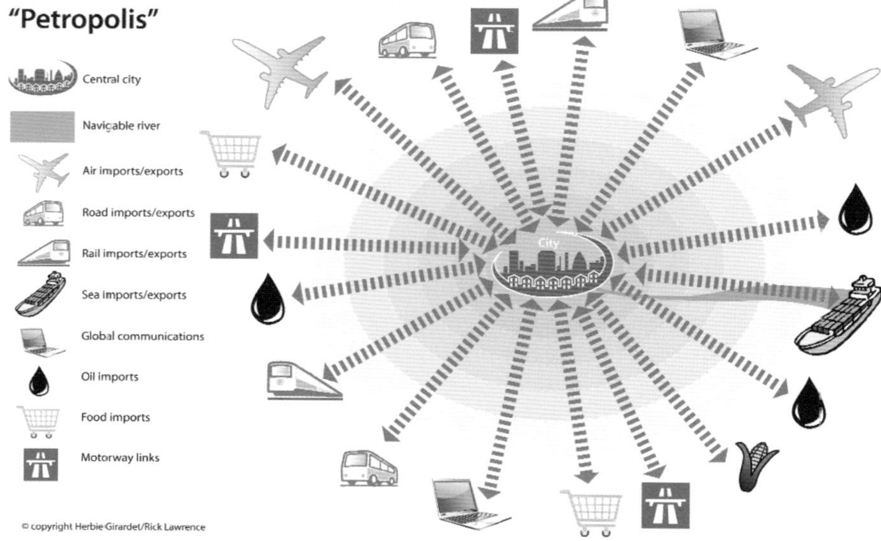

Figure 3.1: *Petropolis, the modern city, systemically dependent for all its functions on a wide spectrum of fossil fuel technologies. Modern transport systems enable it to be globally connected.* ***Source:*** *H. Girardet and R. Lawrence*

I first used the term Petropolis in a report to the World Future Council called 'Regenerative Cities' in 2010. It refers to the fossil fuel-powered city that emerged from the Industrial Revolution, with all its key functions enabled by daily injections of coal, oil and gas. But equally important are its factories and the global supplies of resources and products that are delivered to it by global transport systems. This chapter explores whether Petropolis, with all its interlocking fossil fuel-powered systems, can be a viable home for humanity.

Starting in Britain some 250 years ago, the coal-fuelled Industrial Revolution caused an unprecedented explosion of urban growth.[i] Initially cities grew on the basis of local or regional energy sources, but increasingly they came to run on globally traded fossil fuel supplies. Since the late eighteenth century, ever larger cities have grown on the basis of ever increasing energy supplies from ever larger and deeper coal mines, oil and gas fields, and power stations and refineries.

Petropolis is a gas guzzler *par excellence*. Lewis Mumford stated that the modern city is the product of 'carboniferous capitalism' – its functioning systemically relies on profitable investments in technologies that are dependent on an uninterrupted daily supply of carbon fuels.

Historically, there has never been a city of much more than a million people not powered by fossil fuels. Without coal, oil or gas the growth of large modern cities would not have occurred. Most of the world's energy use occurs in cities or for their benefit. Their construction, transport, electricity supply, services provision and manufacturing all rely on injections of vast amounts of energy. And the food supplies and the long-distance transportation systems they depend on are similarly dependent on fossil fuels.

It took around 300 million years for fossil fuels to accumulate in the earth's crust and we are on track to burning a large proportion of these in just 300 years – now at a rate of well over a million years' worth per year.[ii]

Fossil fuel burning is driven not just by consumer demand, but also by political support: 'Globally, the cost of government subsidies for fossil fuels increased from $311 billion in 2009 to $544 billion in 2012, the IEA estimates. Once lost tax revenues are included, this figure rises to around $2 trillion, equal to over eight per cent of government revenues, according to a recent IMF report.' [iii]

It is well established that fossil fuel combustion causes climate change and that urban fossil fuel use plays a central role in this. Whilst cities all over the world, then, are key agents of climate change, they are also likely to become its primary victims – particularly those located near the sea, in river valleys prone to flooding or in areas vulnerable to droughts. A recent assessment suggests that a one-metre global sea level rise, forecast for the end of the twenty-first century or soon after, will have a direct impact on 150 million people. Indirectly it will affect hundreds of millions more as rising sea levels damage the productivity of farmland in coastal locations.[iv]

According to the Intergovernmental Panel on Climate Change's most comprehensive assessment in seven years, published in March 2014, the impacts of climate change are already widespread and likely to cost up to $100 billion a year to address. But in reality nothing like this figure was being spent to either try and prevent or adapt to the looming global climate crisis.[v]

King Coal rules OK

How did it all start? Deep mining was made possible for the first time by the use of steam pumps, invented by the English engineer Thomas Newcomen in 1712. This enabled access to vast underground stores of metal ores and coal for the first time in history, which were otherwise under water and inaccessible. By 1735, 100 Newcomen engines were installed across Britain, and by 1800 some 2,000 were in operation, including some built by James Watt, whose innovations made it possible for steam engines to operate in commercial enterprises and to drive machinery. The modern urban factory had been born.

In Britain the emergence of the industrial, fossil fuel-powered city was driven by technology and finance, as well as government policies. These included the Enclosure Acts of 1776, 1842 and 1875, promoting the enclosure of rural land, and consolidating its ownership in the hands of a small, wealthy elite. In many places it ended the traditional rural people's rights to share strips of farmland surrounding villages and to graze livestock on common land. It caused the, often forceful, ejection of millions of people from their rural habitat. Most had to seek new livelihoods in Britain's expanding colonies or in its new industrial cities. Former peasants became industrial workers, the builders of canals and then railway lines that connected Britain's cities to each other, to the seaports and, ultimately, the colonies beyond.

The exponential growth of industrial cities started from the 1750s onwards. Manchester, for instance, grew 33-fold in 90 years, from 12,000 people in 1760 to 400,000 people in 1850. Birmingham, Liverpool and Newcastle grew at a similar pace. Industry created work for many and wealth for some, but major negative consequences soon resulted as well: unprecedented air and water pollution caused a variety of illnesses. Most workers lived in slum conditions that are familiar today from Third World cities. In Bradford, another boom town, the impacts on people's health were particularly stark: the average life expectancy of just over 18 years was the lowest in Britain, and only 30 per cent of children born to textile workers reached the age of 15.[vi]

Figure 3.2: *Pig-iron smelter. The proliferation of steel-based technologies was at the heart of the Industrial Revolution and the huge variety of new products it gave rise to.* ***Source:*** *Mark Edwards*

Sheffield was yet another booming industrial centre. In 1855 Henry Bessemer revolutionised steel production with his coke-fired Bessemer Converter, which produced high-quality steel from molten pig iron by the controlled addition of carbon. By 1879 Sheffield was churning out 10,000 tons of Bessemer steel weekly. With this technology, Bessemer had reduced the time needed to make steel rails from two hours to 15 minutes. Britain's railway network expanded from 8,000 miles in 1855 to 18,000 miles in 1885. Cheap steel also stimulated the construction of steamers, freighters and warships – and their cannons – which were crucial for extending Britain's global reach. The mobility of people, raw materials and products had reached unprecedented levels.[vii]

Cities as expansive systems

Fossil fuel technology has enabled the expansion of both the physical space taken up by cities and their populations, as well as their access to resources and markets across the world.

What, then, are the spatial factors involved in urban growth? Here we need to differentiate between *urban footprints* – the land surfaces that cities occupy, and which expand through an increase in urban populations and living standards – and the *ecological footprints of cities* – the areas required to supply cities with essential resources from distant territories. The two concepts are often confused. Here is an attempt at clarification:

Urban footprints, then, are the land surfaces required to accommodate a city – its built-up area as well as the space taken up by inner-urban transport arteries, gardens, parks and sports fields. The *ecological footprint of cities*, in contrast, are the land surfaces – outside urban areas – that are required to supply cities and their populations with biological resources such as food and forest products, plus the areas that are needed to absorb the carbon emissions of cities. Ecological footprints, then, are the regional and global 'hinterlands' of cities.

The expansion of actual urban footprints, of course, is closely associated with the desire for space – of families wanting to live on their own plot of land in detached houses. This is the motor car-dependent, low-density urban growth that has been occurring across America, Australia and Europe. The resulting urban sprawl is further driven by the segregation between residential and commercial uses, and other design features brought about by zoning policies.[viii]

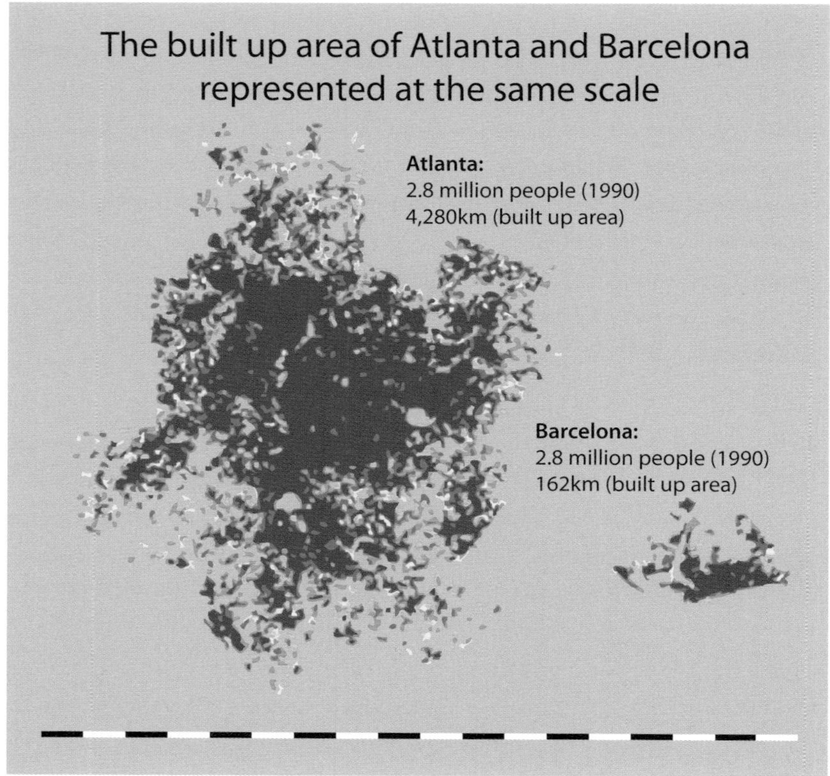

Figure 3.3: *With similar populations, low-density Atlanta has a surface area 26 times larger than Barcelona. Atlanta has mainly suburban low-density housing, whilst in Barcelona low-rise apartment buildings predominate. Atlanta's per capita CO_2 emissions from passenger transportation – mainly private cars – are ten times higher than those of Barcelona with its pedestrian zones and with a highly efficient public transport system.* ***Source:*** *Atlanta Area Data Base and Barcelona Regional Planning Office*

Modern cities have often been established, and are still being established, on former forest and farmland. As cities expand, so do the roads and rail networks that link them to other towns and cities. The loss of farmland as landscapes are paved over and built upon is well documented, and so are detrimental impacts of urban sprawl on areas of wildlife habitat.

Material affluence and urban sprawl go closely together. They are directly linked to people's desire for more living space per person, use of cars for commuting, and the wish to get away from urban noise, pollution and crime. In some places designated greenbelts have prevented urban construction on the peri-urban countryside. The need for extensive infrastructure systems – road and rail, water, gas, electricity and sewage networks, often funded by local authorities – has facilitated commercial housing development in many urban regions.[ix]

In some countries, urban sprawl has become a national issue of concern. To the visitor, a small country like Switzerland could appear to be one vast built-up region. In recent years, new buildings – often private second homes – have been springing up like wild mushrooms almost everywhere. All, of course, require their own road access and provision of services. The rate of construction is being driven by property developers who have taken advantage of historically low mortgage rates: in recent years, repayments have often been less than the rent on an apartment or house.

For many Swiss, the loss of open countryside is becoming a major concern, or even anger. They think that the country currently seems to lack the know-how to ensure sensible land use, and new expertise in environmentally acceptable approaches to infrastructure planning and urban development. The need to limit the spread of holiday homes is a particularly pertinent issue. Switzerland is urgently looking for ways to limit rampant construction in the countryside where every year more of the natural world is being paved over, first in the valleys and increasingly on verdant slopes. The general public increasingly demands that national as well as regional legislation is passed to ensure that only clearly defined zones are released for building development as opposed to areas reserved for nature conservation and agriculture. Any new housing development is to be allowed only on land already classified as building land.[x] Similar concerns prevail in many countries affected by urban sprawl.

Urban footprints can vary vastly, depending on whether cities grow outwards or upwards: for instance, the 2.8 million people in Barcelona – mainly in apartment buildings – live on just 162 km^2, whereas the 2.5 million people in Atlanta live on 4,280 km^2, a ratio of 1 to 26.4. And yet, compact Barcelona, rather than sprawling Atlanta, ranks amongst the world's most liveable cities and most popular urban destinations.[xi]

As cities become larger and richer, fewer resources they use tend to be supplied from their local hinterland, and more and more from nature's global bounty. Managing *urban footprints* via urban growth boundaries and greenbelts has had much greater priority for planners and administrators than dealing with the vast *ecological footprints* of modern cities. They are 'out there', halfway across the planet: they are much less tangible, and they are seen as being largely outside of their control. But they are very real nevertheless, and in a globally urbanising world, they are becoming a major concern. The *ecological footprints* of individual cities can be several hundred times larger than their *urban footprint*.

Figure 3.4: *Due to being made up primarily of apartment buildings, Barcelona is much more compact than low-density Atlanta. Antonio Gaudi's architecture greatly contributes to Barcelona's popularity with visitors from around the world.* ***Source:*** *H. Girardet*

London's growing urban footprint

The connection between the expansion of local urban footprints and the global *ecological footprints of cities* can be vividly illustrated when examining the example of London. It has always primarily been a great trading and distribution centre rather than an industrial location. From 1600 onwards commercial enterprises such as the East India Company played a crucial role in extending Britain's global reach. By 1700 the Port of London was the primary trading hub of Britain's rapidly expanding empire. Its ever growing merchant navy brought in goods such as cotton, sugar, tobacco, silk, spices, tea and porcelain from the Americas and Asia, not only to satisfy domestic demand, but also for re-export throughout Europe and beyond. Fortunes were made and some of the money was invested in magnificent buildings, in new housing as well as in transport infrastructure.

By 1800, with one million inhabitants, London was the world's largest city. But the world had seen nothing yet. A century later London had grown to an unprecedented 6.7 million people, incorporating 32 villages and small towns along the rivers Thames and Lea. From 1863 onwards railway technology further expanded London's urban footprint. It made possible the creation of 'Metroland', new residential suburbs north of London alongside the newly created Metropolitan Railway Line. For millions of people the dream of a modern home in beautiful countryside north of London could be realised for the first time. They could now commute into central London by train from as far as 50 miles away. Elsewhere, new rail and road networks started to stretch like spider's webs across farmland all around London, incorporating many more villages and small towns. London grew and grew, and by 1939 it had an unprecedented 8.5 million inhabitants, with a suburban region accommodating a further four million.

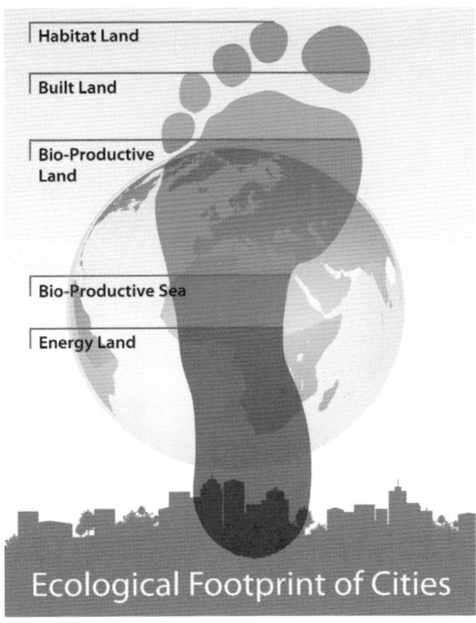

Figure 3.5: *The growth of London's urban footprint was accompanied by the rapid expansion of the global footprint of Britain's empire. From the 1760s onwards, steam power became a crucial factor in Britain's global dominance. Coal as an energy source facilitated an expansionist economy where distances were rendered increasingly irrelevant. As British armies subjugated ancient empires and local tribes, London acquired a global hinterland, or ecological footprint, 'on which the sun never set'.* ***Source:*** *H. Girardet and R. Lawrence*

London, with its financial prowess, became a great centre of culture and creativity, of magnificent buildings and fabulous cultural institutions, and a great market for all kinds of exquisite hand-crafted and manufactured products. But in today's language, London could also be described as a great pioneer of fossil fuel-dependent, unsustainable development. Across the city, the smog from a million coal fires filled people's lungs and darkened the sky. Mark Twain wrote in 1883 that 'in London ... you can't persuade a thing to look new; the coal-smoke turns it into an antiquity the moment you take your hand off it'.[xii]

Apart from importing exotic products from across the world, London needed daily supplies of vast amounts of food for its ever growing population. At first, most of this came from nearby farmland, and from elsewhere in Britain. But the new steam-powered transport made it possible for food, and particularly grain, to be imported from further and further away. After parliament annulled Britain's 'corn laws' in 1846, suspending tariffs on imported food, cheap wheat and barley started flooding in from

Canada, the United States and Russia. Luxuries like tea came from India, wine from France, Spain and Italy, oranges from Spain and Portugal, and sugar from the West Indies.

From 1870 onwards, refrigerated ships brought in lamb and beef from New Zealand, Australia and Argentina for the first time. From 1890 onwards, steam-powered trawlers brought fish from ever greater distances into Britain's fishing ports. Fish came in via the port of Lowestoft in East Anglia and the Great Eastern Railway to London's Billingsgate Fish Market.

As far as the supply of fresh vegetables was concerned, Heathrow was the location of London's primary market garden. Today, even though its sandy soil is largely concreted over by aeroplane runways, Heathrow is still a major supplier, but food is flown in in the bellies of planes. A global harvest offers Londoners – and many themselves are of global origin – great culinary variety, but it requires the continuous input of vast quantities of fossil fuels. By the time air-freighted food reaches a London dining table, it will have used many times the energy that is contained in it as calories.

Over the last 50 years, agriculture in developed countries across the world has become ever more capital intensive, machine and fossil energy-dependent. In the UK, only 1.5 per cent of the population is still producing food. Rural landscapes here increasingly exist for the purpose of meeting the demands of city people for green spaces to visit and for weekend leisure.

In a study I did in 1995 I set out to quantify London's ecological footprint. I calculated that it extends to about 125 times its own surface area of 168,000 hectares, or a total of 21 million hectares. This equates to the equivalent of the entire area of the productive land of England, Scotland and Wales, though in reality, of course, these land areas are located across the globe rather than just in the UK. The figures I compiled break down as follows: for food, London requires about 1.2 hectares of farmland per person, a total of 8.4 million hectares, or around 40 times its surface area. For forest products it needs an area of 768,000 hectares. To sequester its carbon output of about 60 million tonnes of CO_2 about ten million hectares would be required.

My figures were actually incomplete since they didn't take account of food waste, pet food acreage and marine fishing grounds.[xiii] A more recent study, which includes these factors, quantified London's total ecological footprint as covering 293 times its surface area.[xiv]

In 1995, seven million Londoners used around 20 million tonnes of oil equivalent per year, or about two super-tankers a week. But at least the same amount of fuel again is required to bring in goods and products from outside, by freighter, train and truck, and with ever more stuff being flown in from across the world.[xv]

Ecological footprints and rucksacks

Many of the processes of mega-urbanisation that started in London are still unfolding across the world today. As cities in China, India and South America grow, their global resource demands increase at the same time. The ecological footprints of cities now cover much of the world's land surface. If all the world's citizens had resource and energy demands as high as those in London, New York, Los Angeles or Berlin, we would need three to four planets. But it is not easy to make new planets, or to colonise others, and for now there is just this one world for us to inhabit.

According to the WWF Living Planet Report 2012, 'We are living as if we have an extra planet at our disposal. We are using 50 per cent more resources than the Earth can provide, and unless we change course that number will grow very fast – by 2030, even two planets will not be enough'.[xvi]

It is not only the energy input into our food system that should concern us, but also its global land use impacts, particularly on rainforests. In the Amazon rainforests, logging, mining and cattle ranching for faraway markets have been a primary cause of deforestation, facilitated by massive road building programmes. Now soybean production, primarily used as fodder for urban meat supplies, is a primary cause of forest conversion. Since 1950 the world soybean harvest has climbed 14-fold, from 17 million tons to 250 million tons. The world grain harvest, by comparison, has increased less than four-fold. Soybeans totally dominate agriculture in both Brazil and Argentina.[xvii]

Figure 3.6: *Much of the timber used in urban window frames, tables and floor boards originates in rainforests areas such as the Amazon or Borneo. Whilst some of it is now certified, illegal logging continues to decimate pristine ecosystems.* ***Source:*** *H. Girardet.*

In Malaysia and Indonesia, deforestation is primarily for palm oil plantations. Over 11 million hectares of former rainforest areas have been converted from rainforest into palm oil monocultures in the last 25 years. China, India, Pakistan, the European Union and the United States are the primary importers of palm oil, for use in food, transport fuel, cosmetics and 'organic' detergents. The environmental consequences of this are dramatic: loss of habitat for a great variety of living species, destruction of the habitats of indigenous tribes, soil erosion and water pollution.[xviii]

Since the 1970s the concept of *Limits to Growth* – of economies, resource use and human populations – has been widely discussed. But according to the Brazilian theologian and philosopher Leonardo Boff, it would be more appropriate to talk about *Limits to Aggression* against the Earth.[xix] The global resource demands of an urbanising world don't only have huge ecological impacts, they have also had appalling repercussions for indigenous populations, particularly in forest and savannah territories where conversion to logging, mining and commercial farming and plantations has occurred.

The process of urbanisation now significantly contributes to the depletion of biodiversity, loss of soil carbon and of the natural fertility of farmland across the world, as well as to climate change. In the oceans, too, the problems are getting serious. Melting ice and changing albedo in the Arctic, nutrient run-off from agriculture and sewage, overfishing, increased acidity from carbon dioxide dissolving into the sea, and rising temperatures combine to harm ocean ecosystems.[xx]

For better urban planning and resource management we need to learn from ecosystems, as living interactive systems, which are both complex and resource efficient. As effectively circular systems they waste nothing; they redistribute nutrients and energy, and all participant species benefit in their own way. This is true as much of ecosystems on the land as in the sea.

In addition to measuring the *ecological footprints* of cities – their total external territorial requirements – we also need to account for the use of resources that are extracted from point sources such as mines. The quantities of materials involved have been called ecological *rucksacks*. So what are they? The term refers to the total quantity of materials that are extracted from their natural setting, as the goods we use are made. On average, industrial products carry non-renewable resources rucksacks that are about 30 times their own weight if the entire production process, from the 'cradle' to the point when the product is ready for use, is considered.

The *ecological rucksack* concept, then, illustrates the degree of stress exerted on the environment by the process of resource extraction and processing. The concept describes the total material inputs required to generate a given product, minus the weight of the product itself. For example, mining one kilogram of steel carries an 'invisible' ecological rucksack of 21 kgs. One kilogram of aluminium has an 'eco-rucksack' of 85 kgs. Mining of one kilogram of gold typically disturbs 540,000 kgs of materials, such as rock and sand. With diamonds the ratio is an astonishing 53,000,000 to 1.[xxi]

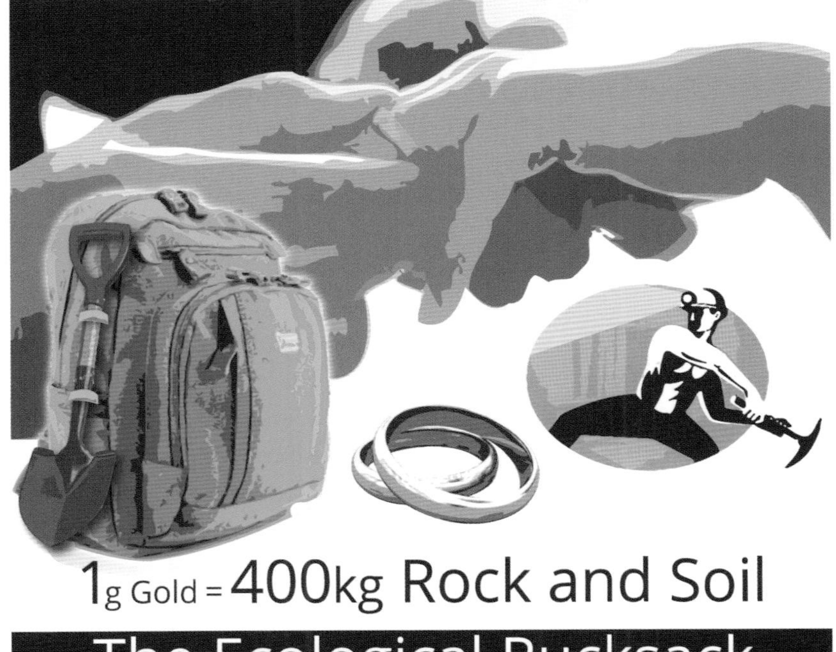

Figure 3.7: *The concept of the ecological rucksack was developed by Friedrich Schmidt-Bleek at Germany's Wuppertal Institute. It states that the materials contained in the products we use are only a small proportion of all the materials that have to be mined or moved to extract them.* ***Source:*** *H. Girardet and R. Lawrence.*

Combining ecological footprints and rucksacks into one 'big picture' helps us to understand the hidden impacts of our resource consumption patterns. These are important criteria for getting to grips with the environmental challenges of our urbanising world.

As cities become the predominant human habitat, urban development needs to undergo a profound paradigm shift. We need to find ways to minimise their systemic dependence on fossil fuels and their profligate use of resources, including luxury food. We need to ensure that urban consumption patterns become compatible with the world's ecosystems. The ecological, economic and social *externalities* of our urban systems need to be assessed and addressed in new ways: cities have to work at developing a regenerative relationship with the world's ecosystems.

Over in the United States

The many new technologies pioneered in Britain during the Industrial Revolution were also eagerly adopted in the United States. Pittsburgh, Pennsylvania, in particular, had all the right ingredients for rapid industrial growth: it was a region rich in coal, and had abundant forests and rivers that provided good access to the Great Lakes and to new manufacturing centres such as Detroit. From 1889 onwards the Scottish-born entrepreneur Andrew Carnegie built his steel company into the largest in the world. Pittsburgh soon called itself the 'steel capital of the world' and also became known as 'Smoky City', or 'hell with the lid taken off'. Carnegie did very well out of vertical integration. He owned iron ore mines, steel companies, locomotives manufacturers as well as railway lines that connected the fast-growing cities of Pennsylvania. He built the first bridge across the Mississippi, opening up the American West. Towards the end of his life his business acumen had its equal in his wide-ranging philanthropic engagement.

New York City is another prime example of a 'Petropolis'. It originated as a small Indian settlement conveniently located at the mouth of the Hudson River. From the late sixteenth century it became the entry point for immigrants from the old world, as destitute European farm workers swelled the queues at Ellis Island. Soon it struggled to keep up with waves of immigration from all over the world. From 1800 to 1950, New York's population grew 100-fold to eight million people, level-pegging with London. By growing higher and higher, it became the most densely populated major city in the United States, located on just 780 km^2.

Using girders made in Carnegie's steel mills, New York became the world's first skyscraper city, growing upwards at breakneck speed, whilst also extending its urban footprint outwards beyond the confines of Manhattan Island. Bridges, train lines and highways facilitated its sprawl. Canals and railways brought in all manner of essential supplies: oil from Texas, wheat from Kansas and vegetables and fruit from California were its existential basis. And as New York grew, so did Chicago, America's premier food city, and Detroit, motor city *par excellence*, home to Ford, General Motors and Chrysler.

Utilising the new fossil fuel-powered transport technologies, cities increasingly 'declared independence' from their local hinterland and became global economic and transport hubs and centres of consumerism. New modes of transportation made it ever easier to supply food, raw materials and manufactured products from ever greater distances. By the late nineteenth century the age of economic globalisation had arrived, facilitated also by the telegraph and the telephone.

Petropolis is, above all else, motor city. The phenomenal changes in human lifestyles made possible by the car – from Ford Model T onwards – have given rise to new concepts of land use planning. The vast, low-density urban landscapes that appeared in the United States and Australia are defined by the ubiquitous use of *petromobiles* – the word *automobile* implies that they are 'self-powered', which clearly they are not.

Figure 3.8: *A substantial proportion of oil is burned in the engines of stationary vehicles. Designing lifestyles requiring a long daily car journey from home to work is a huge waste of human energy as well as fossil fuels.* ***Source:*** *H. Girardet*

Back in Europe

The lure of the power of deep-mined coal was not confined to Britain and the United States. In the 1850s, the Industrial Revolution took hold in Germany, Belgium and France. In Germany, the Ruhr region around Essen underwent a transformation similar to that of Britain's Black Country and the South Wales valleys. From an area dominated by forests, small farms, villages and towns, it was transformed into a predominantly industrial landscape, of mines, steelworks, slag heaps, tenement buildings and railway lines.

Industrial development was driven by companies such as Krupp and Thyssen. From 1852 to 1925 the population of the Ruhr region increased ten-fold, to 3.8 million people. The Industrial Revolution in the Ruhr, in turn, powered Germany's economic development and, ultimately, also the growth of Berlin, which became its capital city in 1871. From 1755 to 1933 its population grew ten-fold, to 4.3 million people.[xxii]

In 1878 the invention of the internal combustion engine by Karl-Friedrich Benz in Germany, followed by the first airplane flight by the Wright brothers in the United States in 1903, gave rise to petrol-powered transportation, shrinking distances as never before, and the world has not been the same since. Today we live in a *mobilisation* rather than a *civilisation* – of natural resources, people and products.

The world's major transport systems start and end in cities. They are the nodes from which mobility emanates, along roads, railway lines, aircraft routes and telephone lines. Cities sprawl ever outwards along urban motorways and railway lines to their suburbs and shopping malls and beyond, whilst their centre is often devoid of life outside business hours. They are both the origin and the destination of this *mobilisation* that has come to define our new existence as *amplified humans*, powered by energy technology.

Figure 3.9: *Open cast lignite mine near Aachen, Germany. The days of labour intensive deep underground coal pits are largely over. This excavator, operated by one man, is the largest machine on earth. Lignite, a very sulfur-rich fuel, powers many European cities.* ***Source:*** *H. Girardet*

Energy and capital

Since 1900, and particularly since 1950, fossil fuel-dependent urbanisation has been spreading inexorably across the world. The global economy is controlled from a few 'global cities' such as London and New York which are the staging posts of the global economic system and which also happen to have the largest average per capita income.[xxiii] Urbanisation, and the growth of economies, transportation and communications, is driven above all else by footloose finance in search of the highest possible return on investment. Financial institutions in New York, London, Hong Kong, Tokyo and Singapore are intimately connected with the growth of industrial and trading cities across the world.

Today there are 22 megacities of over ten million people. Their numbers rose from none in 1950 to five in 1975, to 19 in 2000, with 16 of them in developing countries. By 2015, there will be some 23 megacities, of which 15 will be in Asia.[xxiv] It is important to point out, however, that only about 10 per cent of people live in megacities with ten million inhabitants or more; by far the majority live in cities of a million people or less.

In 1950, most of the world's workforce was employed in agriculture; by 1990 most people worked in urban services.[xxv] Since then the global economy has grown many times and, under the auspices of neo-liberal capitalism, which knows no boundaries, it is becoming ever more integrated. The main beneficiaries are a new urban middle class who take the global supply of unprecedented quantities of resources and industrial products for granted.

Neo-liberalism, the world's dominant commercial ideology, is primarily responsible for creating a type of city that is increasingly defined by urban elites and consumerism:

Neoliberalism and urbanisation

1. *The global patterns of urbanisation, with a few large 'city states' at the helm, are a direct expression of neo-liberal economic policies.*
2. *Neo-liberal economic activity favours cheap production in low-wage countries (and cities) for consumption and accumulation in suitable global markets.*
3. *Corporate-led neo-liberalism favours free trade, privatisation of services and minimal government interference in business.*

4. *Corporate global capital seeks to minimise the regulatory reach of national policies in its quest for the most profitable investments.*
5. *Global capital encourages international government agreements that ease market entry and minimise control of competition.*
6. *Transfer of economic control from the public to the private sector is regarded as key for the economic health of nations and cities.*

The existential vulnerability of modern industrial and fossil fuel-dependent cities becomes apparent when looking at Europe and the United States. Cities such as Sheffield, Liverpool, Glasgow, Gelsenkirchen, Pittsburgh, Detroit, Chattanooga and many others have contracted or even collapsed as their industrial economies withered under the pressure of globalised trade in industrial products. Some have been able to reinvent themselves as university and cultural centres, or by developing a variety of service centre functions. Some have benefitted from regeneration funds from their national governments or bodies like the European Union. But others, such as Detroit, still have to find a plausible future base. Will the new industrial cities in countries like China and India suffer similar fates in the decades to come?

Notes

i *Industrial Revolution and Public Health*, www.myuniversalfacts.com/2007/06/industrial-revolution-and-public-health.html.

ii *UNEP, Resource Efficient Cities*, www.unep.org/newscentre/default.aspx?DocumentID=2688&ArticleID=9179.

iii www.economist.com/news/finance-and-economics/21593484-economic-case-scrapping-fossil-fuel-subsidies-getting-stronger-fuelling.

iv UNEP, *Ice and Sea Level Change*, www.unep.org/geo/geo_ice/PDF/GEO_C6_C_LowRes.pdf.

v www.ft.com/cms/s/0/12d4b5d0-b65b-11e3-905b-00144feabdc0.html#axzz2xMNLSFOh.

vi www.observatory.bradford.nhs.uk/Documents/Public-health-annual-report-2012.pdf.

vii Archives Hub, Edinburgh Uni. Library, www.archiveshub.ac.uk/news/02101803.html.

viii Wikipedia, *Urban Sprawl*, http://en.wikipedia.org/wiki/Urban_sprawl.

ix Wikipedia, *Urban Sprawl*, http://en.wikipedia.org/wiki/Urban_sprawl.

x www.swissinfo.ch/eng/politics/internal_affairs/Swiss_seek_to_limit_urban_sprawl.html?cid=32339240.

xi http://lsecities.net/media/objects/articles/measuring-the-human-urban-footprint.

xii Gordon, R. and Malone, P. (1997) *The Texture of Industry: An Archaeological View of the Industrialization of North America*, Oxford University Press, Oxford.

xiii Girardet, H. (1999) *Creating Sustainable Cities, Schumacher Briefing 2*, Green Books, Dartington.

xiv *City Limits, London*, www.citylimitslondon.com/downloads/Complete%20report.pdf.

xv Joplin, J. and Girardet, H. (1997) *Creating a Sustainable London*, Sustainable London Trust, London.

xvi WWF (2012) Living Planet Report, http://awsassets.panda.org/downloads/1_lpr_2012_online_full_size_single_pages_final_120516.pdf.

xvii Earth Policy Institute, www.earth-policy.org/plan_b_updates/2009/update86.

xviii *Palm Oil*, http://en.wikipedia.org/wiki/Social_and_environmental_impact_of_palm_oil#Environmental_issues; http://wwf.panda.org/what_we_do/footprint/agriculture/palm_oil/environmental_impacts/biodversity_loss/.

[xix] Boff, L. (2012) *Sustainable Development: A Critique of the Standard Model*, http://leonardoboff.wordpress.com/2012/02/06/sustainable-development-a-critique-of-the-standard-model.

[xx] *International Programme on the State of the Ocean* (IPSO), October 2013.

[xxi] GDRC, *What Are Ecological Rucksacks*, www.gdrc.org/uem/footprints/rucksacks.html.

[xxii] *Berlin's history*, www.berlin-geschichte.de/Historie/.

[xxiii] Sassen, Saskia (1991) *The Global City: New York, London, Tokyo*, Princeton University Press, Princeton, NJ.

[xxiv] World Resources Institute Washington, *Urban Growth*, www.wri.org/wr-98-99/citygrow.htm.

[xxv] N'Dow, Wally (1997) An Urbanising World, in Kirdar, Uener, ed., *Cities Fit for People*, United Nations Publications, New York.

Chapter 4

Petropolis goes global

China's urban-industrial explosion

No country in history has been transformed from rural to urban and 'mega-urban' as quickly as China has in recent years. But it all started differently: After 1949 China deliberately prevented rural–urban migration under a closed-city policy. Mao envisioned a country of village industries, collective farms and regional self-sufficiency. Urban growth was largely prevented by deliberate policy, and for 30 years population mobility was minimised by issuing local-only passports which determined a person's place of residence by their role in the local labour force.

Figure 4.1: *In 35 years Pudong has turned from an area of urban farms into Shanghai's Manhattan and a major force in the global trading and financial system.* ***Source:*** *Shanghai City Archive*

All that changed after Mao's death in 1978. Deng Xiaoping's new socialist market economic policies threw China's doors wide open to foreign investment, causing a boom in new export-oriented urban industries. The energetic basis of this development depended on a massive increase in energy use, and the expansion of China's coal mining. The figures speak for themselves:

From 1979 onwards, China experienced the largest rural–urban migration in human history. By 1995 there were some 80 million migrants in China's major cities. By 2012 the figure had swelled to over 300 million. Peasants became factory, construction, restaurant and transportation workers, and some also tend greenhouses on peri-urban farmland. But by no means are they always welcome. Migrants are often held responsible for traffic congestion, housing shortages, competition for jobs and increasing crime. Many city dwellers want to slow down urban growth for these reasons and because of lack of adequate investments in sewage, energy distribution, water supply and waste management infrastructure.

Since 1978 many Chinese towns and cities have multiplied their populations. Shenzhen, a former fishing village on the border with Hong Kong, has become an industrial production centre. It is probably the fastest growing city in history: from 1980 to 2013 it grew from a few thousand to 11 million people. The transformation of Pudong in Shanghai from urban farmland to a new Manhattan is another symbol of China's astonishing transformation.

In China, urban growth and financial/economic globalisation are intimately connected. Not surprisingly, Shanghai has joined the elite ranks of the world's premier financial service centres. Its economic boom is symbolised by its vast new container terminals well as its huge stock market. Pudong has turned from an area of urban farms into an Asian Manhattan. Megacities such as Beijing, Shanghai, Chongqing, Guangzhou and Tianjin, with their new factories, warehouses and shopping malls, have wide, new roads full of new cars, and a skyline dotted with cranes alongside newly built tower blocks.

A special feature of China's urban-economic growth is the central role of global investment capital, though this is rapidly being replaced by locally generated capital. Gradually, cheap labour has become more expensive and a new middle class, with increasing spending power, is emerging. As Chinese labour loses its competitive advantage, other Asian countries, such as Vietnam, Laos and Cambodia, are becoming favoured new destinations for foreign investors.

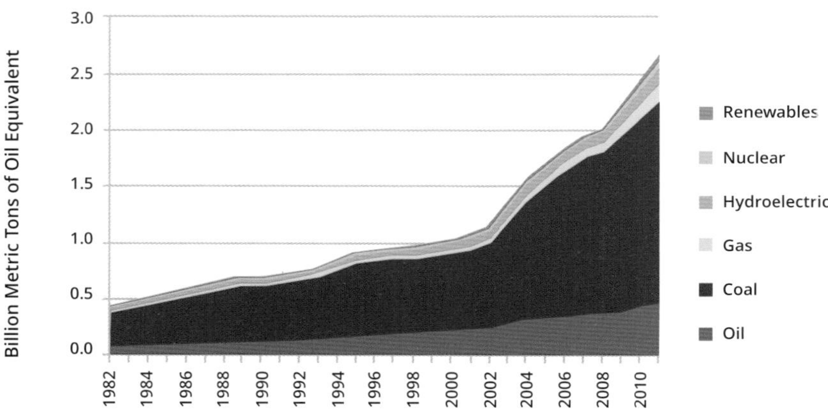

Figure 4.2: *This forecast suggests a relatively slow growth in renewable energy in China. Other forecasts project a much faster increase.* ***Source:*** *International Energy Agency*

Since the 1990s the world has watched China with fascination and trepidation, as pictures of vast factories, gleaming skyscrapers, fast railway lines and urban motorways clogged with cars hit global television screens. China's centrally planned coal-, oil-, nuclear- and hydro-powered urbanisation is probably proceeding faster than in any other country in history. For two decades, China's economy has grown at over nine per cent per year, and its cities have developed at a similar pace. By 2010 China was about 50 per cent urbanised, with dozens of mega- and multi-million cities, and some 400 new smaller cities.

In recent years China's export-led manufacturing boom has been matched by the inexorable growth of a domestic consumer society. A quarter of the country's population has moved from rural ground-level dwellings to high-rise blocks of flats and dormitories, well-equipped with hi-fis, TVs and washing machines. Fridges are stocked with supermarket food, and meat consumption is growing fast. As we have already seen, country people switching from rural to urban lifestyles greatly increase their per capita resource use.[i]

China is now producing a greater variety of industrial products than any other country in the world. What are the environmental impacts of urban-industrial development in China? Not surprisingly, the use of hazardous materials has become commonplace. They end up in industrial effluents. Storage tanks for diesel, gasoline, ammonia, chlorine, sulfur compounds and chemical cleaning agents are proliferating, and sometimes spring a leak.

Sulfur dioxide, nitrogen oxides and soot have turned the air in China's cities into smog, and urban sewage, fertiliser and pesticide run-off from farms and industrial chemicals are poisoning its rivers. Its carbon dioxide emissions have overtaken those of the United States. Meanwhile, the number of demonstrations by rural people against air and water pollution, and against the encroachment of cities, factories, power stations and highways on farmland, is going up year by year.

The protests also reflect public concern about soil pollution: in December 2013 China's Ministry of Land and Resources reported that as much as eight million acres of farmland, an area the size of Belgium, or two per cent of China's arable land, is now too polluted with heavy metals and chemical residues to safely grow crops. A particularly worry is cadmium in rice crops. In Guangdong Province, where rice paddies and factories are now cheek by jowl in many places, cadmium contamination of rice has made much of it unsuitable for human consumption. Solutions are not cheap: Cleaning up factories and rehabilitating polluted land are both immensely expensive. [ii]

Can industry-based urbanisation in China be reconciled with the country's acknowledged goal of sustainable development? There has been some political lip service to 'harmony between humanity and nature' and on building 'a conservation-oriented and environment-friendly society'. But until now China has undergone the same old 'dirty' development known from Europe and America, with smoke clouds above cities, with acid rain downwind, and with polluted effluents in the country's rivers damaging irrigated crops in rural areas.

It remains to be seen whether China will learn to respect the environmental limits to growth. Gradually, legislation on pollution is being tightened. Its electricity supply is gradually shifting from coal-fired power stations to gas, nuclear, hydro and wind, with solar panels supplying a substantial proportion of hot water in tower blocks and apartment buildings (see Chapter 7 for more on this).

China's rapid urban-industrial growth has significant land use implications – domestically as well as globally. It is living further and further beyond its environmental means and the implications are significant. A rapidly growing middle class is pushing up demand for meat, and particularly pork. In 2012 Chinese ate five times more pork than in 1979, half the world's total. Since China has 21 per cent of the world's population but only nine per cent of its cultivated land, it can't feed its 460 million pigs from its own farmland. China now requires 60 per cent of the world's soybean exports, and Chinese companies are resorting to buying up more and more farmland overseas.[iii]

Figure 4.3: *The land elsewhere: Mato Grosso, on the southern edge of the Brazilian Amazon, used to be savannah and forest land. Today it produces soybeans for urban consumers around the world, with enormous inputs of fertiliser, pesticides and fuel oil. Soybeans are primarily used as animal feed to satisfy the growing global demand for meat, particularly in countries such as China.*
Source: *Paulo Fridman*

India is next

In India, too, urban areas are growing very rapidly, with 90 million new residents added from 2004 to 2013. While India is still a mainly rural country, dominated by villages, it actually has the world's second largest urban population, after China.[iv]

In 1947, only 60 million people, or 15 per cent of the total population, lived in urban areas. Since then, India's population has grown 2.5 times, but its urban population has grown five-fold. By 2011, some 380 million Indians lived in nearly 3,700 towns and cities, about 32 per cent of the country's population. 71 million people, or about one-third of urban India, lived in metropolitan cities of a million or more. Their number has increased from just one in 1901 to 40 in 2001. By 2030, a further 280 million people are expected to become urban dwellers.[v]

Much of the growth is not occurring in city centres but on the urban fringe, following the relocation of industrial enterprises: India's largest metropolitan centres – Mumbai, Delhi, Bangalore, Kolkata, Chennai, Hyderabad and Ahmedabad – experienced a 16 per cent loss of manufacturing jobs from 1998 to 2005, while in rural areas up to 50 km from these large urban centres, manufacturing jobs increased by 54 per cent.[vi]

In India, too, per capita increase in energy use – driven primarily by coal mining – is a key factor in urban-industrial growth, though not quite on the same scale as China. But power cuts are an endemic problem, with peak electricity supplies falling short of demand by some 10 per cent. The bulk of electricity is produced by coal-fired power stations, but their construction tends to lag behind the ever growing demand. Interestingly, a lack of reliable power supplies has limited the development of high-rise social housing developments that are such a common feature of Chinese cities, though middle-class high-rise buildings that are now appearing in many cities tend to have their own diesel-based electricity generators.

In spite of the growing economic strength of India's large cities, population pressure and deterioration in the physical environment are serious problems. Unlike in China, urbanisation is proceeding in rather haphazard ways, with slums growing in and around all major cities. Nearly one-third of the urban Indian population live below the poverty line, and about 50 per cent have no sanitary facilities. In most cities traffic congestion is endemic, with inadequate road space and lack of adequate public transport provision.

Across urban India, the gap between demand and supply of essential services and infrastructure has been widening in recent years.[vii] Water supply is a particularly serious problem. In most Indian cities water supplies are intermittent, and people in poor districts often have to buy expensive water from tanker lorries. Even in wealthier neighbourhoods piped water usually circulates for only a few hours a day. When water pipes are depressurised, sewage effluent from adjacent pipes often penetrates into leaking water pipes. As a result, digestive diseases, 'Delhi belly', are a common problem.

Across East Asia, rapid industrial development has contributed to income growth, and poverty has certainly been reduced. According to World Bank statistics, between 1965 and 1990, East Asia's industrial sector grew nine times, by an average of nine per cent a year. Nearly a third of the region's population lived in poverty in 1970 compared with only ten per cent now. Along with income growth, population growth has fallen markedly: it was 2.3

per cent a year from 1965 to 1990, and is expected to fall to 0.7 per cent a year by 2030. But how environmentally sustainable is India's urban-industrial development, driven as it is by the massive growth in the use of non-renewable resources, and particularly fossil fuels?

Latin America and Africa

Latin America, like many other regions, has changed dramatically in the last 50 years, from mainly rural to predominantly urban. City populations have been growing by over three per cent a year. At first national capitals grew fastest, but then secondary urban centres followed suit. In 2013, 74 per cent of Latin America's population was urban, with 80 per cent living in just 600 towns and cities.

In recent years, Latin America's international role of exporting raw materials and importing manufactured goods has changed significantly. New global trade agreements negotiated during the 1990s resulted in large reductions of import tariffs for capital goods. As a result, large cities such as Sao Paulo, Mexico City and Buenos Aires have become manufacturing centres as part of a globalised system for the assembly of industrial products.

Africa is changing rapidly as well. Currently, urban growth is most rapid in sub-Saharan Africa.[viii] It is often driven by acute crises in rural areas, without offering adequate employment opportunities in cities. In a 2013 report, the World Bank states that in the last 30 years the number of Africans living in extreme poverty has risen from 205 million to 414 million. In October 2013 the research group Afrobarometer reported that urban-economic growth was primarily benefitting a small elite.

A major change in recent years has been that Africa is gaining increased access to international capital. Foreign direct investment into Africa increased from $9 billion in 2000 to $62 billion in 2008. Relative to GDP this nearly matches foreign capital flow into China. In fact, China herself has been a major investor in mining and oil exploration in Africa. Whilst the continent's resources sectors have drawn the most foreign capital, money has also flowed into tourism, textiles, construction, banking and telecommunications.[ix] Invariably, much of foreign capital ends up in Africa's cities.

In Nigeria, Lagos, Africa's largest city, is truly a 'Petropolis' – the premier port city of one of the world's major oil exporters. Until the 1950s Lagos had less than 100,000 people. But when oil was discovered in the Niger Delta, major investments were made by oil companies such as Shell and everything changed. Lagos grew at an astonishing rate, from nearly 700,000 people in 1963, to eight million in 1990, and to around 15 million people in 2003.[x]

Lagos handles most of Nigeria's oil and gas shipments, which account for 98 per cent of export earnings and 83 per cent of federal government revenue. But instead of its people becoming wealthy, unemployment and poverty are rife.

Figure 4.4: *Oil from the Niger Delta has generated an estimated $600 billion since the 1960s. But the majority of the Delta's population live in abject poverty, with minimal social infrastructure and endemic conflict as land and fishing grounds have been polluted.* ***Source:*** *EcoNigeria*

A tiny elite has been the main beneficiary of Nigeria's oil revenues, with few of its citizens seeing tangible financial benefits. From 1996 to 2005 poverty in Lagos increased nearly nine-fold, from 6.27 to 53 per cent in 2004, according to Nigeria's Federal Office of Statistics. This increased poverty rate is closely connected with massive migrations of people from other parts of the country. Despite being a country rich in oil and other resources, Nigeria stubbornly holds a very low position on the Human Development Index – 142 out of 172 in 2010.[xi]

Apart from poverty there are other major problems: endemic traffic congestion means that it can take people three hours to travel 20 kilometres. And despite the region's substantial endowment of water, Lagos lacks adequate water supplies. Lack of adequate sewerage means that human wastes are still mostly discharged through open ditches onto off-shore tidal flats. But at least 90 per cent of Lagos's population have steady electricity supplies, unlike much of the rest of Nigeria.

Lagos is not Africa's only major oil city. Elsewhere, Angola's capital Luanda and South Sudan's capital Juba have both become oil centres as well. And as recently discovered oil reserves in Ghana, Kenya, Mozambique, Uganda and Tanzania are starting to be exploited, it remains to be seen whether oil revenues will be spent at home – building up domestic infrastructure such as roads, railway lines, power- and sewerage networks – or whether corrupt officials will squirrel them away in foreign bank accounts.

In 1991 the then World Bank chief economist, Larry Summers, stated in an infamous memo that he had 'always thought that under-populated countries in Africa are vastly under-polluted'.

Since then, Africa has been playing catch up. At around five per cent, Africa's economic growth in the last decade has been faster than in most other regions. Air and water pollution have been increasing rapidly, and both are affecting urban populations disproportionately.

Living conditions for a billion or more city people in developing countries are often worse than they were in the cities of the European Industrial Revolution, with people forced to breathe polluted air, drink dirty water and live in cardboard or tin shacks infested by flies, lice, cockroaches, rats and disease-carrying mosquitoes. In cities such as Nairobi, squatter settlements accommodate up to half of the urban population.[xii] A UN-Habitat Report found that Africa has its fair share of the nearly one billion people worldwide who live in slums, about a third of the world's urban dwellers.[xiii] They scratch a living from petty trading, waste picking, mechanics, carpentry, masonry, plumbing and tailoring, and sometimes urban agriculture and fishing.

In many developing cities, waste pickers provide a valuable service since they may provide the only solid waste collection service. The primary incentive for waste pickers is the inherent value of the materials they collect which end up in a chain of reuse and recycling. Some waste pickers live in poverty, but others earn substantially more than their country's minimum wage. As cities develop, the role of waste pickers is often supplemented or replaced by formal waste collection services.

Poorer cities in developing countries often cannot afford to install appropriate infrastructure technology, and this problem is often amplified by corruption. Because squatter settlements or slums tend to lack services such as water supplies and sewage disposal, major epidemics of diseases such as cholera, typhoid and TB are often prevented only by the availability of antibiotics.

Air pollution, local and global

And what about air pollution linked to urban growth? This is a problem that affects the largest cities the most. The inhabitants of megacities such as Lagos, Mexico City, Beijing or Chongqing are exposed to horrendously polluted air, causing high incidences of bronchitis, pneumonia and lung cancer. Such problems often result in vigorous demands efforts for reform. But there is often less concern about detrimental effects of acid fumes such as sulfur and nitrogen oxides on forests and farm crops downwind from cities and power stations since these are outside people's everyday experience. And the greenhouse gas emissions affecting the global climate are even lower down the ladder of priorities: impacts on *human health* have much greater policy priority than impacts on *planetary health*, and yet these are of the greatest concern for the future of humanity.

Figure 4.5: *Smog over Singapore. Large cities in emerging economies are invariably victims of air pollution – mostly from intra-urban and peri-urban coal and oil combustion, but also from forests being burned to clear land for food and palm oil crops, as here in neighbouring Malaysia. Such local air pollution also significantly adds to global climate problems.* ***Source:*** *H. Girardet*

If Africa has been 'under-polluted' from local emissions until recently, as 'famously' suggested by former World Bank chief economist Larry Summers in 1991, transcontinental air pollution all the way from Europe and America may have affected the climate and livelihoods of Africans for decades in surprising ways. According to a recent study by scientists at the University of Washington, decades of drought in central Africa reached their worst point in the 1980s. They argue that this greatly contributed to Lake Chad, a shallow desert lake, on which more than 30 million people in Cameroon, Niger, Chad and Nigeria depend for water supplies, shrinking by 95 per cent. Aerosols emanating from coal-burning power stations and factories in North America and Europe had a cooling effect in the Northern hemisphere. Tropical rain bands shifted south, and rains no longer reached the Sahel region just below the Sahara desert. Only when clean-air legislation was passed in the United States and Europe, reducing aerosol emissions there, did the rain bands shift back, reducing the Sahel drought.[xiv]

More recently, the prolonged drought in the Horn of Africa in 2010 and 2011 is also attributed to climate change. It caused a widely reported severe food crisis, affecting around ten million people in northern Kenya, Ethiopia, Djibouti and Somalia. Rains failed over two seasons, having a dramatic impact across the east coast of Africa.[xv]

About half the cumulative man-made CO_2 emissions between 1750 and 2010 have occurred in the last 40 years. Most developing countries are already affected by climate change and according to the IPCC, fossil fuel combustion in the rich, highly urbanised countries will invariably hit the poorest countries hardest. Much higher temperatures could reduce the length of the growing period in some parts of Africa by up to 20 per cent, with major implications for urban food supplies. [xvi]

Arabian Gulf cities: the ultimate Petropolis

Nowhere is the growth of modern cities dependent on daily injections of fossil fuel energy more apparent than in the Arabian Gulf, where half a dozen large cities have sprung up over the last 50 years. The super-fast growth of cities such as Dubai, Abu Dhabi, Doha and Jeddah, with their amazing collection of skyscrapers, their artificial islands and their low-density desert suburbs, has been making newspaper headlines across the world. The Gulf region may have vast oil and gas reserves, both for export and for domestic use, but their utter dependence on desalinated water and imported food is an existential issue that can't be overlooked.

A century ago, the Gulf region, the world's largest peninsula, was sparsely populated and consisted of a few sheikhdoms that controlled vast – mainly desert – areas, including several oases and a few small coastal settlements. Migrant lifestyles were the norm. Economic and population growth were severely limited by the region's harsh environment and lack of water. Qatar,

Kuwait, Manama, Muscat, Dubai and Abu Dhabi were small fishing and pearling ports with well-established trade connections beyond the region. The seas around the peninsula, with their large coral reefs and fertile fishing grounds, were an important resource.[xvii]

In the port towns, small, sedentary populations developed their own specific architectural and urban designs. Streets and lanes were narrow and shaded, and buildings had thick gypsum walls to keep the cool in and heat out. Their cooling towers harnessed the harsh summer winds and helped to keep rooms at pleasant temperatures. Houses never faced south and were arranged around courtyards to best take advantage of prevailing breezes.

Until the 1930s, the pearl industry was the region's most important economic sector. But when Japan started to flood the world market with cultured pearls, the Gulf's ancient pearl industry collapsed.[xviii] However, this coincided with the discovery of oil below the desert sand and very quickly everything started to change. The Gulf peninsula was found to contain the world's largest oil deposits and soon oil pumpjacks began to dot the desert landscape, and new pipelines started to fuel the region's rapidly growing coastal cities and their economies.

Most of the cities of the region have become major ports, oil storage and transport hubs. In the last 75 years the huge revenues from oil and gas production have transformed the region. In today's Gulf cities narrow, shaded pedestrian streets have given way to wide, multi-lane urban motorways on which the car is king. Glass, concrete and tarmac are the predominant construction materials.

The region's new cities have become synonymous with urban sprawl. Gulf cities like Riyadh, Jeddah, Dubai, Doha, Manama, Dammam, Abu Dhabi, Muscat and Kuwait City are growing by up to 5 per cent a year, and their downtown urban landscape is defined by soaring towers and shopping centres, as well as ambitious education, research, cultural and sports facilities.

Today, over 80 per cent of the region's people live in large, modern cities. Its population – residents as well migrant workers – numbers around 80 million. The huge oil and gas revenues provide for Gulf citizens' basic needs, and many people have become wealthy without too much effort or risk.

On the Arabian Peninsula, per capita use of fossil fuels – and greenhouse gas emissions – is among the highest in the world. But the finite nature of oil and gas supplies and the limited availability of water are becoming a growing concern.

Figure 4.6: *The old town of Jeddah, with its traditional climate-adjusted architecture, is being allowed to fall into decay. Few of the old houses are being preserved as new air conditioned, high rise, concrete and glass buildings rise into the sky.* ***Source:*** *H. Girardet*

Meanwhile rising temperatures due to climate change are increasingly being felt across the region and annual rainfall is showing a significant decreasing trend.[xix] In the cities the large surface areas covered in concrete and tarmac are contributing significantly to an urban heat island effect, with rising temperatures requiring ever greater reliance on air conditioning.

The general aim of urban planning in the Gulf seems to be to create cities that look similar to established global cities such as New York, Hong Kong or Singapore, and with similar functions, but these are increasingly seen as unsuitable for the region's hot climate.

Given the abundance of oil and gas in the region, it is not surprising that Gulf cities are the epitomy of fossil fuel dependence. All urban transport in the Gulf runs on oil. Car-based transport accounts for over a quarter of total energy use and greenhouse gas emissions, with impacts both on the health of local people as well as the global climate.

Cities in the Gulf region could probably be classed as some of the world's least sustainable cities. According to 2008 World Bank figures, Qatar has the world's highest CO_2 emissions, a total of 49.1 metric tons per person/year. Kuwait with 30.1 tons and the United Arab Emirates with 25.5 follow closely.[xx] Between them they also have the largest per capita ecological footprints – far exceeding other countries.

If every human lived like a Qatari, humanity would need five planets.

Figure 4.7: *Dubai is the ultimate Petropolis. Will this huge new city, planted in a desert location without any natural water or local food supplies, be able to exist in a world in which cheap oil and gas can no longer be taken for granted?* ***Source:*** *Dubai City Council*

Water equals oil

The Arab region as a whole, consisting of 22 countries, accounts for 6.3 per cent of the world's population, but only 1.4 per cent of its fresh water supplies. Despite this, water consumption in the Gulf countries, at around

300 litres per person, is among the highest in the world. Lack of consumer education is a major concern, and many residents seem to have no awareness that water is in short supply. Vast expanses of green on golf courses and the lawns of gated communities give the impression that water is plentiful.

Most water is actually supplied by oil and gas powered desalination plants, costing some $1 per cubic meter to produce and consuming eight times more energy than groundwater supplies. Desalination accounts for up to 20 per cent of the region's total energy consumption.[xxi]

Desalination is highly problematic not only because the fossil fuels it depends on are a finite resource, but also because much of the brine produced is flushed back into the Gulf, affecting coral reefs and fish stocks. The UAE, Qatar, Bahrain, Saudi Arabia, Kuwait and Iran have 120 desalination plants between them. Apart from brine, these plants flush nearly 24 tons of chlorine, 65 tons of pipe antiscalants and around 296 kgs of copper into the Gulf waters every day.[xxii]

Whilst water is a scarce and precious resource, few people in the region are asking why water of drinking quality standard is used for flushing toilets. Grey water is only utilised for irrigating golf courses and city trees, but nowhere is it used for growing food crops.

Food supplies

Only oases and some coastal regions of the Gulf were traditionally used for farming. But in the course of drilling for oil, fossil water was also found in various parts of the desert. To make the desert fertile, fossil groundwater is pumped up from depths of up to 1,000 metres and distributed via rotating arms. 'Centre pivot' irrigation in the Saudi desert is typical of many groundwater irrigation projects across the arid regions of the Earth. The circular fields can produce of a great variety of crops, from alfalfa to wheat to vegetables. They can have a diameter from a few hundred metres to as much as three kilometres.

The fossil water mined in these projects accumulated over tens of thousands to millions of years and is not being replenished in this arid region. In Saudi Arabia the area under cultivation grew from 400,000 acres (1,600 km^2) in 1976 to over eight million acres (32,000 km^2) in 1993. But in 2008, the Saudi government abruptly curtailed wheat production as the water was getting scarcer and more saline. In that one year, Saudi wheat imports increased by an astonishing 1,600 per cent!

But modern food systems are global. If irrigation water for growing wheat in the Arabian desert runs out, grain for bread making is imported from Canada instead. If Australian soybean fields erode or suffer drought, chicken produced with soy from Argentina or the Brazilian Amazon is eaten instead. If fish from the Arabian Gulf or the Red Sea runs out, fish from the Pacific will take its place. Yet sooner or later the world will hit the limits of such highly energy-dependent global food supplies.

Figure 4.8: *Centre pivot irrigation using non-renewable fossil water is an exceptionally unsustainable method of supplying food to cities, yet it is still expanding in arid regions of the planet.* ***Source:*** *NASA*

A recent development, under the term 'land grab', has been accelerating around the world: this refers to the globalisation of land acquisition for food supply to countries and cities deficient in nearby farmland. For instance, a Saudi conglomerate has recently acquired two million acres of farmland in eastern Sudan to produce food for Saudi Arabian cities such as Riyadh, Jeddah and Dammam. This is causing much concern among traditional Sudanese cattle herders and farmers. A website called 'Farmlandgrab' also highlights land acquisition by other Gulf countries such as Dubai, Abu Dhabi and Qatar in places such as the Ukraine or Uganda.[xxiii]

Similar developments are occurring on the Omo River, a tributary of the Blue Nile in Ethiopia. The Gibe III hydroelectric dam that is being built there, close to the border with Sudan, will block the south-western section of the river, so ending its natural flood cycle. The Mursi are one of several local tribes who have lived there for time immemorial. The dam will prevent their flood-retreat cultivation methods which rely on the fertile soils being deposited on the river banks by annual floods in the Ethiopian highlands. The Mursi are being evicted from the traditional lands to make way for irrigated cash crop and biofuel plantations, to supply electricity to Addis Ababa, one of Africa's fastest growing cities.

Petropolis and global boomerangs

We are seeing ever more extraordinary contraptions appear across the face of the Earth to extract fossil fuels from the Earth's crust, to refine them and to deliver them into our cities and homes. With much of the 'easy' coal, oil and gas now used up, new kinds of highly problematic extraction and processing methods have come to underpin the existence of our urban systems. In West Virginia mountain tops are being removed for open cast coal mining. In Alberta, tar sand mining pollutes vast bodies of water from the process of extracting the oil contained within the sand. Across the United States, fracking has temporarily produced a glut of gas for use in power stations and trucks. In the Gulf of Mexico, off-shore platform operators are now pumping up oil from as much ten kilometres down in the Earth's crust in ever more hostile waters. Is the systemic dependence of modern cities on such fuels a viable proposition?

The impacts of fossil fuel-dependent urbanisation are reverberating across the world. Climate change is a particular concern: a large part of the increase of carbon dioxide in the atmosphere is attributable to combustion in and on behalf of the world's cities.[xxiv] Two hundred years ago atmospheric CO_2 concentrations were around 280 parts per million (ppm), but by 2014 they had risen to nearly 400 parts ppm. Some people still prefer to think that such increases of pre-industrial concentrations are of little consequence, but there is overwhelming scientific consensus that we are heading for trouble. A recent report, published not by an environmental NGO but by the World Bank, warns that we are on track for a 4°C warmer world, marked by extreme heat-waves, declining global food supplies, loss of ecosystems and biodiversity, and life-threatening sea level rise.[xxv]

In recent years the most dramatic growth has occurred in giant coastal cities, particularly in Asia and Africa in locations well suited as container terminals. Of the 22 megacities of over ten million people around the globe, 14 are located in coastal areas. The expansion of global trade has led to coastal populations and economies exploding on every continent. 40 per cent of the world's cities of one to ten million people are also located near coastlines. This has had major environmental consequences: careless development practices have degraded or destroyed important habitats such as wetlands, mangrove forests, coral reefs, seagrass meadows and estuarine fisheries.

But there is a catch: sea level rises of up to a metre this century could well cause major coastal conurbations such as London, New York, Shanghai, Calcutta, Dhaka and Lagos to become the primary victims of global urban greenhouse gas emissions, with huge impacts on property values as well as human living conditions. But communicating the dangers of such *boomerang effects*, which could soon undermine the very existence of our major cities, is still a major challenge.

There is no question that the fossil fuel supplies on which Petropolis depends are, most definitely, finite. It is a *dependent system*. And what goes in must come out again: whilst relying on vast amounts of external inputs for its sustenance, Petropolis also discharges huge quantities of solid, liquid and gaseous wastes into the global environment without much concern about the consequences.

The dependence of contemporary urban systems on non-renewable resources is ecologically, economically and geopolitically precarious. The systems conditions that define Petropolis need to be fundamentally re-assessed before resource shortages, food insecurity, savage storms, sea level rises and other environmental impacts start to undermine its very existence. We need to think about the multiple risks associated with a fossil fuel-powered urban age from a long-term perspective. Otherwise nightmare scenarios of films like Mad Max may yet become a haunting reality.

Philippines Typhoon Haiyan, November 2013

Science tells us that climate change will mean more intense tropical storms. As the Earth warms up, that would include the oceans. The energy that is stored in the waters off the Philippines will increase the intensity of typhoons and the trend we now see is that more destructive storms will be the new norm. To anyone who continues to deny the reality that is climate change, I dare you to get off your ivory tower and away from the comfort of your armchair. I dare you to go to the islands of the Pacific, the islands of the

Caribbean, and the islands of the Indian Ocean and see the impacts of rising sea levels; to the mountainous regions of the Himalayas and the Andes to see communities confronting glacial floods; to the Arctic where communities grapple with the fast dwindling polar ice caps; to the large deltas of the Mekong, the Ganges, the Amazon, and the Nile where lives and livelihoods are drowned; to the hills of Central America that confronts similar monstrous hurricanes; to the vast savannas of Africa where climate change has likewise become a matter of life and death. Not to forget the hurricanes in the Gulf of Mexico. And if that is not enough, you may want to pay a visit to the Philippines right now.

(Yeb Sano, lead negotiator from the Philippines at Cop 19, Warsaw, November 2013, links Typhoon Haiyan to climate change)

Notes

i Worldwatch Institute (1997) *The State of the World*, Earthscan, London.

ii www.chinadaily.com.cn/china/2013-12/30/content_17205018.htm

iii Footprint Network, www.bbc.co.uk/news/world-asia-19797989; www.footprintnetwork.org/images/article_uploads/China_Ecological_Footprint_2012.pdf.

iv Government of India (2006) *Health and Living Conditions in Eight Indian Cities*, www.measuredhs.com/pubs/pdf/OD58/OD58.pdf.

v Indian Census 2011, http://censusindia.gov.in/.

vi World Bank, www.worldbank.org/en/news/feature/2013/10/21/india-urbanization-report-beyond-sustainable-cities.

vii www.teindia.nic.in/mhrd/50yrsedu/15/8P/81/8P810D01.htm.

viii UN (1999) *World Urbanisation Prospects*, United Nations, New York.

ix McKinsey, www.mckinsey.com/insights/economic_studies/whats_driving_africas_growth.

x Abiodun, J. O. (1994) *The Challenges of Growth and Development in Metropolitan Lagos*, www.unu.edu/unupress/unupbooks/uu26ue/uu26ue0i.htm.

xi www.proshareng.com/news/44.html.

xii Hardoy, J., Mitlin, D. and Satterthwaite, D. (1992) *Environmental Problems in Third World Cities*, Earthscan Publications, London.

xiii UN Habitat (2003) *The Challenge of Slums: Global Report on Human Settlements*, Earthscan, London.

xiv Hickey, H. (2013) *Pollution in Northern Hemisphere Helped Cause 1980s African Drought*, www.washington.edu/news/2013/06/06/pollution-in-northern-hemisphere-helped-cause-1980s-african-drought/.

xv Lawrence, F. (2011) *Guardian*, 4 July, www.theguardian.com/world/2011/jul/04/drought-east-africa-climate-change.

xvi http://report.mitigation2014.org/spm/ipcc_wg3_ar5_summary-for-policymakers_approved.pdf.

xvii Wikipedia, *Arabian Peninsula*, http://en.wikipedia.org/wiki/Arabian_Peninsula.

xviii Wikipedia, *Arab States of the Persian Gulf*, http://en.wikipedia.org/wiki/Arab_states_of_the_Persian_Gulf.

xix *International Journal of Climatology*, Vol. 32, Issue 6, www.onlinelibrary.wiley.com.

xx Worldbank, http://data.worldbank.org/indicator/EN.ATM.CO2E.PC.

xxi Alarabiya, http://english.alarabiya.net/articles/2012/01/23/190093.html.

xxii MEDRC Series of R&D Reports, www.ifh.uni-karlsruhe.de/science/envflu/research/brinedis/brinedis-finalreport.pdf.

xxiii Farmlandgrab, www.farmlandgrab.org.

xxiv Earth Magazine (2012) *Carbon and the City*, 22 May, www.earthmagazine.org/article/carbon-and-city-tracking-emissions-megacities.

xxv *World Bank Climate Change Report 2012*, http://climatechange.worldbank.org/content/climate-change-report-warns-dramatically-warmer-world-century.

Chapter 5

The urban metabolism

The urban metabolism

In an urbanising world, the planning of new cities, as well as the retrofit of existing ones, needs to undergo a profound paradigm shift. For a safe urban future, it is crucially important to quantify the flow of energy and resources within cities, and between cities and the world beyond, i.e., the *metabolism* of cities.

The prevailing way in which modern cities use resources is highly problematic. They have an essentially linear, unidirectional metabolism, with resources flowing through the urban system without much concern about their origin, or about the destination of wastes. Inputs and outputs are treated as largely unconnected. Fossil fuels are extracted from rock strata, refined and burned, and the waste gases are discharged into the atmosphere. Raw materials are extracted, processed and assembled into consumer goods that ultimately end up as trash which cannot be beneficially reabsorbed into living nature. In distant forests, trees are felled for their timber or pulp, but all too often forests are not replenished.

Figure 5.1: *We tend to forget that cities are not just made up of buildings, public spaces and roads. The hidden pipes and cables underneath our feet are visible only when major repairs are needed. Most of what flows through them originates from far-away locations.* ***Source:*** *H. Girardet*

Similar processes apply to the urban food system: nutrients and carbon are removed from farmland as crops are harvested, and then processed and eaten. The resulting sewage, with or without treatment, ends up in rivers and coastal waters downstream from population centres, and the plant nutrients it contains are rarely returned to farmland. Rivers and coastal waters all over the world are 'enriched' by a potent mix of urban sewage and toxic effluents, as well as the run-off of mineral fertiliser and pesticides applied to the farmland used for feeding cities.

Cities and entropy

The creation of innumerable large cities across the world that rely on daily injections of fossil fuel energy would seem to be a remarkable exercise in short-sightedness. Petropolis is subject to the second law of thermodynamics which states that the use of energy is an irreversible process. Usable energy is irretrievably turned into unusable, dispersed energy. As energy does 'useful work' it will inevitably end up as waste, pollution or *disorder*.

Petropolis is a giant heat engine: the energy used to run power stations, pumping engines, transport systems, factory conveyor belts, cranes and internet server farms can be used only once, and thus the energy content of non-renewable fuels is turned into low-grade heat and waste gases.

Cities are vast interconnected systems designed for turning energy into 'work' or motion, flowing along their roads, rails, wires and pipes. As fossil energy is used and raw materials are processed, their quality inevitably deteriorates. Order, which is established in the form of cities, causes disorder elsewhere in nature. So concentrating or ordering human activities in high-energy cities means increasing the level of disorder, waste and pollution for the planet as a whole.

As they currently function, then, cities are 'entropy accelerators' – they deplete and downgrade the resources they depend on in the process of using them. The limited availability of low-entropy energy is the ultimate constraint on urban systems and their long-term well-being. Local air pollution and global climate change is the most topical 'high-entropy expression' of burning fossil fuels to power the highly organised urban lifestyles we have created.

Modern cities are the home of the 'amplified man'. Whilst we are essentially biological beings, our 'amplification' via a huge array of technologies defines our identity as never before. This point can be vividly illustrated by our energy use. As purely biological creatures our energy output – derived from the food we eat – is a maximum of 100 watts per person. (Our brains use about 30 watts.) If the electricity is generated in a typical coal-fired power station, it takes about 325 kg of coal to power a 100 W light bulb for one year.[i]

But the total amount of energy we use today is actually about 6,000 watts for an 'average' European, and about 11,000 watts for a North American. This means that Europeans, as primarily urban citizens, use at least 60 times more energy from technical than from purely biological energy sources. Europeans have sixty 'energy slaves' working for them day and night. This is an astonishing and unprecedented reality.

The amount of energy US citizens use in their predominantly urban lives today is a vivid demonstration of this point: they use 14 times more per capita than their ancestors used before the Industrial Revolution.[ii] But as such high-energy lifestyles are copied across the world, there is also an ever growing awareness that we live in a world of limits: The more fossil fuel energy is used today, the less will be available tomorrow.

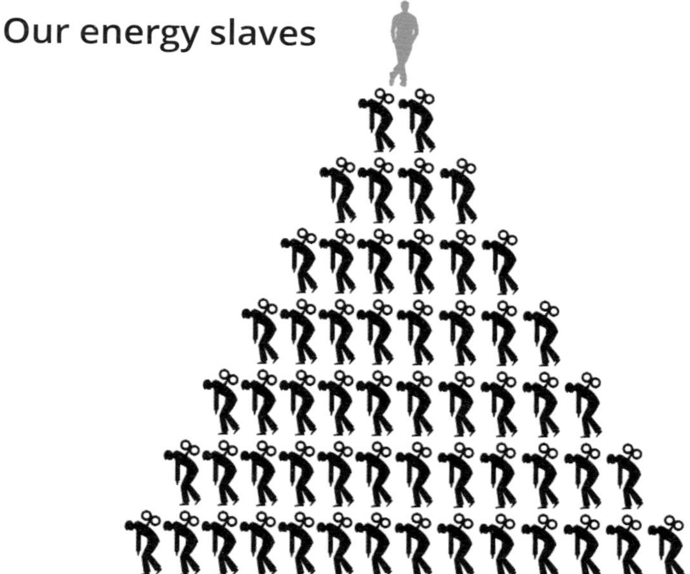

Figure 5.2: *The concept of energy slaves was first used by Buckmister Fuller in 1944. One energy slave is the equivalent of the technologic-mechanical energy that a healthy human youth can deliver during 250 working days in a given year. Each European today has about 60 energy slaves, represented by the output of the motors and engines working on our behalf. For Americans and Australians the figure is nearly twice as high. Fossil fuels are the main energy source. Energy efficiency and renewable energy are essential for curtailing our highly problematic dependence on fossil fuel energy.* ***Source:*** *B. Fuller, H. Girardet, R. Lawrence*

Energy sufficiency

Factor-four to factor-five (75 to 80 per cent) reductions in CO_2 emissions in the developed world over the coming decades are widely seen as necessary if catastrophic climate change is to be avoided. Thus, very deliberate limitations on energy use are required.

If we are serious about keeping the Earth from warming by no more than 2°C, we can only burn a quarter of its oil, gas and coal reserves. This is the startling conclusion of a study by Myles Allen of the University of Oxford. Humanity has to stick to a carbon budget, of burning a maximum of a trillion tonnes of carbon if we want to avoid runaway climate change.[iii]

Since the Industrial Revolution humanity has burned about 500 billion tonnes of carbon fuels. Says Myles Allen:

> ***We can afford to burn only 250 billion tonnes more – or perhaps 500 billion tonnes if we are willing to run the higher risk ... It took 250 years to burn the first 500 billion tonnes. On current trends we'll burn the next 500 billion in less than 40 years.***[iv]

This perspective has been scrutinised and endorsed by the Intergovernmental Panel on Climate Change (IPCC). A few developed countries, such as Britain, have committed themselves to factor-five, or 80 per cent, improvements in energy productivity by 2050, and in highly urbanised societies the major improvements have to be made primarily in the energy use of cities. For newly urbanising countries the challenge is to implement best global practice in the design of new cities to ensure maximum energy efficiency.

It is clearly evident that the American and Australian model of low-density urban sprawl is simply not fit for purpose in a carbon-constrained world, though it is still being copied in places such as the Arabian Gulf.

What can cities do to minimise their systemic dependence on fossil fuels and to ensure high energy efficiency standards? Much can be done to improve the energy efficiency of existing buildings and to achieve high efficiency standards for new buildings. Buildings typically use about 40 per cent of total energy consumption. In many countries appropriate measures are now being taken to improve the energy performance of buildings.

In a recent study by the World Business Council for Sustainable Development (WBCSD), energy use by building type was analysed for millions of existing and new buildings, accounting for differences such as climate and building design. The WBCSD's $15 million 'Efficiency in Buildings Research Project' shows how energy use in buildings can be cut by 60 per cent by 2050 by the use of better building materials, new approaches to building design and better energy management. The central message of the pioneering four-year study is that immediate action is required to transform the way the building sector prioritises energy. The report makes six principle recommendations:

- **strengthen building codes and energy labelling for increased transparency;**
- **use subsidies and price signals to incentivise energy-efficient investments;**
- **encourage integrated design approaches and innovations;**
- **develop and use advanced technology to enable energy-saving behaviour;**
- **develop workforce capacity for energy saving;**
- **mobilise for an energy-aware culture.**[v]

The evolution of insulation materials

Figure 5.3: *30 cms of fibreglass have the same insulation capacity as 20 cms of polystyrene foam (PU), 12 cms of polyurethane foam (EPS) and 3 cms of vacuum insulation panels (VIPs). This new insulation technology, which is becoming widely available, enables internal insulation on buildings whose facades can't be altered. It has huge implications for improving the energy efficiency of cities.* ***Source:*** *Kevothermal Limited*

The challenge now is to incentivise home owners as well as property developers, who let buildings for rent, to ensure superior energy efficiency standards of their buildings. Their tenants will save money while local air pollution and CO_2 emissions are significantly reduced at the same time.

Transport, of course, is another key focus. The challenge here, above all else, is to reduce the reliance on the private motor car, although this is obviously problematic in cities that have been designed around the car. (The comparison between Atlanta and Barcelona, in Chapter 3, illustrates this problem vividly.) Where new cities are still being built, urban layouts less reliant on private transport are increasingly finding favour with planning authorities.

But car technologies are improving as well. A decade ago car manufacturers could barely imagine making cars that did not run on petrol or diesel. The greatest potential improvements in energy efficiency can now come from a progressive elimination of internal combustion engines: they operate with a maximum efficiency of only 20 to 30 per cent. Electric cars, by comparison, achieve an efficiency of up to around 90 per cent. The widespread adoption of electric cars will transform the energy performance of private transportation.

To achieve an energy-sufficient world, governments, businesses and individuals must adopt new energy scenarios. A multitude of actions are needed to aggressively reduce energy consumption in all sectors. The necessary changes will not come through market forces alone, there need to be well thought out policies to help drive the necessary changes.

Mode	Energy Efficiency (MJ per pass.km)
Car	2.45
Bus	1.05
Metro	0.46
Suburban Rail	0.61
Light Rail	0.56
Tram	0.52

Figure 5.4: *Energy use of transport. Not surprisingly, public transport outscores the car.*
Source: *Peter Newman and Jeffrey Kenworthy*

The 2000 Watt Society

The idea that it is necessary to define a level of global overall limits to energy use beyond which we should not go is rapidly gaining credence – both in terms of 'what is sufficient for us' and in terms of 'what is good for the planet'. In Switzerland a concept called the 2000 Watt Society has been developed.

In this scenario each consumer would cut their total energy use to no more than 2,000 watts – 17,520 kilowatt-hours per year of all energy use – by the year 2050 at the latest. Together with this target, a one tonne of CO_2 emissions limit per person and year was also stipulated. The concept can be scaled up from the household level to the collective energy use of the country.

2,000 watts corresponds to the average consumption of Swiss citizens back in 1960 and is the current world average. Switzerland itself currently uses a per capita average of some 5,000 watts. This compares to 6,000 watts in Western Europe, 12,000 watts in the United States, 3,000 watts in China, 1,500 watts in India, and only 400 watts in Bangladesh.

The concept has been adopted by cities such as Zurich and Basel and envisages the progressive refurbishment of the cities' building stock to best practice standards, further significant improvements in the efficiency of transport, revisioning of energy-intensive materials use and widespread introduction of combined heat-and-power systems, renewable energy and micro-generation.

Warm Zone Kirklees

In the UK, the city of Kirklees pioneered a comprehensive approach to urban energy efficiency from 2009 to 2010. 'Kirklees Warm Zone' was Britain's most comprehensive programme to tackle domestic energy efficiency, fuel poverty and climate change, providing practical energy efficiency support to householders.

In Kirklees an estimated 45,000 householders were in fuel poverty, unable to adequately heat their homes. The Warm Zone helped most of these households to their improve energy efficiency whilst also offering other support services. The main aim was to provide warm, energy efficient homes. Installation of all energy efficiency measures was made dependent on an initial technical survey of the home.

Warm Zone provided:

- free cavity wall and loft insulation for all households;
- free low-energy light bulbs to all;
- free improvements to heating systems for needy households;
- competitive prices for replacement boilers for households that can afford to pay;
- reduced prices for renewable technologies.

Warm Zone worked on a ward by ward, street by street approach. Funding was provided by Kirklees Council, Scottish Power, National Grid, the Regional Housing Board, Scottish Power Energy People Trust and British Gas Energy Trust.

www.kirklees.gov.uk/community/environment/energyconservation/warmzone/WarmZoneReport.pdf

Server farms

The Internet underpins global communications as never before – networks of internet users generate virtual cities. But this does not come entropy-free: server farms use a huge amount of electricity. It is claimed that in 2013 they required more energy than the global auto industry used for producing cars and trucks. If the Internet were a country, it would be in fifth place for using energy and producing greenhouse gas. According to Greenpeace, the global Internet consumes more power than Russia. When functioning at full capacity, Google's eight server farms alone are claimed to use some 476 megawatts of electricity, enough to power San Diego. While the widespread use of the Internet may reduce some physical travel, our global daily 'journeys' on the Internet require huge amounts of energy. Some change is underway: most Internet companies are now investing in greater energy efficiency and some are engaged in switching from fossil fuels to hydro, wind and solar energy, and, in some instances, to locations such as Iceland that have low average annual temperatures.[vi]

Countering the rebound effect

Under the right circumstances, moves towards greater energy efficiency can become a useful tool for dealing with climate change as well as energy shortages. There is a well-documented history of improvements in the energy efficiency of important technologies. For instance, in the nineteenth century the energy productivity of steam engines increased no less than 14-fold.

But the beneficial outcomes of efficiency improvements were being questioned as long ago as 1865 by British economist W. Stanley Jevons in his book *The Coal Question*. His 'Jevons Paradox' states that the conservation of fuel can actually lead to increased fuel consumption: if large numbers of people start conserving fuel, this can lower the price of that fuel which, in turn, will encourage increased consumption. Thus, argues Jevons, increased energy efficiency can result in raising demand for energy in the economy as a whole.

The same can be true at the household level. Whilst every effort should be made to help consumers save energy, this does not necessarily have the desired result: for instance, today's 15W fluorescent lights bulbs use four times less energy than 60W incandescent bulbs, but people may use more lights and leave them on for longer. Or: today's refrigerators use about four times less energy than 1970s models, but they are also likely to be much larger. Or: car engines have become more efficient in recent years, but people now tend to buy bigger, heavier and more powerful cars. By 'taking back' some energy savings, people thus contribute to the rebound effect.

Critics of the Jevons Paradox argue that energy savings are also cost savings and when budgets are tight or when energy prices go up, people will want to save energy after all. And in some instances a new sense of environmental responsibility may also influence behaviour patterns.

This will be further enhanced by government policies aiming to counter climate change, or balance of payments deficits resulting from fuel imports. In order to ensure a safe, reliable, accessible and affordable energy supply, future energy policies therefore need to:

- **define per capita energy sufficiency standards;**
- **remove subsidies for polluting energy supplies;**
- **decouple energy consumption from utility company profits;**
- **promote efficient technologies in buildings and transportation;**
- **use energy performance contracting to retrofit buildings;**
- **shorten distances between energy production and consumption;**
- **develop and implement smart grid technologies;**
- **use eco-taxes to curtail conventional power use.**[vii]

Resource productivity

Energy is just one of many inputs we use. A 2011 report by UNEP's International Resource Panel states that:

> ***By 2050, humanity could devour an estimated 140 billion tons of minerals, ores, fossil fuels and biomass per year – three times its***

current appetite – unless the economic growth rate is 'decoupled' from the rate of natural resource consumption. Developed country citizens consume an average of 16 tonnes of those four key resources per capita (ranging up to 40 or more tonnes per person in some developed countries). By comparison, the average person in India today consumes four tonnes per year.

With the growth of both population and prosperity across the world, the prospect of much higher per-capita consumption of finite resources is 'far beyond what is likely sustainable'. Limits to growth are becoming a reality. Already the world is running out of cheap and high quality sources of some essential materials such as oil, copper and gold, the supplies of which, in turn, require ever-rising volumes of fossil fuels and freshwater to produce. Improving the rate of resource productivity ('doing more with less') faster than the economic growth rate is the notion behind 'decoupling'. That goal, however, demands an urgent rethink of the linkages between resource use and economic prosperity, buttressed by a massive investment in scientific, technical, financial and social innovation, to at least freeze per capita consumption in wealthy countries and help developing nations follow a resource efficient path.[viii]

The infrastructure systems that provide transportation, information, sewerage, water and information distribution will determine to a large extent how resources flow through urban systems. They also play a major role in shaping the consumption patterns of people. Applying 'material flow analysis' is thus an important step towards reaching meaningful outcomes.

The urban world we live in is, above all else, defined by a proliferation of factory-made consumer products. Their manufacture faces another fundamental problem: they, too, are subject to the second law of thermodynamics and entropy. Usable resources, extracted from nature, inevitably degrade into waste. In an urbanising world so strongly defined by ever increasing energy and resources use, this is a major systemic problem.

Entropy, then, is a defining characteristic of contemporary economic and urban development. We are faced with the problem of irreversibility. However hard we try, the pollution and wastes emanating from a factory won't somehow be sucked back into it; or the ancient rainforest tree that supplied timber for a dining table in London or New York won't somehow become a living tree again.

Figure 5.5**: Whilst landfills have been falling out of favour in some countries, much domestic waste still ends up there, such as here in the Saudi desert.* ***Source: *H. Girardet*

The problem of the entropy of materials becomes very evident when we take a searching look at the theory and practice of recycling. Ubiquitous recycling is seen as a key component of a 'sustainable society'. Whilst landfill dumping is on the retreat, and recycling on the rise in many countries, much of it is, in fact, *downcycling*: the materials and products we have finished with are converted into lower-level waste.

Recycling only slows down the degradation process. For instance, metals of various grades are often recycled and smelted together, and a lower-grade composite material results. In plastics recycling the problem is particularly evident: the many types of plastics we use and discard don't mix well, and so lesser quality lower-grade hybrids are the result.[ix]

In the modern world it has become virtually impossible to avoid the use of plastics. But the consequences of dumping plastics as waste are dire. A vivid illustration of the largely unsolved problem of plastics recycling is the great Pacific Trash Vortex, one of five vast garbage patches rotating on ocean currents. About 100 million tonnes of plastics are produced globally every year, of which about 10 per cent end up in the sea where they mix with organic material and are often swallowed by fish, turtles or seabirds. This is just one of many examples of the enormity of the waste problem facing our high-consumption urbanising world.

The challenge is to find ways of preventing the dumping of plastics by up-cycling them into higher value products such as clothing fabrics. Making outdoor furniture or fence posts from mixed plastics is another option.

Figure 5.6: *Outdoor benches, furniture, and fence posts made from mixed recycled plastics: this is the best use, or reuse, for what is a virtually indestructible, long-lasting material.* ***Source:*** *Kedel Ltd*

Paper recycling, too, is a process of downcycling: fibres are shortened in the recycling process, and writing paper ends up as newsprint, cardboard and papier mâché. But at least this can be turned into compost and used as a soil conditioner.

Electronic wastes are the ultimate example of twenty-first century entropy, and here the problem of downcycling is particularly pronounced. Many electronic devices are discarded after a couple of years, and this is the ultimate example of built-in obsolescence. A huge variety of materials are required for the production of computers, printers, hi-fis, mobile phones, TV sets and household appliances. Worldwide, an estimated 50 million tonnes of electronic wastes are produced each year. These usually contain lead, cadmium, beryllium or bromine-based retardants and other toxic substances. Because they also contain valuable materials such as gold, copper or rare earths, they are often partially recycled, primarily in informal centres in China, India or Thailand. The plastics that remain are usually burned, releasing toxic fumes into human lungs and into the atmosphere. And if electronic devices are incinerated, they invariably end up as toxic ash.[x]

***Figure 5.7:** Electronics waste is the fastest growing sector of our throw-away lifestyle.*
***Source:** H. Girardet*

Towards circular systems

There are many systemic problems associated with linear urban waste disposal practices:

- The dumping of technical wastes in landfills is a notoriously problematic land use.
- Recycling, more often than not, is actually downcycling.
- Anaerobic decomposition and uncontrolled burning at landfills emits greenhouse gases.
- Sanitation related diseases are a widespread problem in developing cities.
- Discharging of liquid waste poisons watercourses and wastes plant nutrients.

To deal with these issues is a major task for the evolving science of urban ecology. In Ecopolis, aiming for long-term viability, as discussed in Chapter 6, the environmental externalities associated with urban resource use are systemically addressed. It takes the circular systems found in nature, where all wastes are organic nutrients for new growth, as its inspiration.

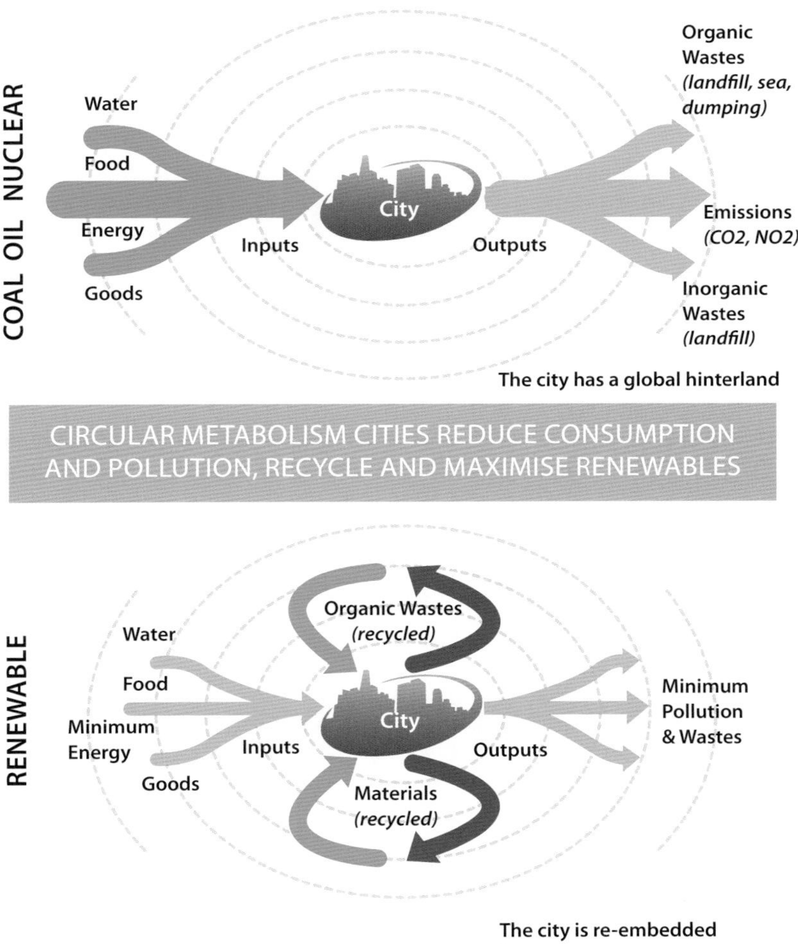

Figure 5.8: *From linear to circular: in an urbanising world the metabolism of cities must become compatible with the ecosystems of planet Earth.* ***Source:*** *H. Girardet and R. Lawrence*

On a predominantly urban planet, cities need to find practical ways to mimic nature's circular metabolic systems. Waste outputs will need to become useful inputs into local and regional production systems. It is particularly important to convert the vast quantities of urban organic waste into compost, and to return the plant nutrients and carbon they contain to farmland that feeds our cities.

Biological resources

A particularly urgent issue that needs to be addressed in an urbanising world is how to capture the plant nutrients contained in sewage. We need to find viable ways of intercepting the vast amounts of nitrogen, phosphates and potassium that pass through urban sewage systems, the main macro-nutrients needed for growing crops. The human metabolism only absorbs a fraction of these nutrients contained in the food we consume.

The uni-directional plant nutrient flow, from the farmland to the city, and never back again, has tangible historic origins. This problematic approach was pioneered in Rome 2,000 years ago with the construction of the 'cloaca maxima' through which much of the city's sewage was flushed into the Mediterranean. The loss of soil fertility of the farmland of North Africa, which supplied grain to the people of Rome for centuries, has been well documented.[xi]

In this context the environmental history of London is of also interest once again: to meet the water needs of millions of people from the late eighteenth century onwards, London had to construct a complex pipe network for circulating groundwater around the city with the aid of steam-powered pumps. But London's water table, as well as the water in the river Thames, was increasingly polluted by overflowing cesspits and industrial activity, and sanitary conditions became intolerable. A cholera epidemic in 1853–4 killed nearly 11,000 Londoners. Eventually, in a pioneering feat of environmental detective work, a medical doctor, John Snow, traced a major cholera outbreak in Soho to well water that was contaminated with human excrement.

By the late 1850s London had developed really serious digestion problems as well. More and more houses installed water closets from which sewage was flushed into the Thames. 1958 was the notorious year of the 'great stink', when sewage pollution of the river became an overwhelming problem, concentrating the minds of the members of the House of Parliament wonderfully. How could the sewage produced by millions of people be dealt with? A passionate debate ensued and various schemes were discussed. One was a recycling system consisting of metal pipes arranged like the spokes of a wheel through which the sewage would be transported to fields on the urban fringe to be used for growing crops.

Justus Liebig, a famous chemist, favoured such a scheme. He was called over from Germany to make proposals for cleaning up the Thames. Liebig's primary concern was to capture the plant nutrients contained in the food consumed by Londoners. If the nitrogen, potash, phosphate, magnesium and calcium contained in sewage were never to be returned to the farmland feeding Londoners, how could it stay productive? In a letter to Prime Minister Sir Robert Peel, Leibig expressed his concerns about London repeating mistakes made by Rome 2,000 years earlier, but on a much larger scale:

> ***The cause of the exhaustion of the soil is sought in the customs and habits of the towns people, i.e., in the construction of water closets, which do not admit of a collection and preservation of the liquid and solid excrement. They do not return in Britain to the fields, but are carried by the rivers into the sea. The equilibrium in the fertility of the soil is destroyed by this incessant removal of phosphates and can only be restored by an equivalent supply ... If it was possible to bring back to the fields of Scotland and England all those phosphates which have been carried to the sea in the last 50 years, the crops would increase to double the quantity of former years.***[xii]

Figure 5.9: *Beckton Sewage Works in South London. Waste water treatment is becoming an ever more sophisticated process, but its main task still is to keep people away from pathogens rather than processing the plant nutrients contained in sewage into organic fertiliser.* ***Source.*** *H. Girardet*

But Liebig failed to persuade the Metropolitan Board of Works to build a sewage recycling system. After much debate, the engineer Joseph Bazalgette was commissioned to build 82 miles of large sewers along the Thames and a network of smaller sewage pipes criss-crossing London. From 1865, 20,000 men worked for 13 years to construct the world's most extensive and expensive sewage collection and disposal system. The 1866 Sanitary Act mandated the connection of all London's buildings to Bazalgette's sewage network, which ended downriver at Crossness and Beckton. From there the sewage was flushed into the Thames estuary – out of sight, out of mind. When the system was up and running, the exposure of Londoners to their own sewage ended for good and cholera became a thing of the past.

But as a direct consequence of London deciding to build a sewage disposal rather than a recycling system, Liebig and other scientists set to work on the development of artificial fertilisers: to find a way to replenish the fertility of farmland feeding cities such as London – and other cities across Europe – by artificial means. The age of chemical agriculture had arrived. I would argue that this historic development significantly contributed to the unsustainability of both agricultural and urban systems today.

On British farms in the late nineteenth century, guano, cheaply available from Chile and Peru, temporarily became the primary source of crop nutrients, until artificial fertilisers, containing phosphates, nitrates and potash, had been fully developed a few decades later.

The decisions on sewage treatment taken in London in the nineteenth century still reverberate around the world today. Most cities have constructed sewage disposal rather than recycling systems, and the farmland feeding them is being kept productive artificially by the use of chemical fertilisers. The result is that coastal waters everywhere are 'enriched' by urban sewage and pollutants from industry and households, as well as the fertiliser and pesticide run-off from farms. There must be better ways to design urban waste-water processing systems, particularly in new cities where major investments in sewage infrastructure have yet to be made.

Berlin, Rieselfelder

In Berlin a different approach was taken. When it started to grow rapidly in the late nineteenth century, becoming the world's third largest city by 1870, with over 800,000 thousand people, the question of how to ensure hygienic conditions and what to do with its sewage became a major concern.

Influenced by Robert Koch's pioneering ideas about urban hygiene and Liebig's circular economy ideas, Berlin went for a sewage recycling system. The city rented permeable land in its periphery for use as 'Rieselfelder' – sewage irrigation fields. The waste water was collected in a city-wide sewage system from which pipes radiated out to the Rieselfelder.

Eventually, a total of 10,000 hectares were used for the dual purpose of treating waste water for hygienic purposes by biological means, as well as using the nitrogen, phosphate and potash contained in the sewage for growing fruit, vegetables and grass. Some of the sewage was also channelled into reed beds where the plant roots took up the nutrients.

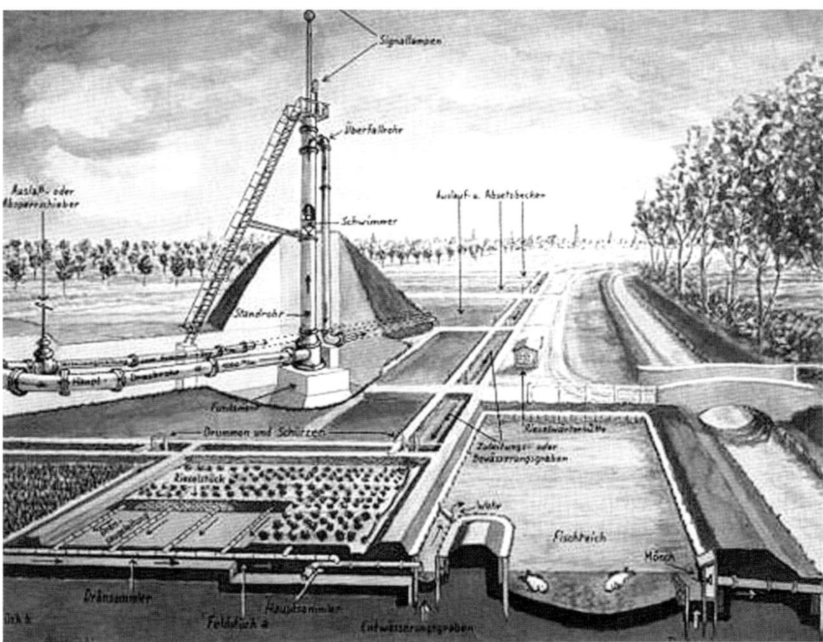

Figure 5.10: *The 'Rieselfelder' sewage systems in cities such as Berlin were designed to capture plant nutrients and to return them to the farmland and orchards feeding cities. Whilst accumulation of heavy metals and chemicals in soils from sewage recycling have been a concern in the past, modern technologies should enable us to eliminate such problems.* ***Source:*** *Berlin City Archive*

The system operated for over 100 years until the 1970s, when it became apparent that the mixing of human sewage with industrial effluents caused a build-up of contaminants in the soil, making it clear that mixed sewage was unsuitable for use as a fertiliser. Technical sewage treatment plants came to replace most of the biologically-based sewage irrigation farms. But in Berlin, and elsewhere, some untreated sewage is still used for sewage irrigation of farmland and forests, or filtered through reed beds or constructed wetlands which are used as nature reserves. The use of wastewater irrigation on farmland near Adelaide (Chapter 7) shows the contemporary relevance of this technology for crop production.

When considering biological waste water treatment for a particular application, it is crucially important to understand the origin of the water to be treated, particular where discharges from factories mix with domestic sewage. The deindustrialisation of many European, American and Australian cities should make sewage irrigation of farmland more feasible once again. The example of the Virginia cropland irrigation system north of Adelaide (Chapter 7) indicates that waste water can now be 'cleaned' sufficiently to allow its use in food production.

Across Europe, many cities have reconfigured their sewage irrigation farms in recent decades. For instance, when a modern sewage plant was built for the city of Münster in Germany in recent years, the former sewage irrigation farm six kilometres outside the city was turned into a nature reserve that offers food and shelter to a large variety of birds throughout the year. Many other European cities have created similar wetland reserves.

New thinking on waste water treatment is urgently needed. The reality is that the soils of many countries that are supplying food to cities are becoming more and more depleted of carbon and plant nutrients due to intensive use of chemical fertilisers and non-sustainable farming practices. Decreasing yields due to loss of soil structure and organic matter are a major long-term threat to global urban food supplies in a climate-challenged world. In arid climates, in particular, poor soil quality is a growing concern. Lack of organic matter has also reduced the water-holding capacity of farmland soils. Farmers have tried to counteract these problems with ever more intensive cultivation methods. The disconnection between cities and farmland, which affects the viability of farming enterprises as well as food supplies to cities, needs to be challenged.

New visions

The vision of the regenerative city incorporates a full circle of waste water recycling and reuse. While considerable progress has been made in organic waste recycling and composting, the loss of plant nutrients from sewage discharge still has to be addressed in an effective manner.

New technologies are becoming available, particularly in decentralising sewage treatment. Waste water can be dealt with beneficially at the level of neighbourhoods or individual buildings for reuse twice: once for use in cleaning and gardening, the second time for sanitation. The result can be a substantial reduction in the waste water volume, as well as the cost and energy required for sewage treatment. A very subtantial reduction in fresh water demand can also be achieved. The key question to be addressed by many cities is this: are they faced with a water *supply crisis* or a water *management crisis?*[xiii]

Limits on available nutrients constrain how well crop plants can grow and how much carbon dioxide they absorb. The various substances originate in different ways: Potash is available in large amounts from mines in many parts of the world. Nitrogen fertilisers are mostly synthesised from nitrogen gas in the air by the use of fossil fuels. But phosphorus, an element without which crops can't be grown, is a much more limited resource. 90 per cent of global supplies are available from mines in only six countries – Morocco, Tunisia, Saudi Arabia, China, Russia and the United States. Within a few decades, this critically important resource could be depleted if the phosphorus discarded in urban sewage is not reclaimed. The challenge now is for cities to close the human phosphorus cycle.

Figure 5.11: *Phosphate plays a vital role in biological systems: its availability may govern the growth rate of organisms. Most phosphorus compounds used today are consumed as fertilisers. The best phosphate deposits have now been largely exhausted, and 'peak phosphate' is looming: a time when the maximum global phosphorus production rate is reached. Capturing phosphate from urban sewage is thus becoming a necessity: Crops to feed cities can't be grown without this mineral.* ***Source:*** *Florida Geological Survey*

Fortunately a number of companies around the world have realised that a potential phosphate scarcity is a new business opportunity. Dutch companies, in particular, have developed technologies for turning phosphate from sewage sludge and municipal organic waste and manure into fertilisers and soil improvement materials. The European Union is developing legislation for both recycling phosphate and for its more efficient use in agriculture.[xiv]

All in all, it is becoming critically important to minimise nutrient outflows from our cities. Sewage recycling can make a vital contribution to assuring urban food supplies from peri-urban farmland as well as reducing the ecological damage caused by discharging nutrient-rich effluent into aquatic and marine ecosystems. A better system for dealing with effluent discharged from our cities is only one of many issues that need to be addressed....

The challenge of decoupling

Many researchers have tried to address wasteful and environmentally damaging production systems in recent years, and to conceptualise viable steps towards creating regenerative use of resources. In this context, the Cradle to Cradle methodology, developed by Michael Braungart and Bill McDonough, is an important conceptual tool. Its starting point is concern about entropy. Importantly it aims to model human industry on nature's processes, viewing materials as nutrients circulating in efficient and waste-free systems. The model applies not only to the design of industrial processes but also to building design, economics and social systems.[xv]

Braungart and McDonough are working with innovative companies on materials assessment, waste and energy balances, lifecycle design and design for disassembly. Their work has great relevance for new approaches to urban systems design. The premise is that we need 'clean' production systems that help to protect and enrich ecosystems. Nature's biological metabolism needs to be enhanced by the circular flow of 'organic nutrients' while industry's technical metabolism must be designed to ensure the circulation of safe, productive 'technical nutrients'.[xvi]

In the UK the Cradle to Cradle concept has been adopted by the Ellen MacArthur Foundation, which makes this statement: 'The linear "take, make, dispose" model relies on large quantities of easily accessible resources and energy, and as such is increasingly unfit for the reality in which it operates. Working towards efficiency – a reduction of resources and fossil energy consumed per unit of manufacturing output – will not alter the finite nature of their stocks but can only delay the inevitable. A change of the entire operating system seems necessary.'

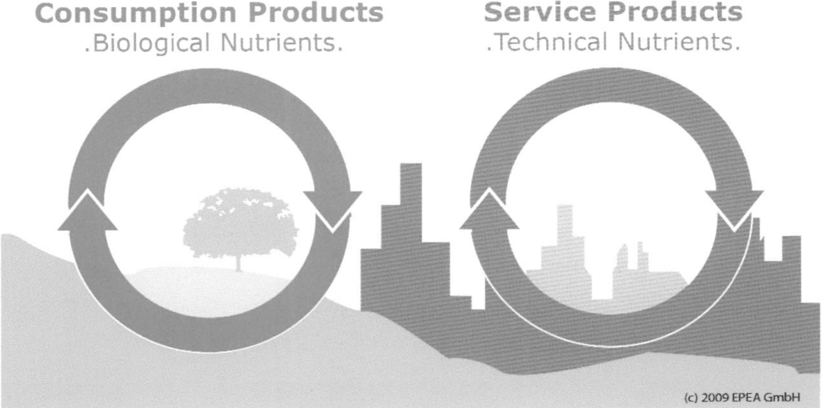

Figure 5.12: *The Cradle to Cradle concept is of critical importance for the creation of regenerative cities and industrial production systems. In recycling, the biological cycle needs to be kept separate from the technical cycle to avoid contamination of the biosphere.* ***Source:*** *Michael Braungart and William McDonough*

Conserving natural capital

The resource use of modern cities requires a fundamental revision, which in turn, requires new approaches to economic theory. The work of ecological economists Herman Daly and Robert Constanza is an important intellectual resource in this context. They state that a minimum necessary condition for future-proofing the relationship between humans and nature is the conservation of natural capital – both renewable and non-renewable:

- **For non-renewable capital the proceeds from resource exploitation need to be re-invested into renewable natural capital such as solar and wind energy.**
- **For renewable capital, resource consumption needs to be limited to sustainable yield levels. This largely applies to biological resources.**

Only in this way can a constant stock of natural capital can be maintained. The preservation of a constant per capita stock of natural capital also requires maintaining stable human populations.[xvii] However, the reality is that population growth continues apace in many developing countries and particularly their cities.

The analysis of Daly and Constanza draws on the work of economist and statistician Nicholas Georgescu-Roegen. Memorably, he stated: 'Our policy toward natural resources in relation to future generations must seek to minimize regrets.'

Georgescu-Roegen's ground-breaking book *The Entropy Law and the Economic Process* outlined the dependence of the economic system on bio-physical systems. He argued that according to the second law of thermodynamics it is impossible to maintain a constant stock of natural capital, since all planetary resources will eventually be degraded or exhausted.[xviii] But he also emphasised that whilst the supply of fossil fuels is limited, there is a great potential to utilise the vast amounts of solar energy that are received by the Earth. Major investments in 'solar energy, organic agriculture, population limitation, product durability, moderate consumption and international equity' could jointly counter entropy.[xix]

Figure 5.13: *Making efficient use of resources is, above all else, an educational challenge. Young people, here in Barcelona, have to become actively involved in discussions about resource consumption and minimising waste disposal.* ***Source:*** *H. Girardet*

This perspective is further amplified by the Austrian scientist Ludwig von Bertalanffy, inventor of the concept of *general systems theory*. During his research in Europe and America he concluded that living systems somehow avoid the inevitable degradation suffered by physical systems. Instead, living systems maintain themselves in a high state of order or 'steady state'.

In his 1932 book *Theoretische Biologie,* Bertalanffy argued that traditional closed system models based on classical science and the second law of thermodynamics were inadequate for explaining living systems. 'The conventional formulations of physics are, in principle, inapplicable to the living organism being open system having a steady state. We may well suspect that many characteristics of living systems which are paradoxical in view of the laws of physics are a consequence of this fact.'[xx]

Thus, living systems maintain themselves in a steady state, and can avoid the increase of entropy, and may even develop towards states of increased order and organisation.[xxi] The crucial point here is that whilst the Earth is basically closed materially, it is open to massive daily solar energy inflows. It thus becomes paramount to base human production and long-term well-being on this virtually inexhaustible solar resource.

James Lovelock, the author of the *Gaia Theory*, came to the same conclusion: he argued that the biosphere has a regulatory effect on the Earth's environment that acts to sustain life. To find signs of life on a planet, one must look for signs of a 'reduction or a reversal of entropy'.

The value of ecosystems services

We cannot manage what we do not measure and we are not measuring either the value of nature's benefits or the costs of their loss. We seem to be navigating the new and unfamiliar waters of ecological scarcities and climate risks with faulty instruments. Replacing our obsolete economic compass could help economics become part of the solution to reverse our declining ecosystems and biodiversity loss.

We need a new compass to set different policy directions, change incentive structures, reduce or phase out perverse subsidies, and engage business leaders in a vision for a new economy. Holistic economics – or economics that recognise the value of nature's services and the costs of their loss – is needed to set the stage for a new 'green economy'.

(Pavan Sukhdev, drawing on his report 'The Economics of Ecoystems and Biodiversity'[xxii])

A realistic response to this perspective is to look at ways in which cities can contribute to countering entropy by increasing their reliance on solar energy and biological processes: enhancing biodiversity and living matter within cities, reforestation to stabilise soils and absorb carbon dioxide, composting organic wastes and incorporating them in soils to enhance their vitality, purifying and reusing liquid waste flows, and reviving streams, rivers, lakes and coastal waters to enhance their biological health and vitality.

Cities need to be understood, first and foremost, as organic living systems. Above all else, this requires ecological literacy – a new understanding of the need for a regenerative relationship between cities and ecosystems. Good urban design should mimic low-entropy natural systems. We would be well served to learn from the metabolism of nature's closed-loop systems in which all wastes are recycled into resources for future growth.

City people are well placed to respond to the looming urban resource use crisis. Many new environmental, cultural and social initiatives in recent years have been initiated by NGOs based in cities. As centres of finance, economic and political power and the media, they are also particularly well-placed to implement change.

Notes

i *Wikipedia, Coal,* http://en.wikipedia.org/wiki/Coal.

ii Post Carbon Institute, http://energy-reality.org/energy-fueled-economic-growth/; *Wikipedia, Tonne of Oil Equivalent,* http://en.wikipedia.org/wiki/Tonne_of_oil_equivalent.

iii www.nytimes.com/2013/09/28/science/global-climate-change-report.html.

iv Brahic, C. (2009) Humanity's Carbon Budget Set at One Trillion Tonnes, *New Scientist*, 29 April.

v WBSD *Efficiency in Buildings Research Project,* www.wbcsd.org/transformingthemarketeeb.aspx.

vi Planet Save, http://planetsave.com/2011/10/27/how-much-energy-does-the-internet-consume/#kVkWpMz3WvCtWbow.99.

vii Leidreiter, A. (2012) *Renewable Energy Regions*, World Future Council, Hamburg.

viii UNEP, www.unep.org/resourcepanel/publications/decoupling/tabid/56048/default.aspx.

ix *Wikipedia, Downcycling,* http://en.wikipedia.org/wiki/Downcycling.

x *Wikipedia, Electronic Waste,* http://en.wikipedia.org/wiki/Electronic_waste.

xi Seymour, J. and Girardet, H. (1986) *Far From Paradiese: The Story of Man's Impact on the Environment*, BBC Publications, London.

xii Liebig, J. (1976 edition) *Agriculturchemie*, Friedrich Vieweg und Sohn, Braunschweig, pp. 88–92.

xiii Girardet, H., Leidreiter, A. and You, N. (2011) *Towards the Regenerative City*, UN-Habitat Urban World, www.unhabitat.org/downloads/docs/UW-RegenerativeCityCC.pdf.

xiv UPI.Com, *Delayed EU Phosphorus Plan Coming Soon,* www.upi.com/Business_News/Energy-Resources/2013/03/11/Delayed-EU-phosphorus-plans-coming-soon/UPI-14571362974700/#ixzz2TGryBd3D.

xv *Wikipedia, Cradle to Cradle*, http://en.wikipedia.org/wiki/Cradle-to-cradle_design.

xvi McDonough, W. and Braungart, M. (2002) *Cradle to Cradle: Remaking the Way We Make Things*, Jonathan Cape, London.

xvii Costanza, R. and Daly, H. (1992) Natural Capital and Sustainable Development, Conservation Biology, 6(1).

xviii Georgescu-Roegen, N. (1971) *The Entropy Law and the Economic Process*, Harvard

University Press, Cambridge, MA.

xix Georgescu-Roegen, N. (1993), www.landecon.cam.ac.uk/up211/SD/reading/SD_ISEE.pdf.

xx www.informationphilosopher.com/solutions/scientists/bertalanffy/.

xxi Bertalanffy, L. von (1969) *General System Theory*, George Braziller, New York, pp. 39–40.

xxii Sukhdev, P. (2008) *The Economics of Ecosystems and Biodiversity, Routledge*, Abingdon.

Chapter 6

Ecopolis

The regenerative city

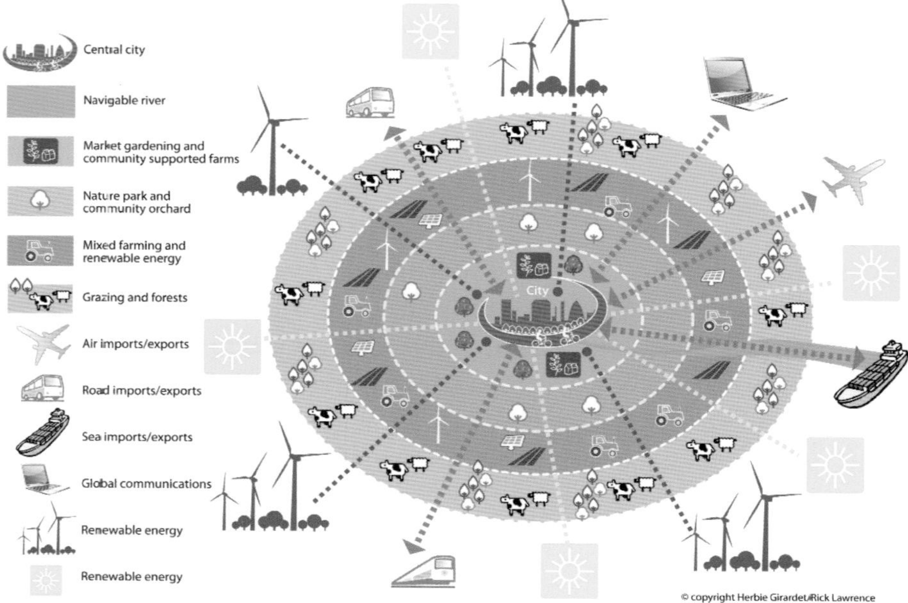

Figure 6.1: Ecopolis – the city that reconnects to its local hinterland, utilising new renewable energy and regenerative, soil restoring food production systems. ***Credit:*** *H. Girardet and R. Lawrence*

In an age of climate change and peaking oil supplies, Petropolis is an outmoded model of urbanisation. Whilst fossil fuel powered cities are still growing and spreading throughout the developing world, there is little doubt that Petropolis has a profoundly uncertain future. The feast of energy and resource consumption we are engaged in is an exercise in accelerated entropy – it is up against non-negotiable natural laws and limits.

This chapter seeks to present the alternative concept of Ecopolis, the idea of regenerative urbanisation, aiming to address these questions:

- **Can cities minimise fossil fuel dependence and switch to renewable energy instead?**
- **Can they reduce their vast, sprawling, global ecological footprints?**
- **Can they reconnect to their local countryside for efficient food supplies?**
- **Can they implement a circular metabolism to regenerate regional soils and ecosystems?**
- **Can they facilitate the creation of new green business and job opportunities?**

In this chapter I use the terms Ecopolis and Regenerative Cities interchangeably. My proposals are intended to be relevant to both existing and newly built cities: in developed countries there is an urgent need for the *ecological refurbishment* of existing cities. In developing countries Ecopolis could be a useful concept for the design and management of newly emerging cities.

In recent years, the term 'Ecopolis' has been used by several writers, mainly in Germany and Australia. Rüdiger Lutz used the term in a book published in 1987.[i] Eckhart Hahn (1993) developed the concept of the 'ecological refurbishment of cities'.[ii] Paul Downton (2009) further developed the concept of Ecopolis in Australia.[iii] It is a twin of the term 'Ecocity', which was formulated and popularised by Richard Register (1987) in the United States.[iv] The challenge now is to turn tentative proposals into a tangible reality.

Beyond sustainability

Since the 1992 UN Rio Earth Summit, the many problems associated with urban and industrial growth are meant to be dealt with by the implementation of sustainable development (SD) as a guiding principle for collective human action. But is it still fit for purpose? The official definition, originating in the Brundtland report, is well known: 'Sustainable development is development that meets the needs of the present without compromising the ability of future generations to meet their own needs.'[v]

Sustainable development is a concept to which few people would object. Most of us would agree that we should try not to live as though there was no tomorrow. But the fact is that since 1992, SD has come to mean just about anything: from the pursuit of the 'triple bottom line', to the efforts by companies to secure sustainable profits, to the worship of 'Gaia'. For business, sustainability tends to primarily be about improving the operating efficiencies of production processes, often linked to useful cost reductions, with reductions of environmental impacts as a secondary concern. For governments, SD has become an issue to be referred to in important speeches but largely ignored in policy making. In a broad sense, SD has become subject to intellectual entropy – being devalued and degraded by the interpretations of specific interests. It has become a rubber band that can be stretched in many directions.

It is probable that the world today is a little bit more sustainable than if SD had never been defined and, supposedly, adopted by the world community. But, by and large, human impacts on the world's life support systems are getting ever greater. Sustainable development has not got to grips with the prevailing ideology of never-ending economic and urban growth in a materially finite world. There is little evidence of the richer countries providing *sustainable development* aid to emerging countries.

Old-fashioned economic growth, powered by fossil fuels and contributing to ecosystems depletion and climate change, is still being fervently pursued across much of the world. While the developed countries are desperate to restore economic growth at times of great financial upheaval, the emerging countries, with well over half the world's population, have been playing catch-up, growing at seven per cent or more a year with little concern about resulting environmental impacts.

I would argue, then, that because so much damage has been and is being inflicted on the world's ecosystems, and solutions need to be found to actively reverse these impacts, we need to move on from *sustainable* towards *regenerative* development. If cities are to be our primary habitat, their long-term viability depends on powering themselves with renewable energy, on developing a circular metabolism, and on regenerating soils, forests and watercourses – rather than just aiming to sustain them in a degraded condition.

Vigorous public pressure is required to ensure that policy makers and the commercial sector act long term. But to guide this process, the general public needs to develop a clear understanding of the huge challenges we face. It could therefore be useful to show how integrated, regenerative urban development can offer plausible new opportunities to all concerned.

Cities tend to exist for a long time and their infrastructure systems can stay in place for hundreds of years. And yet too often they are dependent on the whims of politicians who may only be in power for a short few years and who will tend to make decisions accordingly. In a world dominated by short-termism, a primary challenge is to find realistic ways for long-term perspectives to prevail and to make our cities function in an environmentally responsible, regenerative manner.

Infrastructure investments

An important issue in this context is the need for very substantial investments in the infrastructure of cities. A recent report by Booz Allen

Hamilton, the global strategy and technology consulting firm, suggests that the world's urban infrastructure systems need an astonishing $40 trillion investment 'to bring them up to date'. According to the report, the vast and complex systems used to deliver water, electricity and transport services in urban areas are inadequate in both older cities that are suffering from decaying infrastructures, as well as in newer cities that are still developing their infrastructure systems. The report says that to ensure maximum synergies, water, sewage and electricity schemes should be developed jointly rather than separately.[vi]

This report only talks about the basics. It does not even take account of the vast challenge and opportunities inherent in retrofitting cities to enhance their environmental performance rather than simply to improve service provision. To meet the environmental challenges of the twenty-first century, and to make cities truly compatible with the Earth's ecosystems, requires a global investment programme driven by a new set of priorities: less concrete, more compost; less tarmac, more cycle routes; less large power stations, more local renewable energy; less imported food, more local food.

To this end, the general public needs to exert democratic pressure on local and central governments, based on plausible proposals. It needs to insist on forward-looking practices that ensure the long-term viability of cities. We need a compass to set new urban policy directions, change incentive structures, phase out perverse subsidies, and engage political and business leaders in the creation of a thriving green economy. To this end, the use of eco-feedback technology is needed to provide people with information flows about their environmental impacts and how these can be reduced.

Urban regeneration and regenerative cities

In recent years there have been a great many urban regeneration initiatives in shrinking, run-down cities of industrialised countries. Europe and the United States have their fair share of these, particularly in former coal mining and steel producing areas. These initiatives aim, above all else, at restoring the urban fabric – the 'intra-urban' environment. Some have also been concerned with improving 'peri-urban' areas – turning brownfield sites – coal slag heaps or derelict factory sites – into landscape parks or new housing developments. Such regeneration projects have quite rightly received much funding and media attention, and they have improved the lives of millions of people.[vii]

The idea of creating *regenerative cities* builds on such initiatives but it goes further: it is about a wider horizon, about linking comprehensive measures for improving the conditions of city life with measures for creating an environmentally enhancing, restorative relationship between humanity and the natural world.

Regenerative cities have to be created from the inside out: people need pleasant spaces for life, work and play; they need urban environments that are free from pollution and waste accumulation; they need to benefit from bringing urban energy systems and economies 'back home'; but they also need to live in the certainty that their daily lives are not detrimental to the ecosystems on whose health their cities depend.

New cultural, social and environmental initiatives usually originate in major cities, where NGOs, and research, information and communication clusters are concentrated. Financial, economic and political power is also based there and needs to be directed towards regenerative development. With the right policy and financial stimuli, the creation of new, dynamic green urban economies and lifestyles should be feasible.

Figure 6.2: *To change their consumption patterns, people need eco-feedback. In the Brazilian city of Curitiba, electronic display boards inform the public about how their recycling of paper and cardboard has reduced the numbers of trees that had to be cut down.* ***Source:*** *H. Girardet*

Beyond petroleum: renewable energy, smart cities

Given worldwide concerns about climate change, and given that fossil fuels are a finite resource, with peak oil looming on the horizon, coal, oil and gas can only be the primary energy source for cities for limited periods of time. Can we move out of Petropolis and make ourselves at home in Ecopolis instead? Can cities wean themselves off their daily fix of fossil fuels and power themselves by renewable energy (RE)?

It is clear that the high-energy density of fossil fuels has made them the favourite candidate for powering cities. However, the potential for much more efficient use of energy, as already discussed in Chapter 6, and the many breakthroughs in renewable energy and energy storage technologies should allow for a smooth transition away from fossil fuels over the coming decades.

Many cities have expressed this ambition – led by Scandinavian cities such as Copenhagen and Stockholm. The renewable energy revolution is well on its way. Depending on their geographical location, a variety of options are available. Use of geothermal energy is a realistic prospect in some places. And many cities can often draw on substantial amounts of biogas: combined heat-and-power systems powered by biogas produced from waste material have been and are being implemented in many cities.

But renewable wind and solar energy are prime candidates for powering cities and they are making great advances in many places. Their efficient use makes cities less vulnerable to rising oil and gas prices; it encourages innovation and creates local businesses and jobs; it stimulates the smart use of energy; and it reduces air pollution and urban carbon footprints.

In many parts of the world, solar rooftop installations for electricity as well as hot water are particularly suitable for use within cities. Solar thermal technology has been used for many years in the sunny Mediterranean, and its use is most widespread in both Israel and Palestine, where the costs are fully competitive with fossil fuel energy. The technology is being refined all the time and is also becoming commonplace in less sunny countries. It has found a remarkable expression on some landmark buildings.

Figure 6.3: *In the Chinese city of Dezhou the main employer is Himin Solar, the world's largest producer of solar hot water systems. This iconic building is the company's headquarters. Most of Dezhou's buildings are equipped with solar hot water systems.* ***Source:*** *Himin Solar*

China is the world leader in solar thermal technology. By 2013 China had over 1,000 manufacturers with revenues of over 20 billion yuan ($3 billion) which employed 600,000 people. Some 25 per cent of its buildings now have solar thermal systems – often on houses whose inhabitants never had the benefit of hot water before. By 2010 the number of solar water heaters installed in China equalled the thermal equivalent of the electrical capacity of 40 large nuclear power plants. In 2012 Beijing, with its huge air pollution problems, passed regulations obliging all new residential buildings of up to 12 floors – as well as hotels, schools, hospitals and swimming pools – to install solar thermal systems. Globally, solar water heaters produce as much energy as 140 nuclear power stations.[viii]

The rapid strides that have been made with the development of renewable energy (RE) technologies have not happened by chance: many breakthroughs have been facilitated by government policies. Denmark was the first nation to introduce feed-in tariffs (FITs) for wind energy in the 1980s. At that time 50 KW wind turbines were the norm, but by 2013 their potential output per turbine had risen 100 times to five megawatts or more.

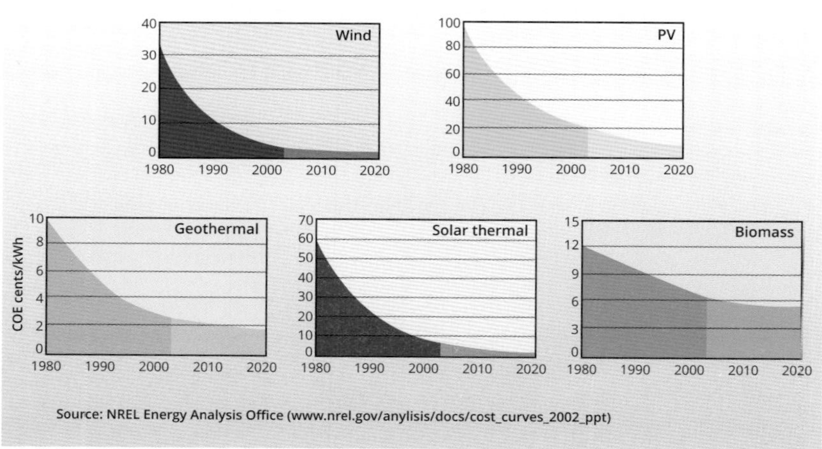

Figure 6.4: The cost reductions of all RE technologies have been dramatic in recent years and this trend will continue, with cost competiveness with fossil fuel systems moving ever closer. ***Source:*** *National Renewable Energy Laboratory*

Solar PV, too, has undergone an astonishing transformation, mainly due to the introduction of feed-in-tariffs in countries such as Denmark, Germany and Australia. They are the electricity part of what is also sometimes called

'Clean Energy Cashback' – paying people a favourable tariff for creating their own green electricity. Additional costs for these programmes are borne by all electricity consumers proportionally. FITs have been introduced in over 50 countries and regions across the world. They have massively increased the uptake of RE, have greatly accelerated innovation and production volumes, and have brought about a dramatic cost reduction of RE technology across the world.

In many cities, retrofitting the roofs and facades of buildings with solar energy systems has huge potential. For cities consisting primarily of tall buildings, it is becoming particularly important to find cost-effective ways of integrating PV systems in vertical glass facades.

Figure 6.5: *Taiwan's National Stadium in Kaohsiung, designed by Toyo Ito, with a capacity of 55,000, is the world's first solar-powered stadium. It is also a power station that can supply over one gigawatt a year to the neighbouring communities.* ***Source:*** *Kaohsiung City*

While cities are finding out that they can supply substantial amounts of energy from within their own built-up areas, particularly from solar energy, further supplies are needed from elsewhere. A large proportion of RE required by cities should come from peri-urban areas, under a principle that could be called 'energy subsidiarity', meaning that as much renewable energy should be supplied from as nearby as possible, using combinations of various renewable energy technologies.

Wind power is well on its way to supplying a large proportion of Europe's electricity needs. In Denmark, on-shore wind farms developed rapidly in the 1990s because of active government support for wind cooperatives. By 2001 over 100,000 Danish families belonged to government-supported wind cooperatives, which had installed 86 per cent of all the wind turbines. Local people had a direct financial benefit from wind power development, supplying major conurbations such as Copenhagen.

In Germany, too, hundreds of thousands of people have invested in citizen-owned wind farms, and thousands of small- and medium-sized enterprises have been established in the new sector. Community ownership, supported by government legislation, has helped wind power gain high social acceptance, particularly on the North Sea coast with its high average wind speeds.[ix]

In Britain, on-shore wind farms are less popular because many are built by commercial developers on land adjoining villages with no benefit to the local community. Community ownership would probably counter this 'nimbyism'. Meanwhile, large-scale off-shore wind farm development has been initiated, despite the higher cost. Off-shore wind energy has huge potential for powering British cities because most are located close to the coast.

Figure 6.6: *In the UK, wind power is making rapid strides. In 2013 the London Array, in the Thames estuary off the coast of Kent, was the world's largest wind farm. With its 175 turbines it has the capacity to power 500,000 homes.* ***Source:*** *Siemens*

By 2013 there were over 800 turbines in wind farms around Britain's coasts, with a capacity of 2,700 MW. The London Array in the Thames Estuary is a particularly striking example. At the end of 2013 it was the world's largest off-shore wind farm with a maximum capacity of 630 MW. A total of 175 turbines had been installed, capable of powering half a million homes and reducing CO_2 emissions by 900,000 tonnes a year.[x]

Since wind power and solar energy can only be generated when the wind is blowing or the sun is shining – and because supply does not always correspond with demand – back-up and storage capacity is required. A great variety of technologies are being developed for this purpose. In Germany some cities are installing large lithium-ion battery storage systems. Pumped-storage hydropower connected to water reservoirs can play a crucial role in securing a stable RE power supply for Europe, though some of this won't be in the vicinity of cities.

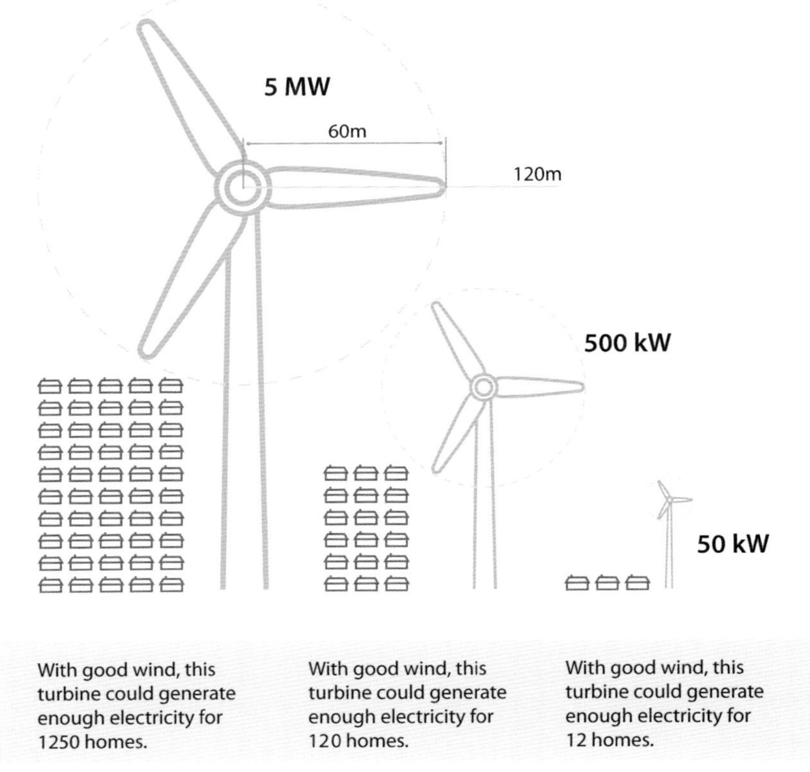

Figure 6.7:** Wind power up-scaling: in the last 30 years wind turbine technology has evolved dramatically, driven above all else by policies such as feed-in tariffs.* ***Source: *H. Girardet, R. Lawrence*

Norway's highly developed hydropower system, with half of Europe's reservoir capacity, could play an important part here. On windy and sunny days, surplus power could pump water from lower to higher altitude reservoirs. This water could then be released to generate power on days when demand is high and RE supplies are low. This cycle can be repeated over and over again.[xi]

Whilst local or regional supply of RE is being actively pursued, longer distance networks of interconnected solar, wind, hydropower and geothermal systems are also being discussed across the world. The Desertec project, supported by major European companies, aims to link RE installations in North Africa and the Middle East with European cities via direct current transmission lines. Other projects aim to transmit RE electricity across North America and Asia via new 'smart supergrids'.[xii]

The options for renewable energy vary greatly according to urban locations and also the size of cities. There is little doubt that it will be much easier to retrofit smaller cities with efficient renewable energy systems than urban areas of many millions of inhabitants.

Large-scale hydro and nuclear

One response to the need to reduce the reliance of cities on fossil fuels has been to supply power from large dams and their reservoirs. It is clear, however, that it would have been impossible to construct the many thousands of dams that already exist across the world without huge inputs of fossil fuel energy, particularly for the vast quantities of cement involved.

The United States pioneered large hydroelectric dams in the 1930s, most notably the Hoover Dam on the Colorado River which supplies electricity (and water) to cities such as Los Angeles, Phoenix and Las Vegas. The Grand Coulee Dam on the Columbia River, completed in 1942, is the largest in the United States. It enabled the growth of Portland and Seattle, as well as creating huge new areas of irrigated farmland. Whilst these dams enabled the growth of major US cities, benefitting their populations, they also deprived local indigenous communities of their traditional fishing and hunting grounds.

In Soviet Russia after the Second World War a series of dams were built on the Volga to supply electricity to Nizhny Novgorod, Samara, Kama, Volgograd and Votkinsk. The Aswan Dam in Egypt, completed in 1976, produces power and water for Cairo. Its electricity is also used to produce artificial fertiliser for farmers along the Nile who no longer benefit from the nutrient-rich silt deposited by the river's annual floods. The 19 million inhabitants of Sao Paulo, too, rely on hydropower. Its electricity supply comes from the huge Itaipu Dam, as well as smaller local dams.

The list of more recent dam projects is long: the Three Gorges Dam in China, on the Yangtze, the world's largest power station, supplies electricity and water to Chongqing and Wuhan; the Theri Dam on the Ganges in northern India was built primarily for Delhi's benefit; the Xiaoshuichi Dam on the Yellow River supplies Lanzhou City; the Grand Ethiopian Renaissance Dam and the Gibe III Dam are being built primarily for the benefit of Addis Ababa. The Great Inga Dam on the Congo, the largest dam project of them all, is supposed to start construction in 2015, and would supply power to cities across central Africa.

Large dams and large-scale urbanisation are closely linked. By the start of the twenty-first century, some 50,000 large dams had been built on more than half of the Earth's major rivers. More are being built all the time. But are they benign? Whilst they ensure electricity and water supplies to cities, the consequences of these massive structures have often been highly problematic. They have displaced tens of millions of people, they have inundated villages and towns and huge areas of wetlands, forests and farmland, and they have wiped out living species and particularly migrating fish populations.[xiii]

Hydropower is listed as a renewable energy source but many reservoirs have limited lifespans because of siltation and flaws in the design of dams. It remains to be seen whether the ever increasing cost-effectiveness of less invasive renewable energy technologies will make large dams a less attractive proposition in coming decades.

And then there is nuclear power. Despite a number of very serious accidents, and despite the huge cost of decommissioning, it still has many advocates. They delight in pointing to the relatively low carbon emissions in countries such as France, with some 75 per cent nuclear electricity supplies. By 2013 there were some 430 commercial nuclear power reactors operating in 31 countries, with over 370,000 MW of total capacity. A further 70 reactors were under construction.[xiv]

Again, there is a close connection between nuclear power and urban energy consumption. Whilst only a few countries still have actively nuclear building programmes, China, with its vast megacities, is pursuing a major nuclear programme, with 28 reactors under construction at the end of 2013. Some people have called nuclear energy a green energy source, but never in history has there been an energy source associated with as many risks and long-term costs as nuclear energy.

***Figure 6.8:** Three Gorges, China, the world's largest hydroelectric dam. Large dam projects have proliferated in the last 80 years, powering cities across the world. However, whilst they often produce huge amounts of electricity as well as irrigation water, they also present a massive, often detrimental impact on local environments and people.* ***Source:** www.news.cn*

Regenerative cities and privatisation

In recent decades, many urban services that were publicly or municipally owned and operated have been outsourced or globalised, and taken over by profit-driven businesses. This makes it harder to generate meaningful change. Creating regenerative cities is a major organisational challenge if city authorities don't have the capacity to operate well-integrated services. In many places energy and water supplies, public transport and waste management are operated by companies for whom the public interest is a secondary concern. The only advantage is that private companies tend to find it easier to raise money on financial markets, which sometimes helps to improve services delivery.

In some places there has been strong opposition to privatisation. In Latin America, privatisation was accelerated in the 1980s and 1990s due to the external imposition of neo-liberal economic policies. Municipal electricity, water, transport and telecommunication suppliers were sold off to international companies. Whilst consumers in some places benefitted from the improvement of some services, politicians and their cronies were often seen to pocket bribes. As a result there was much public resentment. In public opinion surveys across Latin America, 70 per cent of respondents saw privatisation of service companies as a detrimental development.[xv]

In Europe, privatisation of municipally owned services also proceeded rapidly during the same period. Cities have effectively haemorrhaged vast amounts of money that might otherwise have stayed in local circulation. Could the creation of resource-efficient cities, largely supplied with renewable energy from their roof tops and their local hinterland, improve the resilience of urban economies, bring money back into local circulation and create new jobs back in our cities?

In Germany, in particular, this agenda is being vigorously pursued due to public pressure. A large number of city authorities have been buying back municipal energy companies from the private sector. The aim is to create a socially just, climatically beneficial and democratically controlled energy supply from regenerative sources. In many cities privatised energy companies are being taken back into municipal ownership to enable the development of smart, integrated urban energy systems.

However, across Europe many cities face the challenge of precarious finances, often due to the fact that they have very limited tax-raising powers. This often makes it difficult to raise enough capital to take services companies back into public or municipal ownership. It is therefore crucial to initiate steps to redirect money flows by enabling the general public to actively participate in budgeting decisions.

In the Brazilian city of Porto Alegre, which has a population of 1.5 million people, the concept of participatory budgeting has been implemented to great effect since 1989, expanding democratic involvement in financial decision making. All citizens can have a say about what their tax money should be spent on – better schools, better transport, playgrounds, parks, renewable energy installations, and so on. Porto Alegre spends about 200 million dollars per year on such services and this money is subject to participatory budgeting. Through this method Porto Alegre has become a truly dynamic, participatory city. The process involves four basic steps:

- **community members identify spending priorities and select budget delegates;**
- **budget delegates develop specific spending proposals, with help from experts;**
- **community members vote on which proposals they want to see funded;**
- **the city government implements the most popular proposals.**

Following the example of Porto Alegre, participatory budgeting has spread to hundreds of other Latin American cities, and dozens of cities in Europe, Asia, Africa and North America. In India, Arvind Kejriwal, the national conveyor of Aam Aadmi Party, is trying to introduce the concept of participatory budgeting to the whole country. [xvi]

Food for cities

As Chapter 2 indicates, the growth of cities has historically been shaped by the availability of food from their hinterland. Historically, city governments were closely involved in ensuring continuous food supplies to their citizens. But, as we have also seen, industrialisation and transport technology have increasingly disconnected cities from their local countryside. City authorities have stopped managing urban food flows. Food supplies have come to be largely provided by commercial suppliers. Most recently, deregulation and other neo-liberal trade policies have left food supplies to our cities in the hands of vast conglomerates and supermarket chains.

But there are also contradictory forces at work: whilst food is traded globally as never before, there are also strong public demands in many city regions for greater reliance on regional supplies. This is partly due to a growing recognition that whilst the world's demand for food is increasing, its capacity to produce that food is being reduced. As both rural and urban populations on the Earth grow, less and less land is available per person. Greater reliance on local supplies reconnects consumers to local producers and can also help to feed the world's growing numbers of affluent people.

In most of the world's cities, ample food supplies are largely taken for granted. Cities have come to depend on food imported from an increasingly global hinterland. London, as we saw, has a surface area of some 160,000 ha, but its food supplies require over 50 times its own area, or around 8.4 million ha. Much of that land, of course, is located at a distance in countries such as the United States, Canada, Brazil, Kenya or New Zealand.

The largest land surfaces required for feeding cities in developed countries are used for producing grain and animal feed such as maize and soybeans. Today some 30 per cent of the Earth's land surface – or 70 per cent of all agricultural land – is needed for rearing farmed animals, and a third of this is used to produce animal feed. (See also Chapter 4.) A typical meat-intensive diet requires up to 2.5 times the amount of land needed for a vegetarian diet, and five times that of a vegan diet. One hectare of farmland can feed up to 30 people with vegetables, fruits, cereals and vegetable fats. If the same area is used for producing eggs, milk and meat, the number of people fed from one hectare goes down to between five and ten.[xvii]

Figure 6.9: *Traditionally, the few oases in the Gulf region, such as Ala Hasa in Saudia Arabia, with its three million date palms, supplied most of the food consumed by the sparse population of the peninsula. Recently the region's rapid population growth has resulted in a massive increase in food demand from farmland elsewhere.* ***Source:*** *H. Girardet*

A further issue is that the total energy input into the global food system – production, storage, processing and distribution – is vast: as long ago as 1972 more than 20 per cent of the UK's primary energy was devoted to feeding its population, almost a tonne of oil per head. If this was applied globally, 40 per cent of global fuel consumption (in 1972 terms) would be required.[xviii]

Since developing countries are increasingly copying Western urban diets and lifestyles, their land requirements are increasing rapidly. Under current trends we may eventually need three planets, to meet our demand for food and forest products, and to sequester carbon emissions, rather than our one home planet. But it isn't that easy to make new planets, and it seems implausible that we could settle new ones.

Cities take up just 3–4 per cent of the Earth's land surface, but they tend to be built on some of the best farmland. For this and other reasons, good quality farmland is becoming increasingly scarce: World Bank research has established that every year soil erosion, salinisation, climate change and other factors are currently causing some two million hectares of rain fed and irrigated farmland to be lost from production.[xix]

But this research does not make the important link between land degradation and urban food consumption: the problem that cities absorb vast amounts of food without returning plant nutrients and organic matter back to the farmland that feeds them. This is a systemic problem that needs to be vigorously addressed.

According to FAO research, the availability of arable land per person has decreased from 4,307 m^2 in 1961 to 2,137 m^2 in 2007. The main causes are a steadily growing world population, as well as the loss of fertile soils and arable land through prevailing farming practices. Meanwhile, according to Oxfam research, water and food scarcity is causing the deaths of about 24,000 people every day.

And then there is the issue of food waste. In developing countries it is primarily an issue of inadequate food storage, but in highly urbanised countries the main problem is wasteful food consumption: the FAO estimates that one-third of all food produced worldwide – worth around $1 trillion – gets lost or wasted in production, storage and consumption. A study by the UK's Institute of Mechanical Engineers estimates that half of all the food produced in the world – equivalent to two billion tonnes – ends up as waste every year.[xx]

In times of shrinking resources and a steadily growing human population, it is crucial to ensure the maintenance and creation of fertile, humus-rich soils. Compost can play a major role here by improving soil structure. Nutrient- and humus-rich soil can reduce artificial fertiliser use, and can help farmers deal with adverse environmental conditions, such as severe floods and droughts.

Composting organic waste on a large scale can help to tackle some of the world's greatest challenges, such as water and food scarcity, climate change, the loss of soil fertility and even rural–urban migration. Higher organic content of soils also helps to increase its water-holding capacity, and to reduce plant diseases. But while farmers struggle with loss of soil fertility and the threat of decreasing yields, valuable biomass is often dumped and left to rot. In some countries, locally available biomass is not reused while compost is actually imported from abroad.

Composting projects can help to secure the viable existence of farms, stimulate local economies, provide people with regular employment and qualify for emission reduction payments. It is therefore essential to find new ways of using biomass from cities for production of high-quality compost, particularly for use on nearby farmland.[xxi]

Relearning urban agriculture

To reduce the pressure on the world's productive land and to help ensure long-term food security, city people would be well advised to help revive urban or peri-urban agriculture. While large cities will always require some food, and particularly grain, from other places, local food growing should be regarded as an important component of urban living.

We need to find efficient and environmentally enhancing ways of feeding ourselves. To this end, we need to initiate new processes of 'ecological densification' – making good, well-considered use of limited areas of land – to meet increased food demands by increasing numbers of people.

In many countries, large minorities of people grow food in and around cities. In countries where rural–urban migration is prevalent, many people become urban and peri-urban food producers, on a full- or part-time basis. According to the UNDP, some 800 million people were engaged in urban agriculture worldwide in 1999. Of these, 200 million were thought to be market producers, with 150 million people employed full-time.

Cities such as Havana, Accra, Dar-es-Salaam and Shanghai have been studied extensively. But in thousands of other cities people are also quietly getting on with producing food. Urban agriculture in developing countries can greatly contribute to urban food security, improved nutrition, poverty alleviation and local economic development. In developed countries it can contribute to the reduction of 'food miles' – with local distribution via farmers' markets and specialised shops.

In recent years I have had the opportunity to witness urban agriculture in many places. I was interested in this because, among other things, urban agriculture can help cities to put organic waste materials to good, productive use.

In order to survive in a globalising food system, urban farmers must be highly innovative and adaptable. They grow fruits, vegetables, herbs, tree seedlings and ornamental plants, as well as raising animals. They have to cope with city constraints and tap as effectively as possible into urban assets and resource flows.

Whilst often discouraged by local authorities until recently, urban food production is being practised in many places. In recent years its importance has been increasingly acknowledged by researchers, politicians and urban planners for its potential of creating viable livelihoods for urban people.

Urban agriculture often builds on ancient traditions. Historically, most cities 'emerged' out of their own productive hinterland, and some contemporary cities are still deeply 'embedded' in their local landscapes, even in Europe. Many Mediterranean cities are still surrounded by orange and olive groves, vineyards and wheat fields on which a large proportion of their food requirements are grown. They still have very strong relationships with their immediate hinterland.

I found the same in China. China has an age-old tradition of settlements permeated with food-growing areas. Today, at a time of very rapid urban-industrial growth, urban agriculture is still a very important issue for the Chinese. Even megacities, such as Shanghai, with about 15 per cent population growth per year, one of the fastest growing cities on the planet, maintain their urban farming as an important part of their economic systems. A major shift has taken place, however, from 'intra-urban' to 'peri-urban' agriculture. As housing and office developments have grown within the city, farmland there has been lost and food growing has shifted increasingly to the city's periphery.

Tens of thousands of hectares on the outskirts of Shanghai are intensely cultivated with a great variety of vegetables. The Chinese like to cook fresh, locally grown vegetables. Stir-frying wilted vegetables is not regarded favourably. Glass and polythene greenhouses are now much in evidence, producing three to four successive crops a year in Shanghai's warm climate.

Figure 6.10: *In Shanghai much food used to be grown within the city. In recent years peri-urban agriculture has taken over from intra-urban cropping. Whilst some land has been paved over as the city expanded, large areas of peri-urban land are still being set aside for vegetable production for local markets.* ***Source:*** *H. Girardet*

On the outskirts of Beijing, too, vegetable cultivation is much in evidence. But farmers have had to develop ingenious systems to cope with the much colder climate there and with limited water supplies. Greenhouses, too, are much in evidence. During frosty conditions in January and February, they cover their polythene tunnels with several layers of bamboo mats in the evening to keep the heat in at night. Few growers in and around Beijing use coal-fired heating systems in their greenhouses to cope with the icy conditions outside.

In Chinese cities, 'closed-loop' systems, using night soil as fertilisers for urban vegetable growing, are still practised in some places. The night soil is diluted, perhaps ten to one, and then ladled onto vegetables beds. I was told that people prefer vegetables grown with night soil fertiliser because of their superior taste. But most new apartment and office buildings, which are in evidence everywhere, have water closets, and it remains to be seen whether appropriate ways of using their waste water in urban farming can be developed.

In Russia, too, peri-urban food growing is an age-old tradition, with many people retreating to their *dachas* at weekends to cultivate crops in highly productive gardens. In St. Petersburg many people are involved in peri-urban farming: there are some 560,000 plots being cultivated on the periphery of the city. Even in remote places such as Irkutsk in Siberia, with its very short growing season, I have seen people cultivate an great variety of vegetables, including cucumbers and tomatoes, in well-insulated greenhouses, both for home supply as well as for sale in markets.

In South Africa, of course, during the apartheid days it was forbidden for the black majority to grow food on land within and around cities, because that meant people were there to stay. But in today's South Africa a dramatic growth of urban agriculture is underway as people get a permanent foothold in their towns and cities. And throughout Africa, in Ghana, Kenya, Tanzania and elsewhere, much food growing takes places within cities, because they are often still very low density and there is room for food growing. Women tend to be the cultivators in urban areas.

Urban agriculture is an important aspect of the wider issue of urban sustainability, by being able to supply food from close-by as well as offering livelihoods for city people. Another important issue, as already discussed, is the efficient use of nutrients from the urban metabolism that would otherwise end up as pollutants in rivers and coastal waters.

In many cities attempts are being made to use waste water in urban food production. This applies particularly to cities in hot and dry places. For instance, in Adelaide, Australia, tens of thousands of hectares of land on the edge of the city are cultivated using waste water from the city for irrigation, growing vegetables as well as grapes and other fruit. There is some concern about trace quantities of heavy metals that could accumulate in the soil, but it would take decades to cause any problems. Establishing new waste-water crop irrigation systems, as Adelaide has done (Chapter 7), is crucial for regenerative systems of urban agriculture.

Figure 6.11: *Until recently the use of night soil as a source of soil fertility was commonly practised in China and much of Asia. The common use of flush toilets in new housing estates is bringing this traditional practice to an end. Can China find ways of updating its highly effective traditional systems of plant nutrient recycling to ensure the long-term fertility of its farmland?* ***Source:*** *H. Girardet*

Cities and carbon sequestration

A healthy balance sheet matches income and outgoings – in fact, on the balance sheet of a thriving company or household, income exceeds outgoings. But not so in the world's global carbon balance sheet: year after year we are running up ever greater deficits. For instance, WWF's annual Living Planet Reports indicate clearly that in our dealings with nature we are creating ever greater imbalances. We need to deal with the reality that we are consuming the resources that underpin the world's ecosystems services much faster than they are being replenished. Humanity's global ecological footprint now exceeds the world's capacity to regenerate by about 30 per cent.[xxii]

Indisputably, this state of affairs cannot continue. Whilst fossil fuel burning has massively increased in the last 300 years, the capacity of the biosphere to absorb it has been significantly reduced at the same time. Dr Rattan Lal, Professor of Soil Science at Ohio State University, has calculated that 476 billion tonnes (Gt) of carbon have been emitted from farmland soils due to inappropriate farming and grazing practices, compared with 270 Gt emitted from over 150 years of burning of fossil fuels.[xxiii]

Other scientists estimate that 200 to 250 Gt of carbon have been lost from the biosphere as a whole in the last 300 years. These reductions of 'living carbon potential' have resulted from deforestation, biodiversity loss, accelerated soil erosion, loss of soil organic matter, salinisation of soils, costal water pollution, and acidification of the oceans. Can the disruptive impact of an urbanising humanity on nature's carbon cycle, which is causing these ever worsening instabilities, be brought back into balance by deliberate action, and what role can cities play in this process?

An important point in this context is that carbon dioxide should not be simply regarded as a 'bad' that has to be locked up out of harm's way in underground caverns, but that it can be turned into a 'good' that can be used to enhance the well-being of the biosphere and humanity.

Over the course of some 300 million years, carbon was drawn down by living organisms from the atmosphere and 'relocated' in the Earth's crust, ultimately becoming fossil fuel. In the last 300 years we have reversed this process of biological carbon sequestration, and have transferred hundreds of billions of tonnes of carbon back into the atmosphere, with increasingly dire consequences. How can we balance the books? How can we help to re-establish a carbon cycle where income and outgoings are matched?

We must take a new look at how better land-use and forest management can further enhance biological carbon sequestration. There has been much discussion about the feasibility of geo-sequestration of CO_2 from power stations, refineries, etc. However, I think that we need to give priority to *biological* carbon capture and storage or bio-sequestration, through deliberate measures of forest protection, reforestation, the improvement of soil by incorporation of compost and 'biochar', and by restoring ocean vegetation.

It is important to realise that well-thought-out bio-sequestration has multiple benefits for both nature and human society: absorbing surplus carbon also offers significant opportunities for biodiversity protection, soil erosion prevention and, potentially, enhanced food production and poverty reduction in rural areas. This could even help to enhance the economic viability of rural communities in an age in which billions of people have been and are being forced to move to cities to try and earn a better living.

Internationally, the 'Billion Trees Campaign' initiated by UNEP in 2007 recorded that over ten billion trees had been planted by 2010, a quarter of these by urban community groups, NGOs and local governments.[xxiv] Meanwhile IUCN, the International Union for the Conservation of Nature, has started the 'Plant a Pledge' initiative to regenerate no less than 150 million hectares of degraded land across the planet by 2020. Many national and local governments are part of this historic initiative.[xxv]

The regenerative development of ecosystems serving such large cities is a tall order, but must be pursued with vigour. If cities do not proactively regenerate run-down ecosystems – including watershed forests, farm soils, and marine ecosystems from which they draw essential resources, their long-term prospects look bleak. While cities continue to burn fossil fuels, they also need to find ways to sequester their carbon dioxide emissions through 'bio-sequestration' in soils and forests.[xxvi]

Cities have little intrinsic bio-sequestration capacity, and must therefore rely upon territories elsewhere for this.[xxvii] The CO_2 output of cities is far too large for trees within their territories to be able to absorb. Every year we are now discharging over ten billion tonnes of carbon per year, of which four to five billion tonnes are not being reabsorbed into the world's ecosystems but are accumulating in the atmosphere. This is the primary cause of climate change.[xxviii]

In a recent article, NASA climatologist Jim Hansen and others stated that reforestation of degraded land and improved agricultural practices that retain soil carbon, between them, could lower atmospheric CO_2 by as much as 50 parts per million.[xxix] If the carbon sequestration potential of restoring seagrass meadows, kelp forests and other types of aquatic vegetation is added, we can reach fairly optimistic conclusions. However, only joint initiatives on bio-sequestration involving many different groups will ultimately achieve the desired goal of a climate-proof world. There is more about this in the case studies in Chapter 8.

Ecopolis and money

Our current money system continually redistributes wealth from the large majority to a small minority. [xxx] In many parts of the world it also redistributes money from local communities to central government, and, indeed, from consumers to large companies.

A major challenge many cities face are the rules of economic globalisation, not only regarding services provision but also the outsourcing of the production of consumer goods to wherever they are cheapest and most profitable. The ongoing transfer of manufacturing jobs to other parts of the world has shrunk the economic base of many cities, particularly in Europe and the United States. Can their economies be rebuilt under the auspices of regenerative development?

If cities are to ensure that the right approaches to infrastructure and service provision are to be in place by 2050, new financing mechanisms need to emerge. Given the long lead-time for implementing major new infrastructure development, there is a great urgency in defining appropriate solutions. Research into innovative financing mechanisms can be enhanced through online discussions and platforms shared by cities across the world.

In recent decades money has been flowing to the corners of the planet where it could earn the highest possible return, regardless of the wider consequences. The current system favours entrepreneurs who, first and foremost, act in their own self-interest and that of their shareholders, who have little loyalty to particular locations. Environmental externalities can be largely ignored, resulting in a sub-optimal resource allocation. Firms can thus disregard many of the real costs of production, such as pollution of rivers, local air pollution, global climate change, and local job losses. They benefit from the fact that these externalities are difficult to measure and to price accurately. Externalities thus affect resource allocation by distorting pricing mechanisms. And consumers often lack adequate information to make the right choices.

Further work is needed to challenge the perceived financial benefits of economic globalisation. Only if the benefits of economic and financial localisation become clearly apparent, will cities – and national governments – want to act to accelerate measures in this direction.

Figure 6.12: *Many towns and cities across Europe have created their own local currency. They are intended to create a circular financial metabolism, reducing the outflow of money to the global economy, and thus to stimulate local enterprise.* ***Source:*** *Bristol City Council*

The information revolution

Theorists such as Saskia Sassen and Manuel Castells conceptualise global cities as the command and control centres for contemporary global capitalism. Cities such as London and New York have a global sphere of influence; cities such as Tokyo, Hong Kong, Singapore or Shanghai are striving for similar levels of international influence; whereas dozens of other large cities play a less important global role. Small towns, in turn, may only have a sphere of influence of a few dozen kilometres.

According to Manuel Castells, 'the new economy is organised around global networks of capital, management, and information, whose access to technological know-how is at the roots of productivity and competitiveness'. Castells sees the emergence of a global network society: power 'is no longer concentrated in institutions (the state), organisations (capitalist firms), or symbolic controllers (corporate media, churches). It is diffused in global networks of wealth ... information and images, which circulate and transmute in a system of variable geometry and dematerialised geography'.[xxxi]

From a similar perspective, Saskia Sassen has developed a 'global city hypothesis'. She argues that a handful of global cities have become:

- **concentrated command points in the organisation of the world economy;**
- **important centres for finance and specialised producer service firms;**
- **coordinators of state power;**
- **sites of innovative forms of industrialisation and production; and**
- **markets for the products and innovations produced.**[xxxii]

Power and influence grows by the use of new information technologies. The impact of the Information Revolution could be even larger than the Industrial Revolution, profoundly changing the way we live, work, learn and recreate. Networks are replacing communities, with virtual meeting places and markets that are not rooted in place. Global networks are transcending communities based on location and shared experience. The Greek agora, the Roman forum, the town square and the village green are being reinvented in websites and Internet chat rooms. But meanwhile, powerful companies are also using these same technologies to further their own interests outside any democratic control.

> ***We need to understand the functioning of, and possibilities for, changing specific systems of power – economic systems, transportation systems and so on – that entail modes of resource use that are environmentally unsound. The fact that these various systems combine in urban formations is a condition that is analytically distinct from the actual systems involved.***
>
> ***(Saskia Sassen)***

Today, urbanisation and Internet-based economic and financial globalisation are closely intertwined. Cities have become the nodes of globalised production as well as consumption, with unprecedented throughputs of resources and industrial products becoming the norm in the wealthier countries. But in developing countries, too, urban growth is intimately linked to ever increasing per-capita use of fossil fuels and, with it, to impacts on ever more distant ecosystems.

Global cities are the main players in this transformation. They may be economically powerful, but smaller cities may offer more satisfactory living conditions. They tend to be more locally and regionally connected, and because they have better access to their local hinterland, they may find it easier to turn themselves into regenerative cities

Global city networks

These are matters not just for individual cities but for the international organisations that connect cities to each other. Across the world, cities need to work closely together to develop and implement measures for regenerating 'dependent regions' that have been damaged and depleted by their consumption patterns. One or two organisations, such as the Climate Alliance of European Cities, which brings together 1,500 towns and cities across Europe, have made a tentative start at helping cities to take responsibility for their global climatic impacts.[xxxiii]

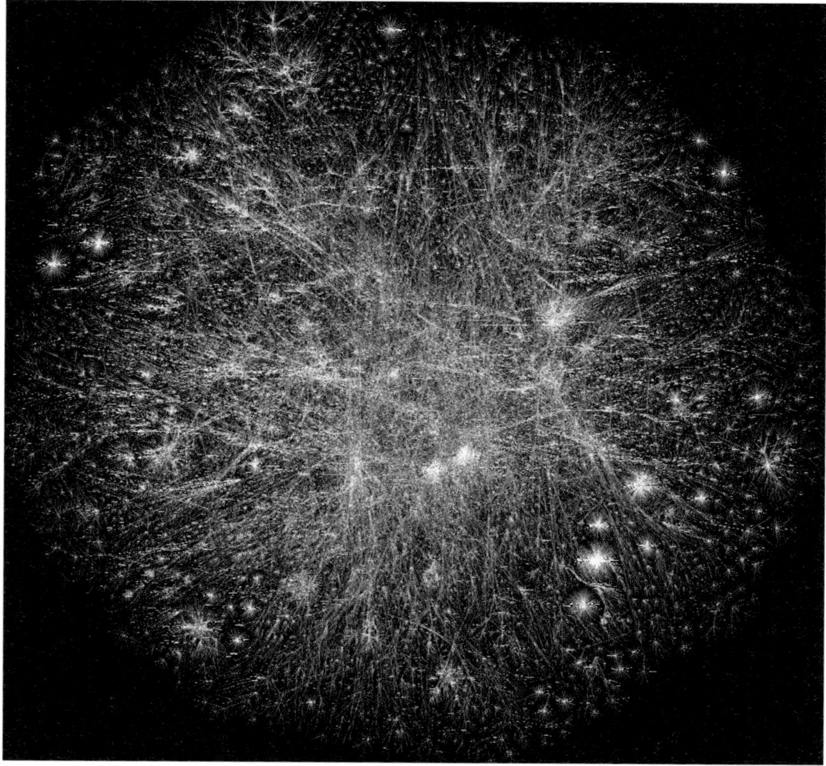

Figure 6.13: *A 'portrait' of the Internet. It connects humanity as never before. The challenge is to create an effective interactive global learning process that truly addresses the huge challenges that humanity faces.* ***Source:*** *National Science Foundation*

There is an ever growing number of organisations that are dealing with environmental concerns: the International Council for Local Environment Initiative (ICLEI), C40, and Energy Cities are just a few of many. The Internet – which in many ways is functioning as a virtual city – is becoming a crucially important tool for spreading information and connecting people to each other across the world. A substantial part of the material presented in this book has been drawn from the Internet.

Internationally, cities are increasingly working together in many different organisations and associations to develop and implement policies for sustainable development across the world. The concept of regenerative cities is implicit in some of their initiatives. The challenge now is to get it widely adopted as a plausible concept that can help to future-proof our urbanising world.

There is no doubt cities cannot possibly act alone to undertake the crucial task of regenerative urban development. But many more policy instruments are needed.

Enabling policy frameworks – nationally, regionally, locally

It is clear that citizens and urban decision makers need to develop a new understanding of the global nature of urban impacts: we all need to realise that today, *urban* boundaries in a urbanising world are effectively *planetary* boundaries, that every city needs to preserve and help regenerate its natural resources base, and that there are tangible benefits to be gained from doing this.

It may be the role of NGOs to point out the crucial importance of a reciprocal 'give-and-take relationship' between cities and natural systems, and to stimulate the introduction of appropriate policy frameworks. Creating environmentally regenerative cities is a new challenge for urban planners, architects, administrators and educators. Implementation tends to fall outside the usual remits of most urban policy makers, and beyond the horizon of most members of the general public. It is crucially important, therefore, for city authorities to set up new departments concerned with the bigger picture, and to combine their likely findings into integrated decision making processes.

In an urbanising world, national governments and international bodies have to work with urban decision makers to ensure that the *triumph* of the city does not end up as a global environmental *tragedy*. Many national governments have already introduced important policies such as waste disposal taxation, circular economy legislation, carbon taxes, energy efficiency ratings and feed-in tariffs for renewable energy which are primarily implemented at the local level. Zero waste policies and support schemes for sustainable local food production are also in place in some countries.

There is plenty of evidence that much can be done to bring substantial sections of urban economies 'back home', particularly by more efficient water, waste and energy management, and widespread use of RE technologies. The World Future Council is lobbying for national agencies for the regenerative development of cities to be established.

The following recommendations are divided between local, regional and national governments.

Local government level

- Set ambitious but realistic goals for regenerative urban development.
- Use cities networks to learn what comparable cities have achieved.
- Set out a roadmap to ensure implementation of policy measures.
- Ensure that achievements are measured, documented and replicated.
- Make sure to engage as many stakeholders as possible.
- Establish a revolving fund to finance regenerative development policies.
- Develop public–private partnerships for large regenerative development projects.

National and regional government

- Recognise the important role of cities in the regenerative development transition.
- Provide suitable financing for innovative model projects at local level.
- Establish a national regenerative development coordination body.
- Expand policies such as feed-in tariffs, green taxes and energy efficiency standards.
- Promote regulations and financial incentives to drive investment in the green economy.
- Adopt new financial tools for quantifying environmental services and costs.
- Withdraw financial support for fossil fuels.

Implementing regenerative urban development is a complex process. It requires creativity and initiative at the local level, but also the creation of appropriate *national* policy frameworks to enable useful things to happen *locally*: suitable measures will involve both 'sticks', such as waste disposal and carbon taxes, and 'carrots', such as feed-in tariffs for renewable energy, and support schemes for local food production. Without national policy initiatives, enhanced by lively public debate, the necessary changes won't happen fast enough, if at all.

Conventional politics tend to be averse to progressive ideas. That is where the importance of green politics cannot be overestimated. In this context the introduction of feed-in tariffs in Denmark and Germany is worth highlighting: in both countries, vigorous public demand for mainstreaming renewable energy was turned into national policy which was then implemented primarily at the local level.

Figure 6.14: *Village migrants on a pavement in Delhi. Rural-urban migration in India is at an unprecedented scale. Can enough new livelihoods in cities be created for village people?* ***Source:*** *H. Girardet*

A future for villages?

Across the world there are about two million villages, many of which originated thousands of years ago. But villages aren't what they used to be – the primary habitat of humanity. The magnetism of the modern city, and the loss of rural employment due to the mechanisation of farming, has taken its toll. The bright lights of Petropolis can't easily be countered by the candle lights or paraffin lamps in a remote village. In many parts of the world rural–urban migration is further amplified by loss of rural livelihoods due to fragmentation of land holdings or deteriorating environmental conditions.

Britain exemplifies these global trends in a particularly vivid manner. With some 80 per cent of people living in cities, only a tiny fraction of the population is still engaged in farming and other aspects of the rural economy. Many villages and small towns, which historically grew out of local landscapes, and were the hubs of farming communities, are now stranded as commuter villages in drive-thru landscapes to which they are barely connected. Similar changes have occurred in much of the rest of Europe.

Because urban growth can have detrimental effects on rural areas, some countries have initiated policies to try to counter rural–urban migration, and to improve living conditions in villages – by rural education and health programmes, improved water supplies and sanitation, road construction, electrification and investment in rural economies. But such policies can also be counterproductive because they tend to introduce urban cultural values into rural areas. The spread of satellite dishes and TV to remote rural communities, in particular, can increase local people's fascination with urban living.

Do villages in 'developed countries' have a future other than as commuter appendages to nearby cities? My first foray into the topic of human settlements was in a book I edited in 1976 called *Land for the People*.[xxxiv] It focused on what I thought of as the imbalance between rural and urban economies in a developed country such as Britain. My chapter in this book was called 'New Towns or New Villages' and the argument was that the time might be right to think of creating new rural livelihoods for people who could no longer get employment in deindustrialised cities or who had simply become disenchanted with city life.

Since the 1970s many attempts have been made to create ecovillages in Europe, North America and Australia. Ecovillages have been defined as a 'human-scale full-featured settlements in which human activities are harmlessly integrated into the natural world in a way that is supportive of healthy human development, and can be successfully continued into the indefinite future'.[xxxv] There is now a vigorous 'Global Ecovillages Network' that spreads know-how on creating new villages, connects ecovillages across the world and also includes many traditional villages that want to reinvigorate themselves with new ideas on permaculture farming, efficient crop irrigation and renewable energy systems.

Findhorn in Moray, Scotland, is the archetypal ecovillage with a permanent population of 350. The Findhorn Foundation is a non-governmental organisation associated with the United Nations. It has 50 years of experience in developing concepts, tools and techniques for creating environmentally-viable human settlements. Findhorn has pioneered innovative buildings made of materials such as local stone and straw bales. It is well known for the stunning fertility and beauty of its gardens and for ecotechnologies such as its Living Machine sewage treatment facility and its electricity-generating wind turbines. It has initiated many social, economic and educational initiatives that are being adopted elsewhere. Findhorn has been recognised for having recorded the lowest ecological footprint for any community in the industrialised world: its average resident consumes only half of the resources and generates one half of the waste of the average British citizen.[xxxvi] In an age in which we need to come up with new ideas for future-proofing human settlements, Findhorn and the Ecovillages Network are making an important contribution.

Figure 6.15: *Findhorn EcoVillage has installed many eco-technologies, including a 'Living Machine' which treats the sewage of up to 350 people. Invented by Canadian scientist John Todd, its tanks contain diverse communities of bacteria, algae, micro-organisms, and numerous species of plants, snails and fish to process the sewage. The resulting water is pure enough to be returned to the local water table or to be used in crop irrigation. The technology has been applied in many places and is suitable for decentralised sewage treatment in communities across the world.* ***Credit:*** *Findhorn*

This book describes some of the environmental consequences of wholesale global urbanisation. Whilst villages have drawn the short straw in the competition with Petropolis, it is time to look at opportunities for making villages a viable part of the future of humanity, particularly in emerging economies. Mahatma Gandhi stated that 'The future of India lies in its villages'. Whilst the sheer pace of urbanisation is running counter to the sentiment of Gandhi's statement, it is finding a new resonance in India. But it is becoming clear that the revival of villages needs to be undertaken with a clear sense of purpose.

In Maharashtra State in western India, Ralegan Siddhi is widely considered as a model of environmental regeneration and conservation. It has some 400 households and a population of 2,300. The village and its semi-arid land cover an area of 1,000 ha. Until the mid-1970s, Ralegan Siddhi was a sorry sight. It had a degraded environment and was afflicted by drought and hunger. Poverty prevailed and many were heavily into drinking liquor. Lack of adequate water supply was a primary issue: the village reservoir, or 'tank', could not hold water as its embankment dam was leaking.

In 1975 Anna Hazare, an Indian social activist, came to head the village of Ralegan Siddhi. As a first step he encouraged the villagers to donate their labour to repair and renew the village tank. Once this was done, the situation started to improve. In the monsoon season of 1975 the tank filled up with water for the first time in living memory. This transformed village life as it provided a secure water supply to the village households as well as irrigation water for their crops.

The villagers then started to dig new irrigation canals. They terraced the fields and planted trees to reduce soil erosion and to supply fruits, nuts and fodder crops for their animals. They also started to install solar PV panels, a wind turbine and a biogas plant: some of the gas was generated from the community toilet. Individual households now have solar lighting, and the village street lights are also solar-powered.

Ralegan Siddhi has a new lease of life: it has water all year, a grain bank, a milk bank and a new school. The World Bank Group has reported that it has been transformed from extreme poverty into one of India's richest villages. By its natural capital and introducing renewable energy, the basis for a new, green economy can be created and village communities can be rebuilt. Ralegan Siddhi is widely seen as a model for the rest of rural India.

In rural Bangladesh the Grameen Shakti (GS) organisation has become very effective and successful by promoting solar home systems (SHS) and biogas technology for low-income households in inaccessible areas. The solar systems are used to light up homes, shops, fishing boats, to run televisions, radios and cassette players, and to charge mobile phones. They are making a major contribution to the viability of villages that are not connected to an electricity grid.

Figure 6.16: *In remote rural areas not connected to the grid, solar energy is becoming an important component of village life. Low interest micro-credit loans have made it affordable for villagers in many places.* ***Source:*** *Grameen Shakti*

GS is one of the largest and fastest growing rural-based renewable energy companies in the world. Its solar systems have become very popular in thousands of villages because they are easy to install anywhere, and there are no monthly bills, no fuel costs, and minimal repair or maintenance costs.

Grameen Shakti enables affordable soft financial credit through affordable installments and an affordable after-sales service. It has made a positive impact on hundreds of thousands of rural people. In addition to solar systems for individual households, it has also introduced a micro-utility model for poorer people who cannot afford their own SHS system. Grameen Shakti also installs biogas plants and promotes the use of organic fertiliser in villages across Bangladesh. By initiating the 'Polli Phone' scheme, it also enables telecommunication through solar-powered mobile phones.[xxxvii]

In the rural areas of many developing countries, renewable energy is widely seen as vital to economic development. The initial investment can be substantial but there are no fuel costs. Localised renewable energy production can liberate and internalise large amounts of capital that would otherwise be required to purchase oil, gas and coal. Oil imports alone for developing countries reached US$100 billion in 2011. According to the International Energy Agency, an annual investment of US$36 billion in renewable off-grid and mini-grid options, would ensure universal access to RE by 2030, and generate millions of meaningful new green jobs, many of these in rural areas.[xxxviii]

Grameen Shakti was established under the umbrella of the Grameen Bank, a community development bank started in Bangladesh that offers micro-credits without requiring collateral to impoverished people whose skills are underutilised. The model has now spread to cities and villages in many parts of the world. The organisation and its founder, Muhammad Yunus, were jointly awarded the Nobel Peace Prize in 2006.

Making ecocities and ecovillages a dominant reality across the world will require a huge shift in perspectives. The two final chapters of this book list a variety of projects which are steps in this direction – starting with initiatives taken within cities and then moving on to discuss projects that aim to complete the picture of what regenerative urbanisation is all about.

Notes

i Lutz, R. (1987) *Ökopolis*, Knaur Verlag, München.

ii Hahn, E. (1993) *Ökologischer Stadtumbau – konzeptionelle Grundlegung*, Lang, Frankfurt.

iii Downton, P. (2009) *Ecopolis, Architecture and Cities for a Changing Climate,* Springer Verlag, Berlin.

iv Register, Richard (1987) *Ecocities – Building Cities in Balance with Nature*, Beverly Hills Books, Berkeley.

v *Our Common Future* (1987) Report of the World Commission on Environment and Development, World Commission on Environment and Development, Oxford Paperback.

vi www.strategy-business.com/press/article/07104?gko=a8c38-1876-23502998.

vii *Wikipedia, Urban Renewal,* en.wikipedia.org/wiki/Urban_renewal.

viii www.treehugger.com/renewable-energy/almost-everyone-has-a-solar-water-heater-in-dezhou-china-video.html.

ix *Wikipedia Community Wind Energy,* http://en.wikipedia.org/wiki/Community_wind_energy#cite_note-emp-10.

x London Array, www.londonarray.com/; http://en.wikipedia.org/wiki/List_of_offshore_wind_farms_in_the_United_Kingdom.

xi www.statkraft.com/energy-sources/hydropower/pumped-storage-hydropower/.

xii Desertec, www.desertec.com.

xiii International Rivers Network, www.internationalrivers.org/problems-with-big-dams.

xiv World Nuclear Association, www.world-nuclear.org/info/Current-and-Future-Generation/Nuclear-Power-in-the-World-Today/.

xv Shirley, M. (2004) *Why is Sector Reform So Unpopular in Latin America?*, The Ronald Coase Institute Working Papers.

xvi *Wikipedia, Participatory Budgeting,* http://en.wikipedia.org/wiki/Participatory_budgeting.

xvii FAO (2006) *Livestock's Long Shadow – Environmental Issues and Options*, Rome.

xviii Leach, G. (1975) *Energy and Food Production*, IIED, London.

xix World Bank, http://web.worldbank.org/WBSITE/EXTERNAL/TOPICS/EXTARD/0,,contentMDK:20452620~pagePK:148956~piPK:216618~theSitePK:336682,00.html.

[xx] Guardian, Environment (January 2013) www.guardian.co.uk/environment/2013/jan/22/reduce-food-waste-campaigners.

[xxi] Soil and More, www.soilandmore.com/.

[xxii] WWF, *Living Planet Report 2008*, www.panda.org/lpr/08.

[xxiii] Jones, C. (2007) *Increased Photosynthetic Capacity Reverses Global Warming*, www.amazingcarbon.com.

[xxiv] UNEP, Billion Trees Programme, www.plant-for-the-planet-billiontreecampaign.org/.

[xxv] Plantapledge, www.plantapledge.com/.

[xxvi] Girardet, H. and Mendonca, M. (2009) *A Renewable World*, chapter 2. Green Books, Dartington

[xxvii] *Wikipedia, Ecological Footprint*, en.wikipedia.org/wiki/Ecological_footprint.

[xxviii] Science Daily, *Global Emissions Speed Up*, www.sciencedaily.com/releases/2008/09/080925072440.htm.

[xxix] Hansen, J., Sato, M., Kharecha, P., Beerling, B., Berner, R., Masson-Delmotte, V., Pagani, M., Raymo, M., Royer, D. and Zachos, J. (2008) Target Atmospheric CO2, Where Should Humanity Aim?, *Open Atmospheric Science Journal*, 2, pp. 217–231.

[xxx] Kennedy, M., www.margritkenney.de.

[xxxi] Castells, M. (1996) *The Network Society*, Blackwell, Oxford.

[xxxii] Sassen, S. (2000) Cities In A World Economy, Pine Forge Press, Thousand Oaks, California; Sassen, S. (2001) Cities in the Global Economy, in Paddison, Ronan, ed., *Handbook of Urban Studies*, Sage Publications, Thousand Oaks.

[xxxiii] European Climate Alliance, www.klimabuendnis.org.

[xxxiv] Girardet, H. (ed.) (1976) *Land for the People*, Crescent Books, London.

[xxxv] Gilman, R. (1991) *The Eco-village Challenge*, Context Institute, www.context.org/iclib/ic29/gilman1.

[xxxvi] www.ecovillagefindhorn.com/news/footprints.php.

[xxxvii] Shakti, G. www.gshakti.org/.

[xxxviii] Biro, F. (April 2011) Chief economist of the International Energy Agency, speaking about the Paris-Nairobi Climate Initiative.

Chapter 7

Case studies, part 1

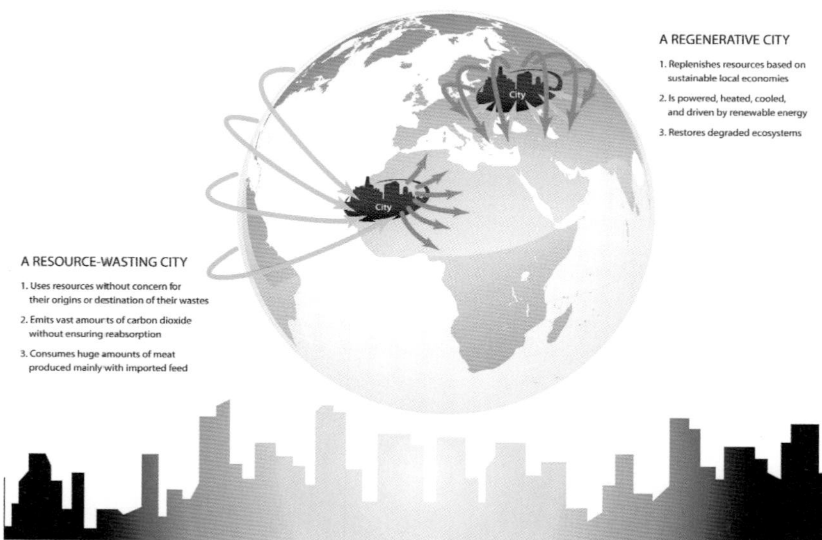

***Figure 7.1:** Perhaps the greatest challenge for our urbanising world is the reduction of the ecological footprints of cities. Can their resource use become compatible with the regenerative capacity of the world's ecosystems? **Source:** H. Girardet and R. Lawrence*

The following case studies show that regenerative urban development is not a utopian pipe dream but that aspects of it are becoming a reality in various places around the world. The spectrum of examples covered here ranges from comprehensive measures taken to improve the performance of whole city regions, to the emergence of urban eco-districts, renewable energy development, circular waste management, regeneration of run-down urban areas, urban agriculture projects, watershed restoration and conservation, and large-scale landscape regeneration.

Adelaide, 2003 to 2013

An urbanising world requires major policy and public participation initiatives to make urban resource use compatible with the world's ecosystems. Metropolitan Adelaide has actively adopted this agenda and is widely recognised as a pioneering regenerative city region. New policies by the government of South Australia on energy efficiency, renewable energy, sustainable transport, waste recycling, organic waste composting, water efficiency, waste-water irrigation of crops, peri-urban agriculture and reforestation have taken Adelaide to the forefront of eco-friendly, regenerative urban development.

Metropolitan Adelaide is a city region of 1.2 million people that has matured over a period of 160 years. The region grew initially by converting territories previously used by the aboriginal hunter-gatherer tribe, the Kaurna people, into farms and pastures. Today Adelaide still has a strong relationship with its rural regions, with its thriving horticultural, wine and mining economy. Hi-tech manufacturing, services and education are playing an important economic role as well. 80 per cent of the population of South Australia lives in Metropolitan Adelaide.

In the 1990s, concern grew about the region's uncertain water supplies and the threat of droughts. The great annual variability of the flow of the Murray River makes Metropolitan Adelaide water-challenged like few other urban regions. After increasingly frequent droughts at the turn of the century, the South Australian government decided that it was time to develop new strategies for 'waterproofing' the city. This stimulated a wider discussion about development trajectories for the region. Were major new initiatives needed? Concern about rising temperatures, and the region's contribution to climate change, were the primary rationale for developing an integrated *urban systems design strategy*, and a targeted programme for implementing this.

A crucially important initiative, taken in the late 1990s, was the construction of a pipeline to take recycled waste water from the Bolivar treatment plant, which treats the waste water of some 600,000 people with state-of-the-art technologies, to an area of peri-urban farmland in a place called Virginia a few miles north of Adelaide. This water, which had previously discharged into the sea, had long been regarded as having potential for irrigating market gardens and vineyards. The Virginia region, with 20,000 hectares, has become South Australia's largest and most diverse market gardening area.[i]

The Virginia pipeline project was funded by a mixture of government equity, private equity and debt. Together with compost supplied from organic waste recycling, as described below, the market gardens of Virginia are a very significant example of regenerative peri-urban land use.

In 2003 I was invited by the then Premier of South Australia, Mike Rann, to be an inaugural 'Thinker in Residence' in Adelaide. This was a unique opportunity to make concrete proposals for a significant further proposal for transforming the city region. During a nine-week period, innumerable seminars and events were held in which a wide cross-section of local people came together to discuss ways in which Metropolitan Adelaide could reinvent itself.

The central theme of my residency was that a vigorous move towards efficient resource use could greatly stimulate South Australia's economy. The reasons for this are quite simple: a city region that takes active measures to improve the efficiency of its use of resources also reduces its reliance on imported resources – it re-localises parts of its energy and food economy and brings a substantial part of it back home. At the end of my residency I published a report called 'Creating a Sustainable Adelaide' which subsequently became the basis for a wide range of new policy initiatives by the government of South Australia.[ii]

The report proposed and elaborated 32 strategies for 'greening' Metropolitan Adelaide. These were scrutinised by a South Australia government cabinet committee during a six-month period and 31 were approved and integrated in government policy in 2004. (Feed-in tariffs for renewable energy were added in 2008 in a speech by the Premier during the 3rd International Solar Cities Conference staged in Adelaide.)

In March 2004 Mike Rann made the following announcement:

> ***Much of what Herbert proposed in his report to the Government after nine weeks in residence studying the way our city works, makes a lot of common sense. That's why we are taking his advice and intend running with his key ideas ... The more we can preserve and improve the environment in which we live, the better positioned we are to build a stronger economy and healthier society.... These measures set a new pace for sustainable development, and set important new precedents for future decision makers.***

Figure 7.2: *Lochiel Park Solar Village is a pioneering low-carbon urban development of 106 houses 8 km from central Adelaide. It boasts highly efficient energy and water use; mandated solar PV and hot water systems; community vegetable gardens; holistic use of locally-produced materials. It is widely regarded as a 'green urban village' of national significance.* ***Source:*** *Cambelltown City Council*

From 2004 onwards, state-level policy frameworks, amplified by lively public debate, and by local creativity and initiative, enabled really useful things to happen. Adelaide set a brisk pace for implementing a wide range of innovative measures which are summarised below. A major transformation was achieved by 2013.

Perhaps most notably from the perspective of regenerative urban development, the composting of organic waste made particularly rapid strides. Compost from urban organic waste is essential for future-proofing the long-term food supply to cities; its incorporation in local soils is of particular importance for regions with poor soil quality and limited rainfall, such as South Australia. The compost enhances the soil's inherent fertility and also greatly improves its water storage capacity.

A large proportion of Adelaide's organic waste is composted by one company, Jeffries. It collects organic waste across the region and processes it at several sites near the city. The matured compost is then returned to farms, vineyards and gardens as soil enhancers. Jeffries has more than tripled its production of compost from some 50,000 to over 170,000 tonnes in the last few years.

Figure 7.3.: *The Jeffries composting facility at Virginia, Adelaide, composts the bulk of the city's organic waste and returns it to nearby market gardens, vineyards and farmland, assuring long-term soil fertility.* ***Source:*** *Jeffries, Adelaide*

Virginia, as described above, is the 'food bowl' of South Australia where a great variety of vegetables, fruit, nuts and vines are cultivated. The region's financial contribution to South Australia's economy includes $120 million of farm gate production, $500 million of food processing, and $474 of interstate income from food trade. There are currently some 2,500 jobs in the industry. A doubling of horticultural output and associated jobs is envisaged over the next 20 years.

Development of renewable energy in Greater Adelaide has also been very rapid in recent years. Following the introduction of feed-in tariffs in 2008, the pace of installation of solar PV roofs was spectacular and exceeded all expectations. Within a few months a large new solar economy was created that employed thousands of people at its peak. The FIT scheme was so successful that in October 2010 the South Australian government felt obliged to scale back the price paid for solar electricity from 46 cents to 16 cents per kWh. Despite this, a total of 120,000 solar roofs were installed or in the process of being installed by the end of 2013.

The South Australian government also set a mandatory wind energy target. The region is particularly well suited to wind farms due to its proximity to the 'Roaring Forties'. South Australia has half of Australia's installed wind power capacity, despite only having 8 per cent of the country's population. By December 2012, South Australia had 13 operational wind farms, with an installed capacity of 1,250 megawatts (MW) and with a further 184 MW under construction. Following some controversy about the location of about wind farms, the South Australian government decided in October 2011 to limit their construction near populated areas.

Metropolitan Adelaide, then, has acquired many attributes of a regenerative city. This is a summary of the transformation that had occurred by December 2013:

- **over 30 per cent of electricity produced by wind turbines and solar PV panels;**
- **photovoltaic roofs on 140,000 (of 600,000) houses, and on most public buildings;**
- **Tindo, the world's first bus running on solar energy;**
- **solar hot water systems mandated for new buildings;**
- **large scale building tune-up programmes across the city region;**
- **60 per cent carbon emissions reduction by municipal buildings;**

- 15 per cent reduction of CO_2 emissions in Greater Adelaide since 2003;
- construction of Lochiel Park Solar Village with 106 eco-homes;
- water sensitive urban development across the city region;
- three million trees planted on 2,000 hectares for CO_2 absorption and biodiversity;
- a zero-waste strategy driven by ambitious recycling incentives;
- 180,000 tonnes of compost a year made from urban organic waste;
- 20,000 hectares of land near Adelaide used for vegetable and fruit crops;
- reclaimed waste water and urban compost used to cultivate this land;
- thousands of new green jobs. [iii]

Figure 7.4: *Adelaide Central Market is where a large proportion of crops grown in the city region are marketed. Hundreds of stall holders share this facility.* ***Source:*** *H. Girardet*

The remarkable story of Copenhagen

In recent decades Copenhagen has done remarkable things towards becoming a liveable as well as a sustainable or even regenerative city. The transformation of much of the inner city into a pedestrian zone was the starting point. This has resulted in a Mediterranean-style ambience where markets, cafes and restaurants proliferate. More people cycle in Copenhagen than in most other cities. And initiatives on energy efficiency, combined heat-

and-power and renewable energy have gone further than almost anywhere in the world and the same goes for waste management. Copenhagen is working to become carbon neutral by 2025!

Public attitudes to resource use have been strongly influenced by vigorous public information campaigns which link people's resource use and climate change.

In the early 1960s traffic congestion in the city centre became a major issue. In 1962 Copenhagen's City Council decided to establish a car-free pedestrian zone in the city's maze of narrow medieval streets and historical squares. The transformation has been remarkable: today, with a total length of almost 3.2 km, it is the most extensive inner-city pedestrian street system in the world.

Figure 7.5: *In Copenhagen, liveability, sustainability and regenerative development have been combined in a very effective way. Pedestrianisation of the city centre goes hand in hand with creation of cycle routes, public transport schemes, combined heat-and power systems, renewable energy development and recycling projects.* ***Source:*** *H. Girardet*

In Copenhagen many urban green solutions, involving large numbers of people, are being implemented. But it has further ambitions: Copenhagen is working to become the world's first carbon neutral capital city by 2025. Its municipal strategic climate action plan combines 50 different initiatives. These have already yielded significant environmental as well as economic benefits. The green sector in the capital region has grown by 55 per cent from 2007 to 2012, creating thousands of new jobs.

Transport

A few decades ago attempts to convince people to use public transport were hindered by massive reductions in travel time for car traffic due to large investments in road infrastructure. Meanwhile, public transport was unreliable and inconvenient because of lack of investment and inadequate integration between transport systems and operators. Copenhagen was faced with the same traffic congestion and pollution problems that have blighted many other cities.

Integrated transport and cycling solutions have changed all that. They have increased mobility and reduced congestion significantly, while benefitting the health of the citizens. Green transport optimises urban space and moves a larger number of people in a more efficient way. It has been shown that within the same amount of space and time, one person can be transported by car, 4.5 persons by bus and six persons by bicycle!

Figure7.6: *Copenhagen has more cyclists than most other European cities due to a highly developed network of cycle lanes.* ***Source:*** *Copenhagen City Council*

By investing in a convenient, reliable and highly integrated transport system it became possible for passengers to move seamlessly between the different modes of transport. Copenhagen now delivers some of the highest levels of mobility in the world. Alongside the traffic itself, congestion and pollution have been reduced to very low levels.

The city's cycle culture has evolved over many years, helped by ongoing investment in cycle tracks and cycle routes. Currently, more than 1.2 million km are covered by cyclists in Copenhagen every day! This amazing number of cyclists constitutes a key part of Copenhagen's identity. 35 per cent of people working or studying in Copenhagen travel there by bike.

Buildings

To enable Copenhagen to become carbon-neutral in the near future, the City is also looking for cost-effective ways to demonstrate the new, green architecture. Being conscious about energy consumption when buildings are erected or renovated is a good investment – for the climate and also for the economy. No less important is the improved quality of life that results from energy efficient buildings. There are huge savings to be made from energy optimisation in buildings, recovering investments relatively quickly.

Energy efficiency over the entire lifecycle of a building is the single most important goal of both new sustainable architecture and retrofitting of old buildings. Although new technologies are constantly being developed to complement existing practices, the common objective is for all buildings to minimise the overall impact of the built environment on human health and the natural environment.

If a house facade is protected and so cannot be insulated on the outside, new materials are used to facilitate internal insulation. Solar panels for hot water and electricity are often integrated in south-facing roofs.

District heating

Copenhagen is a world leader in district heating. Heat supply planning is done by all municipalities. A 160 km hot water transmission system supplies heat to 21 distribution networks in 18 local authorities. The total heated floor area is 60 million m^2. The system is further optimised by shifting to more renewable energy. Rehabilitation of old district heating networks has been carried out for several city districts. Copenhagen Energy also operates district cooling in inner Copenhagen. The facility uses surplus energy from the district heating net and sea water to provide cooling for larger businesses.

Wind-power

A major part of Copenhagen's objective to achieve carbon neutrality by 2025 relies on establishing an interconnected system of wind farms in an around the city. To this end, the Municipality needs to produce 360 MW from more than 100 turbines. The project is being carried out by Copenhagen Energy, a city-owned company.

Like every city, Copenhagen faces challenges regarding wind-power: limited space to implement wind energy on a large scale within the city, and public resistance. The solution to this problem is to create community-owned facilities and to utilise local skills: the city's renewable energy infrastructure is thus being implemented primarily via cooperative ownership. The presence of wind turbines in and around the urban landscape also communicates the need to address climate challenges to businesses, citizens and visitors.

Middelgrunden, off the coast of Copenhagen, was the world's first major off-shore wind farm and consists of 20 windmills placed at 180-metre intervals. Specially designed foundations had to be developed to cope with winter ice. The design had to address factors such as tidal movements, wave and ice loading, metal fatigue and connectivity via submarine cabling. Another key issue was to ensure that the power grid could cope with the intermittent energy supply from the wind farm.

Middlegrunden was an important test bed. Further off-shore wind parks are under construction. The city-owned utility company also plans to build 100 on-shore wind turbines by 2025. A public awareness campaign is helping to convince locals that there will be no significant noise impacts from the project. A recent citizen's survey indicates widespread popular support. Renewable energy cooperatives and individual citizens have the option of buying shares in the new wind parks, with additional funds coming from bank loans and external investments.

The network of turbines in and around the city will play a central role in transforming Copenhagen's energy system from fossil fuel dependence towards renewable energy.

Electric vehicles

The City of Copenhagen wants to spearhead electric vehicles (EVs) as an alternative to gasoline and diesel. If EVs are to be successful in Copenhagen, they must be attractive for EV providers, enterprises and the general public. EVs are exempted from the vehicle registration tax and parking is free of charge.

The city's objective is that by 2015, 85 per cent of the municipality's vehicle fleet should be electric, hydrogen or hybrid powered. The City Council has decided to reserve 500 parking spaces for EV providers to set up and operate charging stations for a period of ten years. As relevant standards and legislation are agreed, the city will offer long-term concessions to ensure the full-scale roll-out of EV infrastructure on public roads.

Smart grid

To meet its target of becoming carbon neutral by 2025, Copenhagen needs to develop an integrated and smart electricity and energy system. It is looking for partners who can assist it in creating a smart grid.

With a 98 per cent connection to the district heating supply, Copenhagen is already a frontrunner in terms of integrated energy systems. Wind power, waste incineration, CHP and biomass will be further integrated. Its district heating system gives it a unique opportunity to create energy storage capacity. Since Copenhagen cannot overcome its climate challenges alone it is cooperating with other municipalities and companies on both the national and international level.

Recycling

Waste management is an important element in Copenhagen's green strategy. Its waste management problems used to be similar to those of most other major cities: in 1988, over 40 per cent of the city's waste was sent to landfill and there was concern that incinerating waste within the city would create dangerous air pollution. National legislation has now provided an integrated solution – a suite of strategies, policies and investments ensures a high rate of recycling and waste to energy. Eight recycling stations are operating within the capital area.

At household level, reuse and recycling has become second nature to Copenhagen citizens through an easy and logical source separation system. Paper, glass, batteries, plastic, metal, electronics, gardening waste, bulky and residual waste are all collected separately, making source separation an easy choice for people. By developing an integrated programme over many years, Copenhagen now sends less than two per cent of its waste to landfill.

National legislation means that waste sent to landfill incurs a tax of €62/tonne while waste sent to incineration incurs a tax of just €7/tonne. In Denmark it is now illegal to send waste to landfill if it can be incinerated. But whilst generation of heat and power from burning residual waste is a core feature of waste management, Copenhagen is looking towards further increasing materials recycling. A holistic approach to waste management is seen as vital for attaining the city's overall green objectives.[iv]

Regenerating the Ruhr region

The Ruhr Region is Germany's most populous region. From the 1850s onwards, after coal mining got underway, the Ruhrgebiet, an area of 4,500 km^2, was transformed from a rural landscape into an industrial region dominated by mines, steel works, slagheaps, tenement buildings and railway lines. The region became Germany's industrial heartland. The new mining and steel industries caused previously small towns such as Essen, Duisburg, Dortmund, Gelsenkirchen and Bochum to grow into a cluster of large, independent cities. But from the 1960s onwards, coal mining declined and heavy industry was increasingly affected by new competition from companies in other countries such as Japan, Korea and China. A social legacy of high unemployment and an environmental legacy of contaminated brown field sites had to be addressed.

In response to this challenge an 'International Building Exhibition Emscher Park' (IBA) was created in 1989 with two primary objectives: to breathe new life into the old industrial buildings, and to regenerate one of the world's most environmentally damaged regions. With a length of 70 kilometres and covering an area of 460 km^2, the Emscher Landscape Park became Europe's largest urban landscape regeneration project. Over the ten-year period of IBA, it facilitated the ecological and economic revitalisation of the Ruhr and Emscher River valleys through collaborative partnerships between various government agencies, the region's 17 local authorities and private investors.

The IBA Emscher Park was a creative laboratory aiming to give old industrial areas a new lease on life. It had five fields of activities: *Emscher Landscape Park* (regenerating urban landscapes between and within the cities), *Regeneration of the Emscher River* (from an open sewer system back to a living river), *Working in the Park* (reusing old industrial sites for new business), *Urban Neighbourhood Development* (both human and ecological refurbishment) and *Industrial Heritage Ruhr* (recognising cultural roots of regional identity).

Funding for the IBA Emscher Park project was provided by a variety of sources. A total of €2.5 billion were invested over ten years – two-thirds from public funds and one-third from private investments. The money was used to transform the region's run-down industrial landmarks for new recreational uses, to give the region a greener identity, and to create a more cohesive community while preserving the area's identity. The project is a highly visible symbol of positive change that intended to have tangible, lasting benefits for the region and its people.

Today, the Ruhr-Emscher region is surrounded by a beautiful green curtain. Former brown field sites have been turned into new forests and green field sites with intermittent historic industrial landmarks. 'Green connectors' link the towns and cities of the region. A new east-west green corridor has been created to join seven other older, but expanded, north-south greenbelts.

Figure 7.7: *The Ruhr region, once the industrial heartland of Germany, has undergone a fundamental transformation. An area of derelict factory buildings, coal slag heaps and rusting gasometres has been revived and turned into a green and wooded landscape.* ***Source:*** *Ruhrverband*

As the landscape has been revived, so have former industrial buildings: many of the region's abandoned industrial sites are now filled with art, culture, housing, commerce and offices. Exhibitions and concerts are staged in the refurbished steel framed structures. Grassy recreational areas, complete with hiking trails and climbing walls, have been sculpted from 26 old coal slag heaps. Former industrial roads and rail lines have been converted into tree-lined paths which link the many different parts of the park. Many innovative new bridges have been built.

The project has greatly increased the local citizens' awareness of the historical significance of their surroundings. And there are other very tangible benefits: with the development of IBA Emscher Park, approximately 5,000 new jobs have been created. The project also includes 25 housing projects – about 3,000 refurbished and 2,500 new housing units have been initiated, which generally include sustainable features such as high levels of insulation and arrays of solar panels.

The region's transformation has been remarkable. Much if it has been turned into a green and pleasant land. Since the IBA expired as a special experiment and a moderating organisation in 1999, the initiatives have been continued by the local towns and by several regional organisations.

Considerable progress has been made with the task of cleaning up the highly polluted Emscher River, which stretches 70 kilometres from east to west and has been the region's primary sewer system since the nineteenth century. For decades, the river has been biologically dead, but now separate underground sewers are being installed to carry sewage and industrial waste water away from the Emscher. Parts of the river have been re-profiled for better flood management, and to slow the speed of the currents. Trees and native plants have also been introduced along its banks. It will take €4.4 billion and 30 years to separate all the waste water from the rainwater, and to create an ecologically healthy river system that complies with the standards of water policy defined by the European Community in 2000. The Emscher project is expected to be completed in the 2020s.[v]

Another milestone was the Ruhr region being awarded the title of European Capital of Culture in 2010. The integration of the regenerated landscape and the refurbished industrial buildings of the region into the exhibition showed all the signs of great creativity and new cultural self-awareness. Thousands of performances, creative events and exhibitions under the general label "RUHR.2010" enjoyed great popularity among local people and audiences from further afield.

Since the end of IBA in 1999 the Emscher Landscape Park has developed further and is managed as a regional park system that connects 53 cities, town and villages. The communities of the Ruhr region are independent entities. From time to time attempts have been made to merge them into one single, giant Ruhr metropolis, but this has never succeeded. In fact, the polycentric structure of this agglomeration of five million people are increasingly seen as a positive feature in which town and country can interact more effectively than in a large mono-centric conurbation. It allows for ongoing new experiments with inter-local and regional co-operation. The European principles of 'multi-level-governance' are being practised and tested in the reality of regional policy in the region. This offers new opportunities for testing integrated, regenerative development.

Faced with the global problems of climate change, the cities and the whole region have recently started to work together to reach joint climate targets. Together they have created a new format called 'Innovation City Ruhr', which is currently being tested in the city of Bottrop. The main idea is to reach ambitious climate targets by converting and retrofitting the city and all its buildings and infrastructures. Comparable to the IBA Emscher Park in the 1990s, this is an experiment that brings together a great variety of institutions. The latest development is the decision of the government of North Rhine Westphalia to organise 'ClimateExpo-NRW. Ruhr 2022' to showcase climate and energy solutions of relevance to developed countries.

The Ruhr-Emscher region is an interesting mix of urban and rural areas, with all towns and cities having fairly easy access to local farm and forest land. Surprisingly, nearly 60 per cent of the Ruhrgebiet is actually farms and forest, and there are some 3,500 farms in the region. One relevant approach to regenerative development being pursued is to link the farmers in the region more closely to its urban population. Already many farmers have developed thriving enterprises growing vegetables and fruit for local urban customers and, in some instances, developing community-supported agriculture projects. Some farms also keep ponies for people from nearby cities. All in all, a thriving relationship between people from town and country is emerging that will now be further enhanced.

In 2014 the management of the Emscher Landscape Park and the regional Chamber of Agriculture started to collaborate on the implementation of new Urban Agriculture and Urban Gardening initiatives across the region. The potential of its forests to sequester carbon from fossil fuel burning is also being investigated.

The story of the transformation of the Ruhrgebiet is a significant example of how the challenges of landscape and building dereliction can be turned into new opportunities. The living and working environment of more than five million people has been upgraded by the ecological and aesthetic regeneration of their local environment. After 25 years of visioning, planning and implementation, the transformation of the region has become a tangible reality, linking urban regeneration with the broader features of regenerative development. At the same time, the Ruhr region has preserved its unique identity and branded itself as an 'ancient monument' of the industrial age. The region serves as a vivid illustration of how areas of industrial decline and landscape dereliction in other parts of the world can take steps to regenerate themselves.

Oakland: towards zero waste

The city of Oakland has set a goal of zero waste in its 2006 strategic plan, effectively changing a linear metabolism into a circular approach, which means initiating comprehensive policy frameworks. Oakland has acted both according to the Alameda County and the California-wide Integrated Waste Management policy, mandating the city to achieve a 75 per cent waste reduction requirement.

The concept of zero waste goes beyond recycling discarded materials: it starts with a thorough analysis of the vast flow of resources through our society, and the potential to use wastes that can't be avoided as inputs elsewhere. As a useful first step the city of Oakland, population 400,000, reduced its annual tonnage to landfill from 400,000 tonnes to 291,000 tonnes in four years by returning waste materials to the local economy for reuse and recycling, applying the *reduce, reuse, recycle and compost* waste hierarchy.

Oakland's waste management principles emphasise a closed-loop production and consumption system, moving step by step towards the goal of zero waste:

- **pursuing 'upstream' re-design strategies to reduce the volume and toxicity of products and materials, and promote low-impact lifestyles;**
- **improving 'downstream' reuse/recycling of end-of-life products and materials to ensure best possible reuse;**
- **encouraging reuse of discarded products and materials to stimulate local economic and workforce development.**

According to the city's decision makers, the major opportunities to reduce landfill lie in two key areas: capturing organic waste for composting, and increasing recovery of recyclables from waste materials hauled by private interests, especially the construction industry. In 2008, organic materials, representing 48 per cent of Oakland's total landfill disposal, were by far the largest remaining recoverable material type in all sectors. In addition, 26 per cent of Oakland's total annual landfill disposal, consisting mainly of construction and demolition debris, originates from the non-franchised direct sector, and is hauled to a number of landfills within and outside the county.

In its 2006 agenda report the city council analysed the key challenges that need to be addressed in order to achieve zero waste. It showed that waste management is very fragmented and that regulations are incomprehensive. Options for delivering better solid waste management – whether franchised, contracted or unregulated – were examined. The resulting policy recommendations are in five parts:

1. **A single franchise for citywide garbage and organics collection services capable of maximising diversion of organics and minimising landfill disposal of garbage.**
2. **A single citywide collection and recycling franchise focused on maximising recycling.**
3. **Landfill capacity procured separately from collection and processing services to attract the broadest pool of franchise proposers, by eliminating landfill ownership as a barrier.**
4. **A permit system to regulate long-established independent recyclers, to enforce new best practice standards.**
5. **A non-exclusive franchise system to regulate construction and demolition debris hauling activities, to stimulate broader use of mixed debris processing in the region.**

The example of Oakland shows the complexity of interconnected policy initiatives. While solutions and best policy examples exist, barriers to implementing effective policy frameworks due to a lack of vertical coordination still need to be overcome.[vi]

Waste management in Accra

Accra, Ghana, like most major African cities, has a serious waste problem. Until recently, waste management in the city region of 600,000 people had been limited to collection and dumping. But existing landfill sites had exceeded their maximum capacity, resulting in a severe environmental crisis from improper waste disposal.

An integrated solid waste management system was identified as a solution for Accra by an alliance of national and city governments and international donors. As a result, ACARP, the Accra Compost and Recycling Plant, is being built as a public–private partnership. The ultra-modern facility, using Chinese–German technology, is designed to treat half the daily waste collected from the metropolis. Only a small fraction of waste will still be landfilled. Municipal solid waste will be recycled and organic waste converted into compost. A faecal waste treatment plant will also capture plant nutrients for the thriving urban agriculture sector of the metropolis. When fully operational, the facility will employ some 500 people, with thousands more job opportunities through the supply chain. In addition to developing scientific and technical know-how, ACARP will also share its expertise through waste management training programmes.

The facility will improve on sanitation in Accra by reducing the health hazards created by the present anarchic waste dumping practices, which are regularly causing blocked drainage channels and major flooding problems in the city. ACARP will provide an effective means of recovering recyclable materials to supply local recycling companies with raw materials and with compost. The organic compost will reduce the need to import inorganic fertilisers and will improve the soil quality on local farms.

ACARP will have both ecological and economic benefits. Unsanitary conditions in Accra are a serious problem for Ghana's economy. Improved sanitation will directly contribute to economic growth. Reduction in medical costs for the city's population due to lessened waste exposure will allow more funds to be channelled into economic ventures. The productivity of Accra's workforce will be boosted as the loss of working hours through sickness is reduced. The facility will thus make a significant contribution to the government's tax income. Importantly, it will thus also contribute to the achievement of Ghana's millennium development goals.[vii]

Eco-districts

Despite many initiatives to build new 'fully fledged' ecocities in different parts of the world, none have so far been realised. In the absence of new ecocities, eco-districts in existing cities are a useful second best to test the various features of regenerative urban development. They are often realised by a combination of public demand, the perception of economic opportunity and public policy.

Figure 7.8: *Solarsiedlung, Vauban, Freiburg. These highly energy efficient buildings also produce a surplus of electricity that is sold to the grid.* ***Source:*** *Rolf Disch*

Renewable energy, urban agriculture, resource efficiency and renewable energy are all part of the story of creating truly regenerative cities which help to reduce the dependence on distant ecosystems. There are quite a number of cities that have 'eco-districts' that show what could be done on a larger scale. Examples include 'urban ecovillages' such as the Beddington Zero Energy Development in Sutton, South London; the Solarsiedlung in Freiburg;[viii] Masdar Ecocity, Abu Dhabi;[ix] eco-districts in Nancy; Hammarby Sjöstad in Stockholm; Lochiel Solar Village in Adelaide; Portland's Eco-District initiative; the retrofit of the Empire State Building in New York; and many more.

One important example of an eco-district is the Solarsiedlung in Freiburg, Germany, consisting of 60 dwellings completed in 2007, which shows the feasibility of building houses that can produce surplus energy beyond their inhabitants' own requirements. The highly energy efficient 'plus-energy' buildings with south-facing solar roofs are widely regarded as a model for intra-urban RE production.[x] The Solarsiedlung was made possible by Germany's renewable energy feed-in tariff legislation.[xi] The policy also enabled the retrofitting of millions of houses across Germany that are now making a significant contribution to the country's electricity supply.

Another important aspect of sustainable urban development is the creation of new kinds of eco-efficient housing estates. This concept is now flourishing across Europe. In South London, the pioneering Beddington Zero

Energy Development project was completed in 2002. This housing and workshop project for some 200 people was designed by Bill Dunster, and created by the Peabody Trust and the Bioregional Development Group. All buildings have south-facing facades and 30 centimetres of insulation in walls, floors and ceilings. The apartments require only 10 per cent of conventional heating energy and this is provided by a small wood-chip-fired combined heat and power plant. PV panels are installed on all the south-facing facades and these supply electricity to a small fleet of electric cars. All apartments have their own small roof gardens that are used for recreation and/or vegetable growing.

The Beddington project shows how ideas for making cities eco-efficient can be turned into practical reality. The ideas are further developed in Bill Dunster's new project called Bickleigh Down Eco Village, which will be a new zero-carbon village and exemplar sustainable community, which will act as a pilot project showing best practice for the future growth of south-west England.

Figure 7.9 *The Bickleigh Down Ecovillage project in Plymouth builds on the pioneering Beddington Zero Energy Development in Sutton, South London.* ***Source:*** *Bill Dunster*

Ecocities: are they for real?

In recent years there have been a great many ecocity projects in various parts of the world. But whilst there has been much publicity, few have actually been implemented – innovative ideas on urban planning are still up against a conservative property market. Nevertheless, the concepts for building new, low-impact ecocities relying largely on renewable energy and circular systems of resource use are not going away.

I had the privilege to work on the Dongtan Eco-City project on Chongming Island near Shanghai as a consultant to the global civil engineering company Arup. Dongtan was intended to become a city of some 500,000 inhabitants by 2030. It was to provide a blueprint for ecocity development across the world and particularly China, which is planning to build no less than 400 new cities in the next 20 years. Dongtan's success was therefore seen as being of crucial importance.

It was planned to be built on Chongming Island in the Yangtze River delta on an area three-quarters of the size of Manhattan Island – 86 square kilometres – and linked to Pudong by a road and a bridge.

The master plan for Dongtan was of a compact city consisting of a series of pedestrian villages, each with its own distinct character. The villages were to be connected by a hierarchy of pedestrian lanes, cycle routes and public transport corridors, allowing inhabitants easy access to different parts of the city. The aim was to ensure that people did not have to walk from any part of the city for more than seven minutes to reach a bus or tram stop. All of Dongtan's citizens were to have easy access to green open spaces, lakes and canals. The city's five- to six-storey, highly energy efficient apartment buildings were designed to incorporate solar and green roofs. The city would be largely powered by renewable energy – the wind, the sun and biomass.

Most of Dongtan's waste output was to be recycled. The bulk of its organic wastes were intended to be composted and returned to the farmland surrounding the city to help ensure its long-term capacity to supply much of the city's food needs. Chongming Island's existing local farming and fishing communities would have had significant new marketing opportunities with the development of Dongtan Eco-City, ensuring a high degree of local food self-sufficiency and enhancing the island's long-term environmental viability at the same time.

One reason for the decision to create a new city of minimal environmental impact was the existence of the largest reserve for migrating birds in China on the southern part of Chongming Island. Its wetlands were to provide a strong visitor attraction. Wetland vegetation would also permeate Dongtan, ensuring that it became part of the island's natural habitat rather than a barrier to it.

Dongtan was initiated by the Shanghai Industrial Investment Corporation (SIIC). The city was to be developed in several stages over 30 to 40 years. Dongtan was intended as a local project with a global perspective, aiming to ensure that China would play a key role in the emergence of a world of ecologically and economically sustainable human settlements.

Sadly it was not to be. The project was not implemented due to political and financial problems that could not be overcome. But large parts of Cong Ming Island are now being developed, drawing on some of the key components of the Dongtan Eco-City master plan.

What about new ecocity projects elsewhere? In 2006 it was Abu Dhabi's turn to commission another purpose-built zero-carbon, zero-waste, car-free city to be powered exclusively by the sun. The Masdar City plan, designed by Foster + Partners, proposed building a city for 50,000 people and 1,500 businesses. It draws on traditional planning concepts of a compact, walled Arabian city, but combined with a range of new ecotechnologies, to achieve a carbon neutral settlement. The shaded walkways and narrow streets would create a pedestrian -friendly environment suitable for Abu Dhabi's extremely hot climate.

Figure 7.10: *Masdar Ecocity, Abu Dhabi. The buildings of the Masdar Institute are connected by narrow pedestrian lanes that are partly shaded for much of the day as in traditional Arab cities.* ***Source:*** *H. Girardet*

Masdar would take eight years to build, aiming to be part of an ambitious plan by the government of Abu Dhabi to become a world leader in developing clean energy and human settlement technologies, including Masdar PV, which is aiming to become a major international solar technology company.

Like at Dongtan, the Masdar City master plan envisages mainly low-rise, low-energy buildings. The design seeks to ensure that air circulates freely in the streets but the sun's heat is kept out. Wind towers are meant to ventilate homes and offices using natural convection. Water comes from a solar-powered desalination plant. The land surrounding the city will contain photovoltaic arrays, wind farms and food growing areas. The city would need only a quarter of the power required for a similar sized community, while its water needs will be 60 per cent lower.

By 2014, only one tenth of Masdar City had been built, housing the Madar Institute and some of its students and staff. The reasons for the delay appear to be linked to the 2008 property crisis in the region. The concepts underlying Masdar Ecocity have been scrutinised as it is an eco-city project next to a major international hub airport. What is the rationale for an energy-efficient, solar-powered city that is also a global business hub relying heavily on jet setting transient populations?

Symbiotic Kalundborg

What does a circular metabolism mean in practice? The town of Kalundborg, in Denmark, provides an interesting example of what can be done when energy and waste is used as a resource rather than treated as a nuisance. In Kalundborg 20 companies and the municipality cooperate, exploiting each other's waste and by-products on a mutual basis. Over several decades they have developed a symbiotic, circular system in which each step of the chain makes a profit. The exchange benefits the municipality as well as the local companies in several ways:

- **one company's waste is a cost-effective resource for another company;**
- **efficient consumption of resources benefits the local economy;**
- **reduced discharges of wastes reduce environmental pollution.**

Kalundborg's symbiotic web starts with Asnæs Power Station. It produces both electricity and heat for 4,500 households in Kalundborg. The station also provides process steam for three companies – the Statoil Refinery, Novo Nordisk and Novozymes. The partners have also reduced their oil consumption by 20,000 tonnes per year by using process steam and have reduced their overall water consumption by 25 per cent by letting water circulate between the individual partners. Some of the power station's cooling water is also used by a fish farm that produces 200 tonnes of trout and salmon annually, with the warm water providing ideal growing conditions.

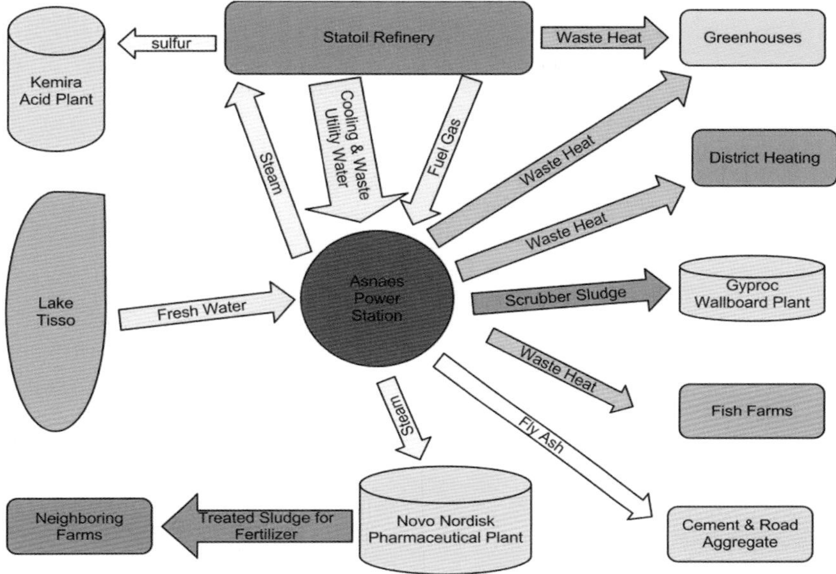

Figure 7.11: *This diagram vividly illustrates Kalundborg as a prime example of 'industrial ecology'. To ensure the continued viability of the whole, it is important that each individual participating enterprise continues to exist. However, the dependence of this interconnected system on fossil fuel technology may be a limiting factor in the long term.* ***Source:*** *Kalundborg Eco-Industrial Park*

The 80,000 tonnes of ash produced by the power station is used in the construction and cement industries. The 200,000 tonnes of gypsum it produces in its sulphur scrubbers is sold to Gyproc, enough for its annual plasterboard production. Excess lime is sold to NovoGro and incorporated in fertiliser for 20,000 hectares of farmland. Novozymes, Asnæs Power Station and Kalundborg Municipality have a joint waste-water treatment facility, with only minimal discharges into the Baltic Sea. Newspaper, cardboard, rubble, iron, glass, green waste and kitchen wastes from the waste stream of Kalundborg and its various companies are all recycled and turned into new products in a 'cradle-to-cradle' production system.

The 'Kalundborg symbiosis' came about through voluntary action by companies primarily for commercial reasons. Other cities have adopted similar resource use strategies using a combination of markets and regulation as the main organising principles. The key issue is to create viable end-markets for remanufactured waste products, and for this purpose regulatory barriers, diseconomies of scale and lack of adequate information need to be overcome.[xii]

London: Crossrail

In London, one of Europe's largest civil engineering projects is currently underway and contributing to a pioneering regenerative development initiative. 26 miles of tunnels are being built below London to create a railway link between Berkshire and Buckinghamshire, and Essex and south-east London, to be completed by 2018. In the process some six million tonnes of soil is being dug up from 20 to 30 metres below the city. It is being transported by train and barge to Wallasea Island in Essex and will be part of a 670-hectare wetland area – a new coastal landscape of mudflats, saltmarshes and lagoons – which will be the largest man-made nature reserve in Europe.

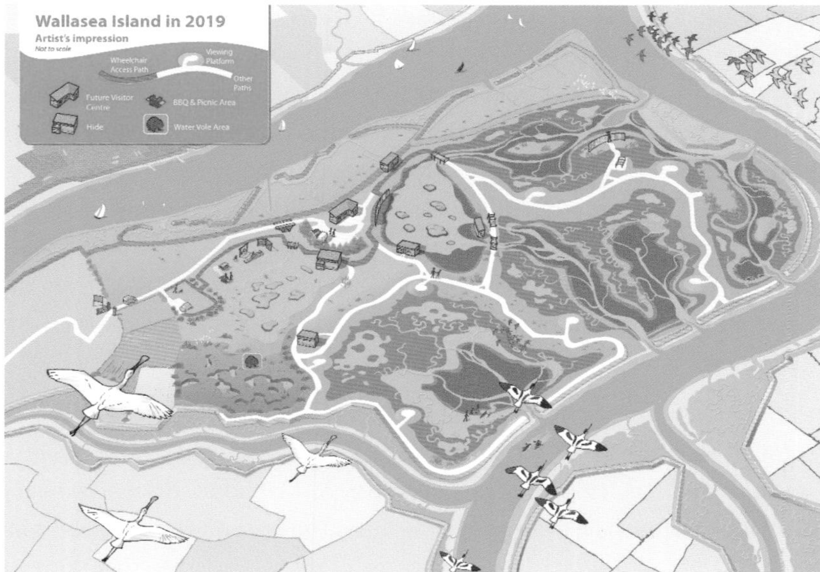

Figure 7.12 *Wallasea Island, Essex, where earth from London's Crossrail Tunnel is being used to create a nature reserve. It will be completed by 2019.* ***Source:*** *Crossrail/ Wallasea Island*

Four centuries ago there were 30,000 hectares of tidal salt marsh along the Essex coast but today just 2,500 hectares remain. The Essex estuaries are among the most important coastal wetlands in the UK and are protected by both national and European law.

Wallasea Island was first reclaimed from the sea by Dutch engineers centuries ago and then turned into farmland. Surrounded by tall, grassy levees, it is now two metres below sea level at high tide and has a high risk of flooding each year. The new nature reserve that is being established on the island will create a habitat for breeding populations of birds such as spoonbills and Kentish plovers, as well as a transit base for migrating flocks of avocet, dunlin, redshank and lapwing, along with brent geese, wigeon and curlew. Saltwater fish such as bass, herring and flounder are expected to use the wetland as a nursery, helping to maintain the small local seal colony. Plants such as samphire, sea lavender and sea aster are also expected to thrive.

There are currently some 30,000 birds living on a small 100-hectare salt marsh in the area, but the new reserve will add a further 670 hectares and will include eight miles of walks and cycle paths for visitors. The island will also help protect other wetland sites on the Essex coast, because the new dams being built will offer protection from the huge currents that would otherwise destroy existing mudflats around the island.[xiii]

The Singapore Water Loop

Cities, directly and indirectly, use vast quantities of water which end up as waste water. Singapore has been importing nearly 40 per cent of its water from Malaysia for its 5.4 million inhabitants. In a quest for greater water self-sufficiency, Singapore has been working in recent years to reduce water imports by improving efficiency as well as boosting the use of three alternative sources: rainfall, desalinated water and treated waste water.

Singapore faced five interconnected challenges: Protecting its own water resources; processing safe drinking water in a cost-effective manner; minimising wastage in water supply system; water conservation; and closing the water loop.

Thanks to public campaigns, the city-state's per capita daily domestic water consumption has decreased slightly, from 165 litres in 2003 to 153 litres in 2013. It has also lowered the unconsumed water lost, for example, through pipe leakages, to about five per cent.

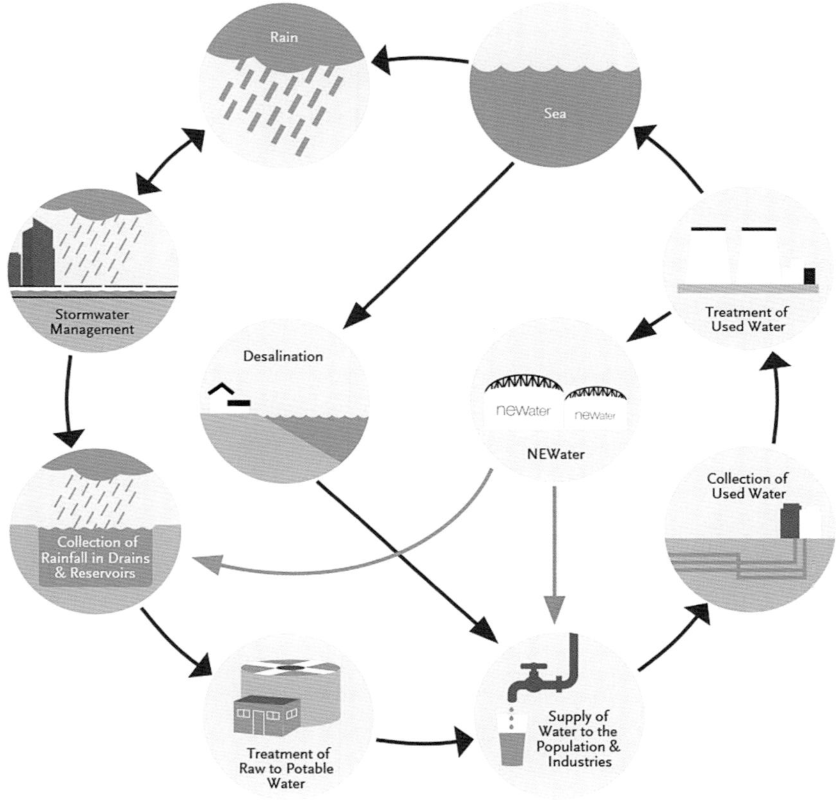

__Figure 7.13:__ The Integrated Water Resource Management System implemented in Singapore. This system is now being copied in other cities, reducing the need to rely on water from further afield.
***Source:** City Council of Singapore*

In recent years Singapore has implemented a highly innovative Integrated Water Resource Management Programme (IWRM). It now collects and treats virtually all its waste water and transforms it into high-quality water which meets the World Health Organization standards for drinking water. This now accounts for 30 per cent of its total water supply. Most of it is used for industrial and air-cooling purposes, but some is combined with reservoir water before being treated for the drinking water supply. What is often seen as a waste output – waste water – is thus reintroduced as an input and helps the city to regenerate its own limited water resources on its own territory.[xiv]

Every drop of water is put to good use. Instead of discharging waste water into the sea, water is now recycled and reused. All inhabitants of the city are connected to this system. Proper accounting of water use, and water metering of all households and businesses, is part of the policy. Its NEWater system uses state-of-the-art membrane technology to remove particles, colloids and macromolecules, ensuring that waste water can be effectively disinfected whilst minimising the use of chemicals. The only major drawback of the use of membranes is the significant use of electricity required for this waste water treatment technology.

Notes

i Dillon, P., Stevens, D., Thomas, R., and White, T. (2005) *Reclaimed Water Management for Horticulture/ Agriculture*, www.wrsv.com.au/virginia/documents/Virginia-Research_mar05.pdf.

ii Girardet, H., *Creating a Sustainable Adelaide*, www.thinkers.sa.gov.au/lib/pdf/Girardet_Report.pdf.

iii Girardet, H., *Regenerative Adelaide*, Solutions Magazine, www.thesolutionsjournal.com/node/1153.

iv Copenhagenet, www.copenhagenet.dk/cph-map/CPH-Pedestrian.asp; http://ec.europa.eu/environment/europeangreencapital/winning-cities/2014-copenhagen/.

v Emscher Park, From Dereliction to Scenic Landscapes, www.dac.dk/en/dac-cities/sustainable-cities-2/all-cases/green-city/emscher-park-from-dereliction-to-scenic-landscapes/?bbredirect=true.

vi *Oakland Zero Waste Agenda Report*, www2.oaklandnet.com/oakca/groups/pwa/documents/report/oak030643.pdf.

vii Accra Compost and Recycling Plant, www.acarpghana.com/.

viii Wikipedia, *Solarsiedlung, Freiburg*, http://de.wikipedia.org/wiki/Solarsiedlung.

ix Masdar, www.masdar.ae/.

x *Solarsiedlung*, www.solarsiedlung.de/.

xi PV Upscale, *Solarsiedlung am Schlierberg*, www.pvupscale.org/IMG/pdf/Schlierberg.pdf.

xii Kalundborg website, www.symbiosis.dk.

xiii Carrington, D. (2012) Guardian, 17 September.

xiv UNEP (2010) Singapore IWRM programme, www.unep.org/gc/gcss-viii /Singapore.IWRM.pdf.

Chapter 8

Case Studies, part 2

Concentrated solar power near Seville, Spain

Across Europe, regional peri-urban RE installations are rapidly growing in number and size. Southern Spain, with its almost permanently blue skies, is pioneering concentrated solar power (CSP) technology. So far the most notable examples are the CSP stations that have been built by the Spanish company Abengoa near Seville in Spain. They feature arrays of mirrors that focus beams of sunlight onto the top of a tower through which liquid is circulated that is turned into steam and powers turbines and generators. The latest versions of these installations can store solar heat in a molten salt solution, which enable them to produce electricity for up to eight hours after dark. Seville is well on its way to becoming the world's first large city to get most of its electricity supplies from solar power stations in its hinterland, as well as from installations within the city.[i]

The Jasper Power project in South Africa, once completed, will be a 96 MW solar photovoltaic plant in South Africa's Northern Cape – one of the biggest solar installations on the continent.[ii]

Figure 8.1: *Sanlúcar La Mayor solar power station, Seville. There are now technologies available to store the heat generated by solar thermal power stations after sunset, ensuring electricity supply late into the night.* ***Source:*** *Abengoa Industries*

The breakthroughs in CSP technology are not confined to Spain. Solana, one of the largest solar power plants in the world, is a 280 MW parabolic trough plant with six hours of thermal storage which is currently under construction. The plant will be located 70 miles south-west of Phoenix, Arizona. Solana began construction at the end of 2010 and began operation in 2013. It will permanently employ some 1,700 people.[iii]

Germany's 100% renewable energy regions

Renewable energy is a key ingredient in the regenerative development of human settlements. In this context the opportunities for smaller communities to generate the energy they consume locally and even become energy exporters to nearby larger towns and cities is increasingly being realised.

Cities and rural communities face different legal, political, financial and topographical challenges and opportunities in trying to initiate their energy transitions. In the transition towards powering cities with renewable energy, regional initatives play a crucial role. Across Germany there are over 100 regions that have implemented – and even exceeded – a 100 per cent renewable energy (RE) target. These so-called 100% RE regions encompass about a quarter of the country's population.

In order to be able to identify, advance and evaluate the potential and dynamics of these initiatives, criteria for 100% RE communities have been developed by the project partners. This is the mission statement: 'A 100%-RE-Ideal-Region covers its energy demand entirely with RE with respect to electricity, heating, and mobility. The region acts very energy efficiently and includes the regional potentials in a comprehensive manner.'

The definition serves as a linking element aiming to create partnerships, interactions and transfer to different communities. In addition to several basic eligibility premises for relevant communities/entities aiming to gain a 100% RE region status, a criteria catalogue has been developed in order to enable a detailed comparison and evaluation. The criteria cover conceptual, qualitative as well as quantitative aspects that are in turn rooted within four major, interrelated dimensions of '100% RE communities':

- **Spatial dimension (building, quarter, village, town, district, region, etc.).**
- **Thematic dimension (local economy, technology, policy, sociology, ecology, etc.).**
- **Normative dimension (actual amounts of RE, 100% target).**
- **Temporal dimension (the stage of development towards 100% RE).**

As many communities are in an early phase of the process towards 100% RE, it is not sufficient to focus on their status quo and the quantity of RE. Hence, other factors are equally taken into account. These may include statements that express the will of the local actors, and ongoing activities within the '100% RE community' are considered within the assessment.[iv]

Municipalities have played an important part in developing renewable energies in Germany and will continue to do so in future. In the energy sector they are the driver of the transformation process towards an Ecopolis. They have far-reaching instruments of control with regard to RE authorisation and installation, enabling local implementation of national energy policies. Local governments and citizens partially fund the installation of RE systems and may even be involved in their operation as lessors through their public works departments. Increasingly, communities are adopting their own renewable energy development goals, forming cooperatives or seeking to attract companies active in the industry to invest in them.[v]

Feed-in tariffs (FITs) especially have played a key role by acting as a connecting framework, linking people, policy, energy and economy. The example of Germany shows that regenerative city regions, actively involving the local community, can play a key role in implementing national energy transition policies. One of the key lessons learnt from Germany is that the pride of ownership should not be underestimated. When local citizens and communities have a direct financial stake in RE projects, social acceptance of these projects tends to be greater, and barriers to implementation are more easily overcome.

With active national government support, potentially everyone can participate in the decentralised development of RE, particularly with public or community-based wind farms or solar systems. Local farmers can produce not only food but also energy for sale as well. The installation, maintenance and operation of RE systems can mostly be carried out by local businesses, e.g. tradesmen, technicians, farm and forest workers. Many small and medium-sized enterprises have the opportunity to benefit from RE development whilst promoting regional added value.

With strong national policy frameworks put in place over the past decade, several towns and regions have already surpassed a 100 per cent renewable electricity target. One example is the town of Lichtenau in Westphalia which produces a 27 per cent surplus of renewable energy and is exporting electricity into the national grid.[vi] The country as a whole reached its **20 per cent RE target in 2011** and is on track to reach 35 per cent by 2020 and 80 per cent by 2050. The German Federal Environment Agency has set an ambitious target of reaching 100 per cent overall RE by 2050.[vii]

National RE policy comprises a wide range of measures:

- **priority for RE's access to the grid;**
- **a FITs policy that compensates RE producers who feed electricity into the grid to recover investment and running costs, plus a reasonable profit;**

- **a low-interest loans programme to accelerate adoption of RE and efficiency improvements.**

The primary challenge for cities all over the world is to find ways of retrofitting existing urban infrastructure, transport systems and individual buildings: energy, water and waste management can often be dramatically improved in line with global best practice. The primary opportunity inherent in all this is to build vibrant new green urban economies, particularly for young people who are eager to create viable livelihoods for themselves.

Figure 8.2: *The largest community-owned solar farm in the UK is the Westmill Solar Coop near Oxford, where 5,000 local people jointly own £16 million of solar PV.* ***Source:*** *www.westmillsolar.coop*

Urban agriculture: a survey

Urban farming is being recognised more and more as an important source of food and income generation in cities around the world. Urban agriculture tends to focus on products that require closeness to the urban markets such as vegetables, poultry and eggs, as well as flowers. Across the world there is a broad consensus now that urban agriculture is an important area for government support at national as well as municipal level, helping to ensure urban food security, creating employment and utilising organic waste. In recent years there has been rapid growth in urban agriculture in both developed and developing countries.

Cuba's great experiment

Havana, Cuba, is often hailed as the world's most remarkable example of urban agriculture development. But before 1989 things were quite different: Cuba's national agriculture policy had emphasised high-input, mechanised production of monoculture crops. Tobacco, sugar and other export crops were produced on large state farms, and most grain and animal feeds were imported. But with the collapse of the Soviet Bloc, and the start of the US trade embargo, things fell apart: the country lost 85 per cent of its export earnings and much of its supply of imported food. And suddenly, the annual supply of a million tonnes of synthetic fertilisers and 35,000 tonnes of pesticides stopped. This meant hardship and hunger for millions of people.

In response, the Cuban people turned a major crisis into an opportunity, regarding both food supplies and food production methods. Cubans of Chinese origin were the initial inspiration behind the urban agriculture revolution that emerged, persuading people to deal with food shortages by growing crops on any surfaces available within Cuba's cities. After some hesitation, the authorities started to support the urban agriculture movement. People from all walks of life were encouraged to learn the skills of organic cultivation, and to enjoy the benefits of tasty, locally grown food. Fresh produce could be supplied with minimal transportation costs and use of fossil fuels, and has become an important source of nutrition, employment and income for many people.

Cuba's urban agriculture programme aims to provide each person with at least 300 grams of fresh vegetables per day – a figure considered by the FAO as appropriate for maintaining good health. Cookery courses at urban farming centres encourage people to share recipes for nutritious and healthy food.

From the early 1990s onwards, urban gardens sprouted up everywhere – on wasteland, at housing estates, schools, community centres, hospitals and factories. The popular, bottom-up urban agriculture movement has become an essential component of Cuba's food policy. The government supports the growers by providing free land and tools, and it subsidises farm inputs. It has helped hundreds of thousands of city people to set up vegetable gardens, to plant fruit trees, and to raise pigs, goats, chickens and rabbits.

Havana has become a world-leading centre for intra-urban organic agriculture. Nearly half the city's 72,800 hectares are now under food crops, and the farms and gardens are often prominently located in and around the city's public parks. Three quarters of the vegetables and fruit required by its people are now produced within the city, using organic compost, biological pest management and simple irrigation techniques. Intercropping based on 'permaculture' principles is widely practiced.

Havana is inhabited by over two million people, nearly 20 per cent of Cuba's population, and is the largest city in the Caribbean. Tens of thousands of people now grow fruit and vegetables, often on plots adjoining their apartment blocks. The crops are usually grown on raised beds which are irrigated with pumped, underground water.

Figure 8.3: *Urban agriculture, Havana, Cuba. This is still the world's best example of intra-urban organic food production, involving large numbers of city people.* ***Source:*** *H. Girardet*

Urban farming comes in three main forms – cooperative gardens (organiponicos), private gardens (huertos privados) and popular gardens (huertos populares). An important source of compost is bagasse trucked in from Cuba's sugar cane fields. Whilst some sugar cane is still grown with artificial fertilisers, the bagasse used as compost on urban farms effectively becomes an organic growing medium.[viii]

Cuba's urban agriculture programme also provides good quality seeds, advice on crop rotations, composting methods and the benefits of earthworms. Urban growers can buy key materials such as seeds, parts of irrigation systems and beneficial insects and plant-based pesticides from government-supported suppliers. There are some 200 'biotechnology centers' across the country, which have developed innovative biological pest control methods, and which advise growers on how to deal with bacterial and fungal diseases without using chemical pesticides.

Cuba's pioneering biotechnology centres have also developed entrepreneurial skills: they have opened a new export market by offering advice on organic cultivation methods in other countries in the tropics and subtropics. They have helped to set up a few Cuban-style organic urban farms in Caracas, Venezuela, though damage to crops by air pollution from cars and factories is an unforeseen, unsolved problem.

Another interesting source of income for Cuba's urban growers and research centres is courses on urban permaculture, which are attended by students from all over the world. The visiting students are often motivated by concern about the highly unsustainable reliance on fossil fuel-powered, long-distance food supplies on which their cities back home currently depend.[ix]

Developed countries

It would be wrong to assume that the Cuban intra-urban agriculture experiment can easily be copied in other cities, particularly those where high land values would make cultivation implausible. But anybody who thinks that urban farming is only a phenomenon primarily of poorer countries, should have a look around parts of New York City. In the Bronx, for instance, an astonishing range of vegetable gardens emerged in the 1980s, primarily in areas where drug-related gang warfare resulted in houses being burned down and gardens left abandoned. With the help of people from New York Botanical Gardens, local people turned dozens of vacant lots into thriving vegetable gardens. Many also grew crops for the sake of their children, who they want to learn about growing vegetables and keeping chicken and rabbits.

In the United States, the growth of farmers' markets has been a remarkable phenomenon in recent years. Despite the enormous dominance of supermarkets, farmers' markets have been of extraordinary success, not only in California, where the growing conditions are best, but also in New York. In 2013 there were some 6,000. In both New York City and LA there are over ten farmers' markets in operation. In the UK, too, there has been a resurgence of farmers' markets, from nothing 20 years ago to about 500 in 2013. And allotment growing has maintained its popularity within cities, though today it is done less and less by retired men, but increasingly by women who want to grow some vegetables for their families.

In the UK there is also urban food production. For instance, in Nazeing in Essex, just outside London, one can see how farming has come under pressure. Like Heathrow, Nazeing used to be a major centre for vegetable growing, in a landscape full of greenhouses. But few growers could compete with cheap, imported vegetables and many had to abandon their plots. The few that are left now grow only one crop: cucumbers. These are grown hydroponically in greenhouses that look as clean as operating theatres. The growers are mainly second-generation Italians. That is because the people who used to own these greenhouses couldn't make them pay any more. The Italian prisoners of wars who had been their labourers during and after the war, took over the last remaining greenhouses, partly because they could draw on additional supplies from Italy. When it isn't cost-effective to grow cucumbers in the winter in England, they will truck them in from Italy instead.

On the outskirts of Bristol, organic market garden schemes have been operating for some time. For instance, at Leigh Court outside the city, an organic vegetable box scheme was set up in the 1990s. But it is not easy to compete with cheap, imported crops – three-quarters of the organic vegetables consumed in Britain are actually trucked and flown in from elsewhere, at great energy cost. But steps to revive peri-urban agriculture are now being taken in many places.

New York, Chicago and Detroit

New York City is not a place where one would expect urban agriculture to thrive – a city of 8.3 million people, it is one of the most densely populated cities in the United States, with some of the highest real estate values. And yet, urban agriculture is doing well here too, though on a much smaller scale than in Havana. What started as the 'green guerrillas' urban farming project in the 1970s has become a mainstream movement supported by city officials, support organisations and foundations. The fact is that there is a lot of vacant land, and large expanses of flat roofs are also suitable for food growing. There are many eco-entrepreneurs in New York, and quite a few have become involved in urban farming and gardening projects. They take over suitable land or roof surfaces, compost food waste, run community food

campaigns, and train youth and unemployed people. New York's urban agriculture community now numbers in the thousands and includes food growers, school staff and pupils, sanitation workers, building owners and public housing residents.[x]

***Figure 8.4:** Urban farmer in the Bronx. **Source:** H. Girardet*

New York is a boom city, whereas Detroit is not. Once a city of two million people, it has contracted to less than 900,000 people mainly due to the decline of the automobile industry. It has a surface area of 139 square miles, more than San Francisco, Boston and Manhattan combined. Vast areas of derelict, vacant land have become available for 'intra-urban' agriculture initiatives, and many are being actively supported by city officials, the general public and local businesses. In a recent report, the American Institute of Architects states that 'Detroit is particularly well suited to become a pioneer in urban agriculture at a commercial scale'.[xi]

Urban farming is being developed by a variety of community groups. But now big business is also becoming involved, and this is stirring controversy. One entrepreneur, John Hantz, has been buying up abandoned lots, and removing derelict houses and abandoned cars – things that the bankrupt city authority cannot afford to do any longer. Hantz wants to plant a forest on many thousands of derelict acres and to start large scale intra-urban commercial farming. Some people in Detroit see him as a visionary, but others argue that he has started a major land grab.[xii]

In Chicago, probably the United States' most innovative urban food production programme has been established in a former meat packing factory – but crops are being grown indoors rather than outdoors. Called 'The Plant', the project is being financially supported by Chicago's city government. Salad crops are being grown on trays on stacks of shelves, using LED and strip lights and a hydroponic growing medium. The project consists of a combination of non-profit and for-profit companies that interact with each other for mutual benefit.

The organisers are trying to show what resilient urban food production and economic development can look like. By turning the outputs of one business into the inputs of another, The Plant is making efficient use of materials that would usually be thrown away. By incubating small craft food businesses, by growing salad crops, making bread and brewing beer, and doing it all using renewable energy generated on-site, the project is setting new standards for regenerative urban food production. The Plant is creating some 125 jobs in Chicago's economically distressed Back of the Yards neighbourhood.

One-third of The Plant is used for an 'aquaponic' crop growing systems and the other two-thirds to incubate a variety of sustainable food businesses by offering low rent, low energy costs, and a shared kitchen. The project requires no fossil fuels but meets all its heat and power needs from a renewable energy system that converts 10,000 tonnes of food waste and organic trash into biogas.[xiii]

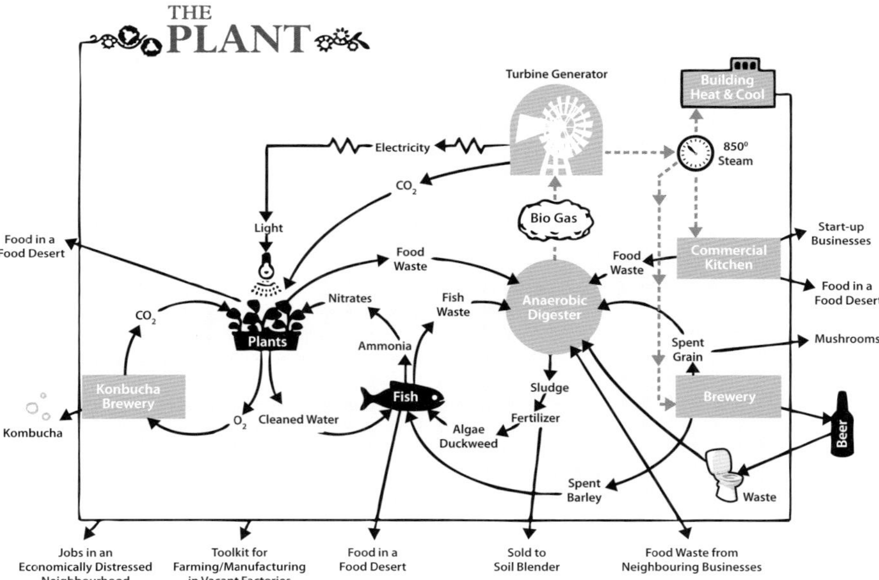

Figure 8.5: *The Plant, in Chicago, is a new kind of highly integrated organisation. By reusing a previously derelict building as a vertical indoor farm and food business operation, it indicates what might be possible in many other cities with underused commercial buildings.* ***Source:*** *Plant, Chicago*

All major US cities have thriving urban agriculture projects. Farmers' markets are doing well everywhere, with growers supplying substantial amounts of the vegetables and fruit from intra- and peri-urban land. However, grain and animal fodder have to be brought in from farms further afield.

Shanghai and Beijing

Today in Asia urban agriculture is a thriving activity in many cities. In China, until recently, highly intensive urban cropping systems made many cities self-sufficient in vegetables. This policy was pursued systematically by Mao Zedong and has been modified only to a limited extent since the changes introduced by Deng Xiaoping.[xiv] Despite China's rapid industrial development, food production is being purposefully maintained on peri-urban farmland administered by city authorities. In Tianjin 20 per cent of people work in farming, in Shanghai 15 per cent and in Beijing 12 per cent, as compared with about 45 per cent working in industry.[xv]

The Shanghai city authorities administer an area of about 600,000 hectares of land: 300,000 of these are built-up areas within the city itself. But as a deliberate policy, some 300,000 hectares of land on the city's periphery are deliberately maintained as farmland for feeding the city. Most of this land is used to supply vegetables, chicken and pork. Wheat and rice for Shanghai are mainly grown further afield in rural areas. Animal feeds such as soybeans, particularly for pork and beef produced in US-style feedlots, are now increasingly imported from far-flung places such Mato Grosso in the southern Amazon.

Shanghai is China's most important industrial, commercial and financial centre, a metropolis of some 15 million people. The total land area administered by its authorities extends to 634,050 hectares. About 58 per cent of this land is occupied by the city itself, whilst 42 per cent, mainly on the periphery, is devoted to intensive agriculture. On 12,700 hectares of peri-urban land, 1.3 million tonnes of vegetables are produced per year, or 4,000 tonnes per day, supplying around 60 per cent of the city's vegetable needs. However, all is not well. Chinese cities can only raise revenue by selling land and there is pressure on urban authorities to raise funds by selling farmland for housing development.

To make land use more efficient, hydroponic, soil-less vegetable cultivation in greenhouses is now strongly supported by the city authorities. But traditional raised-bed cultivation is still predominant, with polythene tunnels much in evidence. I found that the traditional practice of using night soil as fertiliser continues to be practised. Growers use large earthenware jars to store the night soil, which is diluted with water and then ladled onto the crops. However, the apartment blocks now springing up all over China have flush toilets, making this practice difficult to maintain.

Shanghai has entered the fast lane of urbanisation, but the city administration has also realises that that the city will not be able to develop without agriculture ... The city authorities are aiming for a considerable level of agricultural production within the city to ensure a stable food supply for the urban population.[xvi]

Some 800,000 people work on the city's own peri-urban farmland, producing vegetables, fruit, milk, eggs, chicken, pork, carp and catfish meat.[xvii] A further two million work the land in the rural areas to the south of the city growing wheat and rice. The city's policy is to produce at least a million tonnes of grain locally, ensuring a high degree of regional self-reliance.

Some of the growers in and around Shanghai are older local people who continue a lifelong farming practice, but many are migrants from rural areas, doing jobs that have become unpopular with the people of Shanghai.

Figure 8.6: *Peri-urban farming in Beijing. Whilst new office buildings and housing development encroach on city-owned farmland, urban peri-agriculture still plays a crucial role in Beijing's food supply.* ***Source:*** *H. Girardet*

In Beijing, much the same approach to urban farming as in Shanghai is in evidence. The city authorities there, too, administer large areas of farmland. But because the winter months are much colder there, farmers use ingenious methods to cope, maintaining cultivation with very little dependence on artificial heat, despite the icy weather that prevails for several months. To keep the heat in their polythene greenhouses at night, they cover them with several layers of bamboo mats. The growth of Beijing to a city of some 11 million people has swallowed some arable land in recent years, reducing its area from 408,000 to 300,500 hectares between 1991 and 2001. On the other hand, the area used for orchards has gone up substantially during this period, from 50,000 to 85,000. This is because they require less water and fertiliser, making them a highly sustainable cultivation system.[xviii]

Throughout China, city authorities are required by central government to ensure the production of substantial amounts of food from the land they administer. This policy is being maintained despite rapid urbanisation. The

Chinese authorities are also keenly aware of the importance of including agriculture in planning their *new* cities. A vigorous stand has been taken against urban sprawl, by designating 80 per cent of China's arable land as 'fundamental farmland'. To build on this land, four different authorities have to give their approval – local, county and provincial governments, as well as the State Council. Illegal development on protected farmland can be severely punished.[xix]

In Japan, too, urban agriculture is still much in evidence. In Tokyo and the surrounding prefectures some 12,500 hectares are arable land. Nearly 4 per cent of Greater Tokyo's labour force, over 670,000 people, is involved in agricultural work of some sort. From the air, a patchwork of rice paddies looks like it was sewn together by thick bands of roads. Similar patterns of peri-urban faming can be observed throughout Asia, in industrial countries such as South Korea and Taiwan, as well as in developing countries such as Cambodia, Laos and Vietnam.[xx]

Vertical gardening

Figure 8.7: *Vertical farming on a substantial scale is becoming a reality in many cities. This is one way to supply local food, and particularly vegetables, for local consumption. However, grain supplies will require much more extensive areas of farmland beyond city regions.* ***Source:*** *Farmiculture, US*

A survey of bio-sequestration potential

Forests for life

Global forest cover extends to nearly four billion hectares, or 30 per cent of the world's land surface.[xxi] The UN Food and Agriculture Organisation (FAO) has recently done a Forest Resources Assessment which states that the world's forests contain 638 Gt of carbon – which is more than the total carbon contained in the atmosphere.[xxii]

Forest ecosystems are crucially important components of the global carbon cycle in several ways. They remove some three billion tonnes of carbon every year through net growth, absorbing nearly 30 per cent of all $C0_2$ emissions from fossil fuel burning and deforestation.[xxiii]

Healthy forests play a crucial role as global ecological life-support systems. Reports such as UNEP's Millennium Ecosystem Assessment make it clear that the goods and services provided by forests are worth trillions of dollars to the global economy. In addition to carbon sequestration, they provide a wide range of 'ecosystem services' of benefit to all life: they are wildlife habitats, biodiversity centres, climate regulators and watershed protectors – not to mention medicine cabinets and cosmetics counters. By and large these services are regarded as free benefits of no cost to human society and they are absent from society's balance sheet. Thus their critical contributions to the viability of life on earth are largely overlooked in decision making. This problem needs to be urgently addressed: only if we recognise forests as important natural assets with economic and social value can we do what is necessary to promote their protection.

As human populations and their economies grow, so do the resource demands imposed on ecosystems and the impacts of our global ecological footprint. But society is coming to realise that as ecosystem services are threatened across the world, there is an urgent need to evaluate both their immediate and their long-term benefits to humanity. Increasingly, researchers have been able to quantify the economic value associated with ecosystem services based on assessing the cost of replacing these with 'man-made' alternatives.

We urgently need international policy measures to restore soils to their previous levels of fertility and water-holding capacity and to stop the ongoing release of carbon stored in soils, the world's second largest carbon sink, and potentially the world's most effective carbon capture and storage option.

The impacts of soil erosion and carbon loss on world food production have been masked to some extent by an ever-greater array of technologies used in farming which have produced higher yields – however unsustainably. But now we need to find ways to sequester much more carbon from the atmosphere by developing bold initiatives on renewing the world's living systems, including life in the soil. It is time to find ways of replacing the one-way *linear* systems of resource depletion, consumption and pollution that have prevailed in the recent past with *circular* systems which can replenish nature and ensure a sustainable human existence on earth.

It is becoming apparent that the restoration of wastelands, degraded or desertified soils and ecosystems can dramatically enhance soil organic carbon content and soil quality. Such management practices include:

- **organic farming;**
- **conservation tillage;**
- **application of mulch, manure and compost;**
- **use of cover crops;**
- **agroforestry practices;**
- **improved pasture management.**

Farmers need support to alleviate agriculture's contribution to climate change by reducing tillage, increasing organic soil matter, improving grassland management, restoring degraded lands, planting trees and improving animal husbandry systems. These sorts of practices not only enhance soil fertility but also the water storage capacity of soils, and thereby increase the productivity of farmland and grazing land. Restoration of soil organic matter can reverse land degradation, which is urgently needed in many parts of the world. Not only can this help increase food security, but it can also reduce the use of fossil fuels and its associated GHG emissions.

The FAO states that soil carbon sequestration can take effect very quickly and is a cost-effective win-win approach which combines mitigation, adaptation, increased resilience and the promise of more reliable and increased crop yields.

Soil carbon storage was hitherto left out of international negotiations because of envisaged difficulties of validation of amounts and duration/permanency of sequestration. However, in addition to the undisputable multiple benefits of soil carbon storage, soil sampling for

verification purposes is less expensive and more accurate than the indirect estimation of carbon stored in living biomass.

The FAO has recently prepared a Global Carbon Gap Map that identifies land areas of high carbon sequestration potentials and is developing local land degradation assessment tools that includes a simple field measurement of soil carbon. FAO is also working on tools to measure, monitor and verify soil carbon pools and fluxes of greenhouse gas emissions from agricultural soils, including cropland, degraded land and pastures.[xxiv]

All in all, the potential for soil carbon sequestration is very large indeed and deserves to be linked with international policies. With populations expected to grow to nine billion by 2050, and with increasingly uncertain oil and water supplies, well-thought-out new approaches to securing carbon-rich organic soils can help to secure the food supplies of future generations. We need policies to renew the world's soils in closed-loop, low-input farming systems based on a sustainable relationship between urban food consumers and rural farming communities.

A potential major additional benefit of measures to support soil quality and carbon sequestration could be to halt or even reverse migration of people from rural areas to cities. Funding for enhanced soil carbon sequestration could thus have major environmental as well as economic and social benefits.

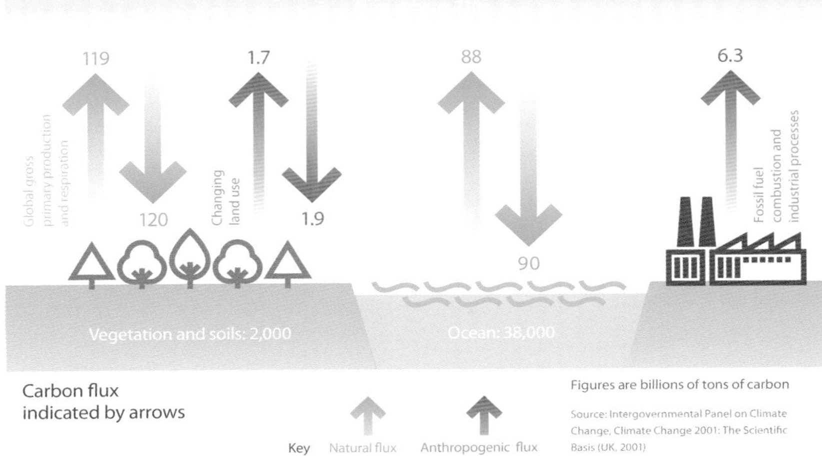

Figure 8.8: *This diagram indicates that at present only half the CO_2 emissions emanating from human activity is actually being sequestered by the biosphere. What can be done to enhance the earth's carbon sequestering potential across the world whilst simultaneously financially benefitting local communities and countering soil erosion?* ***Source:*** *IPPC and Wilf Whitty*

Carbon and the oceans

The oceans absorb about one-third of the CO_2 emitted into the atmosphere from the burning of fossil fuels – mainly through the growth of plankton. However, this valuable ecological service comes at a high price – the acidification of the oceans. When CO_2 dissolves in seawater, it forms carbonic acid and the pH of the water decreases as a result. Since the Industrial Revolution began, it is estimated that surface ocean pH has dropped by nearly 0.1 units, equating to approximately a 25 per cent increase in acidity. This rate of change is a great cause for concern as there is no evidence that the world's oceans have ever acidified so rapidly. By the end of this century, pH could be three times lower and the change could be 100 times faster than that experienced during the transitions from glacial to interglacial periods.[xxv] The effects of ocean acidification are predicted to put maritime ecosystems at major risk and there is an emerging scientific consensus that every effort possible must be made to prevent the pH of surface waters from dropping by more than 0.2 units below the pre-industrial value.[xxvi]

The full ecological consequences of ocean acidification are still uncertain, but it appears likely that many calcifying species, such as corals and shellfish, will be affected. This could have adverse effects on climate change, both by reducing the bio-capacity of the oceans and by decreasing the Earth's albedo via the effect of their bio-productivity on oceanic cloud cover. Global reductions of carbon emissions, with simultaneous efforts to enhance the earth's bio-sequestration capacity, are clearly urgently called for.

Meanwhile, there are other aspects of what is happening to the oceans that have received much less attention from climate researchers. The massive growth of cities along rivers and in coastal regions all over the world has also led to a tremendous increase in the discharge of sewage into coastal waters. This represents a tremendous transfer of both carbon and plant nutrients from rural areas into the sea. All over the world polluted coastal waters cloud sea bed vegetation, reducing its bio-productivity. At the same time, surplus nutrients produce algal blooms that remove oxygen from the water and further affect its productivity.

All over the world coastal waters are polluted and clouded by sewage effluents. Capturing the nutrients and the carbon they contain is necessary for a sustainable world. Cleaning these sewage plumes is also crucially important for enhancing the productivity (and carbon sequestration capacity) of coastal waters.

According to a new survey by the US National Academy of Sciences, seagrass meadows, an important habitat for marine life, have been in rapid decline due to coastal development and pollution. From 1940 to 1990, the annual loss of seagrass meadows accelerated from 1 to 7 per cent and there are only 177,000 square kilometres left globally. The survey indicates that seagrass meadows are as badly affected as coral reefs and tropical rainforests.

Seagrass meadows are presently under greatest pressure in the Pacific and the Indian Ocean due to rapid coastal development. In some places, such as in Florida, seagrass beds have rebounded due to improvements in the quality of water flowing into the sea and due to restoration efforts. Restoration was first undertaken on a large scale in 1973 in Florida's South Biscayne Bay by Prof. Anita Thorhaug of Yale University. Subsequently, seagrasses have been restored on other continental shelves.

Says Thorhaug:

> ***An evaluation of marine macro-plant sequestration potential by national and international carbon communities is urgently needed. The order of magnitude of carbon sequestered is potentially as great for marine macro plants restoration as for forests. Unlike with forests there is little man-made competition for space for restoration.***[xxvii]

The urbanisation of California, too, has led to a huge increase in nutrient pollution in coastal waters, resulting from sewage discharge and use of nitrogen-rich fertilisers from farms. This is thought to be to be the main reason for the dieback of seagrass there.

In the past there were large otter populations in the area, but they were hunted to near-extinction by the early twentieth century, and were subsequently suppressed because they were thought to impinge on fisheries in the area. But then a ban on hunting sea otters along the coast of southern California was lifted a few years ago. Almost immediately it was found that the seagrasses were recovering.

To their surprise, scientists found that the return of sea otters to an estuary on the central Californian coast appeared to improve the health of seagrass and that their reintroduction is helping to increase seagrass populations, even in the face of very nutrient-rich water. The researchers assessed the increases and declines of seagrass levels over the past 50 years in Monterey Bay. They looked at various changes in the aquatic environment, but the only factor that matched the changes in seagrass was sea otter numbers.

They theorised that sea otters were eating the crabs which prey upon small invertebrates in the water. These invertebrates eat a type of algae which blooms when there are more nutrients in the soil. It grows on the leaves of the seagrass, shading them from sunlight and causing them to die back. To compound their findings, the researchers compared similar estuaries with and without sea otters.

Brent Hughes, lead author of the study, says:

This estuary is part of one of the most polluted systems in the entire world, but you can still get this healthy thriving habitat, and it's all because of the sea otters. It is almost like these sea otters are fighting the effects of poor water quality.

Seagrass also acts as a nursery habitat for many species of fish and absorbs CO_2 from sea water and the atmosphere, thus potentially helping with climate change. Not only that, it acts as protection for the stability of the shoreline. It is a foundation species, like kelp forest, salt marsh or coral reef. A major problem is that seagrass is declining worldwide. And a major cause is nutrient inputs from anthropogenic sources, via agriculture or urban run-off.

Says Hughes:

There are a lot of degraded estuaries in southern California because of all the urban runoff from places like Los Angeles and San Diego. Coastal managers will now have a better sense of what's going to happen when sea otters move in to their systems. There's a huge potential benefit to sea otters returning to these estuaries, and in to these seagrass beds that might be threatened.[xxviii]

It seems evident that vigorous efforts to minimise sewage discharges into coastal waters and to enhance their bio-productivity need to be considered as an integral part of any strategy to enhance the bio-sequestration capacity of planet Earth. Together with initiatives to reduce the acidification of the oceans, these are matters that need to be addressed urgently.

New York: the Catskills watershed

A growing number of cities are taking significant ecosystem regeneration and protection initiatives beyond their urban boundaries. The measures initiated by New York City in the Catskills watershed are a prime example. The Catskills is the largest unfiltered water supply in the United States and is one of New York City's most important natural resources, providing about 1.3 billion gallons of drinking water to roughly nine million people every day. Because artificial filtration for that much water would have been prohibitively expensive, New York City decided to invest millions of dollars to protect and regenerate the watershed instead, and to maintain its high water quality.

Throughout the United States all watersheds are subject to regulations which govern activities that could degrade water supply such as impervious surfaces, sewer collection and storm water discharges. Before entering City pipes, drinking water usually has to be treated with chlorine, fluoride and other chemicals. In New York water quality and infrastructure are overseen by the city's department of environmental protection (DEP) in coordination with New York State's department of health.

In the densely developed Croton watershed, which contains extensive NYC suburbs, development pressures and the high cost of land have limited the DEP's ability to undertake protection mechanisms such as land acquisition. As a result the City had to spend millions of dollars to construct a filtration plant to ensure that the Croton supplies comply with surface water regulations.

In contrast, the Catskills/Delaware watershed, which supplies 90 per cent of New York City's water, makes do without any artificial filtration. The system is the largest naturally filtered water supply in the United States, covering 1,600 square miles. Maintaining quality standards for such a large water supply without artificial filtration is a tremendous challenge that requires millions of dollars each year. This money is not spent on technology, but on outreach and education, land management and acquisition, and joint initiatives between watershed NGOs and municipalities.

Given the statutory requirement to maintain the highest water quality, it might seem that a combination of filtration and disinfection would have been a simpler way to achieve the required standards. Yet, the DEP concluded that watershed protection was the better option.

To begin with are the costs involved: the construction cost for a filtration plant large enough to support the Catskills/Delaware system would have cost between six and ten billion dollars, with an additional $110 million annually in operation and maintenance.

In addition there are the health and safety issues that would have arisen: without pre-emptive land protection, significantly higher levels of disinfecting chemicals would have been required to purify the water. Their use is in fact limited by federal law because by-products from these chemicals are known to pose serious health risks. Finally, high levels of chlorination tend to damage the pipe fittings within the water delivery system which add further costs.

In contrast, the total annual cost of watershed programmes in the Catskills is no more than $100 million a year. For all these reasons, it was decided that it was preferable to protect the drinking water at its source.

The DEP uses a combination of regulation, voluntary programmes and partnerships to protect the Catskills/Delaware watershed. Regulation alone cannot guarantee that water quality criteria will be met: with more than 70 per cent of the Catskills/Delaware lands under private ownership, for residential, commercial and agricultural uses, activities can only be constrained to a limited extent.

The voluntary programmes being implemented in the Catskills allow the DEP to work with the local communities to meet water quality criteria while enabling economic and productive use of land by its owners. The watershed programmes fall into three main categories:

Land acquisition

Since 1997, the City has acquired about 70,000 acres of land at a cost of $168 million. Purchases are undertaken selectively, with properties prioritised for purchase based on the presence of natural features such as streams and wetlands, proximity to reservoirs, and potential for development. Land is only purchased from willing sellers, and at fair market prices. Prior to purchasing the land, the City consults with the municipality to ensure the community's interests are taken into account.

Land management

The DEP has devised numerous programmes to encourage private landholders to protect watershed lands. These are operated in concert with watershed municipalities and non-profit partners, including the Watershed Agricultural Council and the Catskills Watershed Corporation. Management programmes include six different, interconnected issues: stream management, wetlands protection, the watershed forestry programme, waterfowl management, agricultural pollution prevention plans and public outreach and education.

Capital programmes

On its own or with its partners, the DEP undertakes numerous capital projects in the Catskills/Delaware watershed designed to preserve and improve water quality. At its own cost, the City has upgraded over 100 small non-city sewage treatment plants. It has also fixed over 2,000 failing septic tank systems and helps cover their running costs. **A stormwater retrofit programme** encompasses infrastructure maintenance, planning and capital expenditures. And working with municipalities in the Catskills watershed, the DEP has also extended sanitary sewers where systems were failing.

All this shows that vigorous efforts are needed to maintain the City's water supply unfiltered. Proof must regularly be submitted that the water continues to meet a set of quality criteria. The EPA has to issue an annual Filtration Avoidance Determination which allows the water to remain unfiltered. New York City's drinking water has maintained its reputation as one of the finest supplies in the United States. The innovative combination of watershed programmes and partnerships has thus minimised the need for filtration and disinfection, proving that 'an ounce of prevention is worth a pound of cure'.[xxix]

Figure 8.9: *The Catskills in New York State are a remarkable example of effective environmental protection and natural ecosystem filtration for New York City's water supply.* ***Source:*** *Green County NY Real Estate*

Manila watersheds

The megacity of Manila, with some 15 million inhabitants, has also realised the crucial importance of protecting and replanting watershed forests. The Marinka Watershed Area, which mitigates flooding in Metro Manila, lost much of its tree cover by decades of logging, slash-and-burn farming, and by charcoal production.

To ensure Manila's water supplies, the Philippine Environment Department has made the Marinka watershed a protected area under the government's green agenda, which aims to expand the country's protected areas for both biodiversity conservation and environmental security. In addition to being an important watershed, numerous species of hardwood trees also provide habitats for a wide variety of endangered birds, mammals and reptiles.

The watershed was declared a protected area after a flood catastrophe caused by Tropical Storm Ondoy, which virtually drowned Manila in 2009. Investigations showed that almost 80 per cent of the watershed had been denuded and that it would take at least ten years to replant the area as a vital first line of defence against floods surging from the uplands down onto Metro Manila.

In the Marinka watershed, the government has put 26,000 hectares under protection, and has banned commercial activities to protect trees and local wildlife in perpetuity. It is reforesting several thousands of hectares of the watershed to enhance its water absorption and storage capacity.

Local governments in the area with jurisdiction over parts of the watershed have pledged to provide alternative livelihoods to settlers and indigenous people to wean them away from charcoal-making and slash-and-burn farming. They have also committed to develop a buffer zone against urban sprawl.

Another area, the Ipo watershed, has also been declared a protected zone. With constant degradation due to illegal logging, soil erosion and landslides had become a major issue. It was found that just 30 per cent of the 6,600 hectares of forest in the watershed had been left intact. Everything else has been destroyed.

The watershed is another critical source of water for Metro Manila and other municipalities. Some 15 million people are dependent on water from the Umiray-Angat-Ipo dams within the watershed, which generates 247 MW of electricity.

A consortium of NGOs and foundations based in Manila was set up to help restore the Ipo watershed. It aims to rehabilitate 4,500 hectares of a total of 6,600 hectares.[xxx]

The Loess Plateau watershed project

Reversing large-scale degradation of ecosystems due to overuse by human activities is a challenge in many parts of the world: nowhere more so than on the Loess Plateau in China's north-west, an area the size of France (640,000 km^2), and home to more than 50 million people. The plateau takes its name from the dry powdery yellow wind-blown loess soil. Centuries of overuse led to one of the highest erosion rates in the world and also to widespread poverty.

Fossil remains on the plateau provide evidence of human activity on the plateau dating back hundreds of thousands of years. This once rich and fertile area of mixed forest and grassland was a cradle of Chinese civilisation, but became increasingly denuded through human activity. Over millennia, trees were felled to create farmland, crops were planted on steep slopes and vegetation was extensively grazed by livestock. The plateau became known for its deep eroded gullies where, each year, one billion tonnes of sediment were washed down into the Yellow River.

For many generations, unsustainable agricultural practices caused the population of the region to be caught in a vicious cycle of ever-worsening degradation. The ecosystem collapsed and people suffered successive floods, droughts and famine. With no vegetation to stabilise the soil, 95 per cent of rainwater ran off, stripping and depositing the top soil in the river, giving the Yellow River its name. With no protection from the wind, soil particles were transported thousands of miles downriver. Moreover, the microclimate was altered and periods of intensive rain and drought were becoming more frequent.

Seeing no alternatives, the region's rural population continued to eke out a meagre living on increasingly marginal land. And without a major change in perspective, experts who visited the region as late as 1992 thought that little could be done to reverse the degradation.

Then, from the year 1995, two projects were set up to restore the Loess Plateau through one of the world's largest erosion control programmes with the goal of returning this poor part of China to an area of sustainable agricultural production.

Figure 8.10: *The regeneration of a degraded landscape. The picture on the left was taken in 1995, the one on the left in 2009. The stabilisation of the Loess Plateau continues today, benefitting local populations as well as inhabitants of cities on the Yellow River.* ***Source:*** *John D. Liu, Environmental Education Media Project, Beijing*

After intensive investigation, pilot projects were set up in several villages to demonstrate that more sustainable practices were possible and had the potential to be scaled up. In collaboration with the local people, a package was drawn up that could be applied to a small watershed. Small dams were built to harvest the rainwater, and large-scale tree planting was initiated to stabilise the soil. Farmers, whose primary interest was to increase productivity to increase their incomes, were paid for their labour. As an incentive, farmers were offered long-term leases to the newly terraced land.

The ecological balance in a vast area had been considered by many experts to be beyond help. But after a decade of hard work and determination by local people, the results are little short of miraculous. Trees, shrubs and grasses have become established, with as many as 50 different species evident on one terraced area. Increased insect and birdlife is evident and gradually villages are becoming hidden within a forest of greenery. The project encouraged natural regeneration of grasslands, tree and shrub cover on previously cultivated slope-lands. Replanting and bans on grazing allowed the perennial vegetation cover to increase from 17 to 34 per cent.

Jürgen Vögele, the World Bank's project manager, has been amazed that the results have been possible within the project period. Within ten years, local people have seen their incomes quadruple as food security and incomes have increased. Moreover, the hydrological balance has been restored, the soil rehabilitated and the flood risk for millions of people along the Yellow River has decreased.

The first phase of the project has lifted more than 2.5 million people in four of China's poorest provinces – Shanxi, Shaanxi and Gansu, as well as the Inner Mongolia Autonomous Region – out of poverty. Through the introduction of sustainable farming practices, farmers' incomes doubled, employment diversified and the degraded environment was revitalised. People in project households saw their incomes grow from about US$70 per year per person to about US$200 through agricultural productivity enhancement and diversification.

In addition, the flow of sediment from the Plateau into the Yellow River has been reduced by more than 100 million tonnes each year. Better sediment control has reduced the risks of flooding, with a network of small dams helping to store water for towns and for farms when rainfall is low.

Employment rates were also increased: more efficient crop production on terraces and the diversification of agriculture and livestock production has brought about new on-farm and off-farm employment. During the second project period, the employment rate increased from 70 per cent to 87 per cent. Opportunities for women to work have increased significantly.

Food supplies were secured: terracing not only increased average yields, but also significantly lowered their variability. Agricultural production changed from generating a narrow range of food and low-value grain commodities to high-value products. During the second project period, per capita grain output increased from 365 kg to 591 kg per year.

Terracing required the development of roads to facilitate access of bulldozers and other vehicles. The new roads have also enabled local farmers to have easier access to nearby markets.

The Second Loess Plateau Watershed Rehabilitation Project, now underway, is intended to further regenerate the Loess Plateau, increasing agricultural production and incomes, as well as improving the ecological conditions in the tributary watersheds of the Yellow River. Additional control dams will help retain sediments and store water for irrigation and domestic water supply. Irrigation will consist of small water cisterns which will catch run-off from roads or small water surface diversions, as well as small-scale irrigation schemes, mostly in Inner Mongolia.

Further cropland improvement includes the conversion of steep slopes to terraced lands, producing higher crop yields while reducing soil erosion and water retention. Vegetation cover will be further increased. Various species of trees, including fruit and nut trees, will be planted on narrow terraces, and marketing will be improved through investments in horticulture.

The transformation of the Loess Plateau in China need not be unique. Whilst many soils, for instance in parts of the Mediterranean, may have reached a 'point of no return', others have a chance of rehabilitation if human impacts on the ecosystem can be reduced.

According to data from the Dartmouth Flood Observatory, over 200 flood events occurred globally in 2007, killing over 8,000 people and displacing tens of millions of others. Whilst it may be impossible to prevent flooding, its impact could certainly be greatly reduced if forests and mangrove ecosystems were restored. But such transformations can only be achieved if communities are made aware of their impact on the environment, provided with alternative livelihood options and enabled to be part of its rehabilitation.

The lessons learnt in the Loess Plateau provide hope for other regions of the world – that given the right policies and investment, ecological regeneration is possible if not left too late.[xxxi]

Seoul and the Gobi Desert

Mongolia is suffering from severe desertification. In addition, it is warming twice as fast as the global average, making life ever more difficult for traditional livestock herders. Overgrazing, droughts, logging, mining operations and expanding populations and farms have turned once fertile grasslands into sandy desert plains. As a result, vast amounts of dust are blowing across Asia.

Over a quarter of China is now officially classified as desert – with up to 400 million people under threat from its fast expansion in the country's western and north-western regions. Intense dust storms have blown across Korea throughout recorded history, but their frequency and intensity have greatly increased in recent decades. Desertification in Mongolia is generating dangerous dust storms thousands of miles away, all the way to Seoul, capital of South Korea.

Seoul imports meat from the herdsmen of the Gobi Desert 800 miles away, but people are less keen to import yellow dust from the Gobi. Winds in March and April carry immense clouds of sand and soil particles eastwards, greatly affecting the people of Seoul. Not surprisingly, desert expansion in China has shot up the agenda in cities downwind. In South Korea government organisations as well as businesses and NGOs are working to create partnerships to combat desertification in Mongolia.

A Seoul-based initiative, Future Forest, is trying to improve matters: it has recruited Korean and Chinese students to help plant millions of trees in the Gobi desert to stabilise eroding land and to try and prevent its eastward spread. The originator of this regeneration initiative is former South Korean ambassador to China, Kwon Byong Hyon. He has helped spearhead an effort to plant trees in the Mongolian desert, hoping to improve both the lives of nomadic desert herders there as well as the air quality that people are exposed to back in Seoul.[xxxii]

Kwon's organisation *Future Forest* is one of several Korean initiatives now working in Mongolia, with the aim of developing environmental cooperation of benefit to both sides. He sees the project as an opportunity to realise the trans-national connectedness to deal with environmental problems.

Another important part of the project was to instigate a policy change for grazing – a highly sensitive issue. The project promoted livestock keeping in pens by feeding of sheep and goats with cut-and-carry fodder, as well as terracing of farmland and development of high-value orchards, vineyards and greenhouses.

Future Forest's biggest project began in 2006 and ultimately aims to plant one billion trees along the border of the Kubuchi Desert, to help to tame the 'yellow dragon'. By 2013 they had planted some four million trees. For his work, Kwon has been named the first 'Sustainable Land Management Champion' by the United Nations Convention to Combat Desertification. [xxxiii]

Notes

i Abengoa Solar, www.abengoasolar.com/web/en/nuestras_plantas/plantas_en_operacion/espana/PS10_la_primera_torre_comercial_del_mundo.html.

ii CNN, Market Place Africa, 10 October 2013.

iii www.abengoasolar.com/web/en/nuestras_plantas/plantas_en_construccion/estados_unidos/.

iv www.100-res-communities.eu/eng/communities/definition-of-and-criteria-for-100-res-communities.

v Renewable Energy World, *Local Development Through Community-Led Renewable Energy*, www.renewableenergyworld.com/rea/news/article/2013/04/local-development-through-community-led-renewable-energy.

vi Lichtenau Stadtinformationen, www.lichtenau.de/42-Stadtinformation-Stadtmarketing-Wirtschaft/427-Energiestadt/430-Energiestadt-Lichtenau/8627,%84Auf-dem-Weg-zur-Energiestadt-Lichtenau%93.html.

vii German Federal Environment Agency 2010: Energy Target 2050: 100% Renewable Electricity Supply, www.umweltdaten.de/publikationen/weitere_infos/3997-0.pdf.

viii Washington Post, 26 November 1999, *Cuba Goes Green*, www.cityfarmer.org/CubaGreen.html.

ix Monthly review, January 2009, *Urban Agriculture of Havana*, http://monthlyreview.org/2009/01/01/the-urban-agriculture-of-havana.

x Five Borough Farm, *Urban Agriculture in New York City*, www.fiveboroughfarm.org/urban-agriculture/.

xi New York Times, *Urban Farmers Crops*, www.nytimes.com/2008/05/07/dining/07urban.html?ex=1210824000&en=9d6a23b0418d45a4&ei=5070&em; CNN Money, *Can Farming Save Detroit?*, http://money.cnn.com/2009/12/29/news/economy/farming_detroit.fortune/.

xii WGBH, *An Urban Tree Farm Grows in Detroit*, www.wgbh.org/News/Articles/2012/12/21/An_Urban_Tree_Farm_Grows_In_Detroit.cfm.

xiii The Plant, Chicago, www.plantchicago.com/.

xiv Sit, V. (ed.) (1988) *Chinese Cities: The Growth of the Metropolis since 1949*, Oxford University Press, Oxford.

xv Choi, S. (1991) Urban Development in China, World Bank, www.worldbank.org/wbi/sdenveconomics/udm/docs/M1S1ChoiSongsuEN&CN.pdf.

xvi Yi-Zhong, C. and Zanghen, Z. (2000) Shanghai: Trends Towards Specialised and Capital-Intensive Urban Agriculture, in Bakker, N., Dubbeling, M., Guendel, S., Koschella, U. and de Zeeuw, H., eds, *Growing Cities, Growing Food*, RUAF.

xvii Liu, E. (1999) Shanghai City Council, personal communication.

xviii Wolf, J., van Wijk, M., Cheng, X. and Hu, Y. (2003) Urban and Peri-urban Agriculture in Beijing, *Environment and Urbanization*, 2.

xix Environmental News Network, Sprawling Solutions, www.enn.com/features/1999/10/102999/sprawl3_5917.asp.

xx Ginsburg, N. and McGee, T. (1991) *The Extended Metropolis: Settlement Transition in Asia*, University of Hawai'i Press.

xxi IPCC (2007) Climate Change, Mitigation Of Climate Change, UNEP.

xxii FAO, Global Forest Resource Assessment 2010, www.fao.org/forestry/fra/en/

xxiii Canadell, J. (13 June 2008) Managing Forests for Climate Change Mitigation, *Science Magazine*, 320.

xxiv FAO, Global Carbon Gap Map, www.fao.org/newsroom/en/news/2008/1000882/index.html.

xxv International Science Symposium (2004) Priorities for Research on the Oceans in a High-CO2 World.

xxvi A Special Report of the German Advisory Council on Global Change (2006) The Future Oceans - Warming up, Rising High, Turning Sour.

xxvii Personal communication, Anita Thorhaug.

xxviii Gage, S. (26 August 2013) BBC report.

xxix Mass, E. (2007) *Drinking Water and Watersheds, Lessons from New York City* www.pwconserve.org/issues/watersheds/newyorkcity.

xxx http://newsinfo.inquirer.net/121923/marikina-watershed-declared-protected-area; www.lcfcsrexpo.com/read-news.php?id=122820121

xxxi World Bank, www.worldbank.org/projects/P056216/second-loess-plateau-watershed-rehabilitation-project?lang=en; New Agriculturalist, www-ag.infow.new-ag.info/en/focus/focusItem.php?a=388.

xxxii Tree Hugger, *Planting Trees in the Mongolian Desert*, www.treehugger.com/natural-sciences/planting-trees-mongolian-desert-fight-dangerous-dust-storms-seoul.html.

xxxiii Tree Hugger, www.treehugger.com/natural-sciences/planting-trees-mongolian-desert-fight-dangerous-dust-storms-seoul.html; www.rtcc.org/2012/04/26/how-korean-organisations-are-combating-desertification-in-mongolia/#sthash.OpDO2gfp.dpuf.

Bibliography

Bibliography

Allen, Adriana and You, Nicholas (2002) *Sustainable Urbanisation, Bridging the Green and Brown Agendas,* DPU, London.

Atkins and UCL (2012) *Future-Proofing Cities*, Department for International Development, London.

Badshah, Akhter (1996) *Our Urban Future: New Paradigms for Equity and Sustainability*, Zed Books, London.

Bakker, N., Dubbeling, M., Guendel, S., Sabel Koschella, U. and de Zeeuw, H. (eds) (1999) *Growing Cities, Growing Food: Urban Agriculture on the Policy Agenda*, DSE, Feldafing.

Barnett, Anthony and Scruton, Roger (eds) (1998) *Town and Country*, Jonathan Cape, London.

Barton, Hugh (ed.) (2000) *Sustainable Communities: The Potential For Eco-Neighbourhoods*, Earthscan, London.

Batty, Michael (2013) *The New Science of Cities*, The MIT Press, Cambridge, MA and London.

Beatley, Timothy (2000) *Green Urbanism: Learning from European Cities*, Island Press, Washington, DC.

Biel, Robert (2013) *The Entropy of Capitalism*, Haymarket Books, Chicago.

Blowfield, Michael and Johnson, Leo (2013) *Turnaround Challenge: Business And The City of the Future*, Oxford University Press, Oxford.

Boardman, Philip (1978) *The Worlds of Patrick Geddes*, Routledge & Keagan Paul, London.

Brown, Lester (2003) *Plan B: Rescuing a Planet under Stress and a Civilization in Trouble*, W.W. Norton, New York and London

Steef, Bujs, Tan, Wedy and Devisari, Tunes (eds) (2010) *Megacities: Exploring a Sustainable Future*, 010 Publishers, Rotterdam.

Carter, Vernon Gill and Dale, Tom (1974) *Topsoil and Civilisation*, University of Oklahoma Press, Norman.

Castells, Manuel (1996) *The Network Society*, Blackwell, Oxford.

Clayton, Antony (2000) *Subterranean City: Beneath The Streets Of London*, Historical Publications, London.

Cockral-King, Jennifer (2012) *Food and the City*, Prometheus Books, Amherst, New York.

Commoner, Barry (1971) *The Closing Circle: Nature, Man, and Technology*, Knopf, New York.

Critchfield, Richard (1981) *Villages*, Anchor Press, Doubleday, New York.

Deelstra, Tjeerd and Girardet, Herbert (2000) Urban Agriculture and Sustainable Cities, in Bakker, N., Dubbeling, M., Guendel, S., Sabel Koschella, U. and de Zeeuw, H., (eds), *Growing Cities, Growing Food: Urban Agriculture on the Policy Agenda*, RUAF.

Desai, Pooran and Riddlestone, Sue (2002) *Bioregional Solutions, Schumacher Briefing 9*, Green Books, Dartington.

Downton, Paul (2009) *Ecopolis: Architecture and Cities for a Changing Climate*, Springer Verlag, Berlin.

Dubbeling, Marielle (2010) *Cities, Poverty and Food*, RUAF Foundation, Practical Action Publishing, Rugby.

Dunster, Bill, Simmonds, Craig and Gilbert, Bobby (2008) *The ZED Book*: *Solutions for a Shrinking World*, Taylor and Francis, Abingdon.

Gehl, Jan and Gemzoe, Lars (2000) *New City Spaces*, The Danish Architectural Press, Copenhagen.

Ginsburg, Norton and McGee, Terry (1991) *The Extended Metropolis: Settlement Transition in Asia*, University of Hawai'i Press.

Girardet, Herbert (1996) *Getting London in Shape for 2000*, London First, unpublished report.

Girardet, Herbert (1999) *Creating Sustainable Cities, Schumacher Briefing 2*, Green Books, Dartington.

Girardet, Herbert (2002 and 2006) *The Gaia Atlas Of Cities*, Gaia Books, London.

Girardet, Herbert (2004 and 2008) *Cities, People, Planet*, Wiley Academy, London.

Girardet, Herbert and Mendonca, Miguel (2009) *A Renewable World: Energy, Ecology, Equality*, Green Books, Dartington.

Glaeser, Edward (2010) *Triumph Of The City*, Penguin Press, London and New York.

Goodwin, Jason (2001) *Otis: Giving Rise to the Modern City,* Ivan R. Dee Publisher, Lanham.

Hahn, Eckhart (1993) *Ökologischer Stadtumbau – konzeptionelle Grundlegung*, Lang, Frankfurt

Hahn, Hermann and Langbein, Fritz (1928) *Fünfzig Jahre Berliner Stadtentwässerung 1878–1928*, Verlag Alfred Metzner, Berlin.

Hall, Peter (1988) *Cities of Tomorrow*, Blackwell, Oxford.

Hall, Peter and Ward, Colin (1998) *Sociable Cities: The Legacy of Ebenezer Howard*, John Wiley, Chichester.

Halweil, Brian (2002) *Home Grown: The Case For Local Food In A Global Market*, Worldwatch Paper 163, Worldwatch Institute, Washington, DC.

Haney, David H. (2010) *When Modern Was Green*, Routledge, Abingdon.

Hardoy, Jorge, Mitlin, Diana and Satterthwaite, David (1992) *Environmental Problems In Third World Cities,* Earthscan Publications, London.

Harvey, David (1989) *The Urban Experience*, Blackwell, Oxford.

Hopkins, Rob (2008) *The Transition Handbook: From Oil Dependency to Local Resilience*, Green Books, Dartington.

Hough, Michael (1984) *City Form and Natural Process*, Routledge, London.

Howard, Ebenezer (1902) *Garden Cities of To-morrow*, Faber & Faber, London.

Jacobs, Jane (1985) *Cities And The Wealth of Nations*, Vintage Books, New York.

Jevons, William Stanley (1965) *The Coal Question*, Augustus M. Kelley, New York.

Joplin, John and Girardet, Herbert (1997) *Creating a Sustainable London*, Sustainable London Trust, London.

King, F. H. (1911) *Farmers of Forty Centuries: Organic Farming in China, Korea and Japan*, Courier Dover Publications.

Knoflacher, Hermann (1993) *Zur Harmonie Von Stadt Und Verkehr, Freiheit vom Zwang zum Autofahren*, Boehlau, Wien.

Kropotkin, Peter (1974) *Field, Factories and Workshops [1899]*, George, Allen and Unwin, London.

Lawton, Richard (ed.) (1989) *The Rise And Fall Of Great Cities*, Belhaven Press, London.

Lehmann, Steffen (2010) *The Principles of Green Urbanism*, Earthscan, London.

Lehmann, Steffen and Crocher, Robert (eds) (2012) *Designing for Zero Waste*, Earthscan, London and New York.

Lutz, Ruediger (1987) *Ökopolis*, Knaur Verlag, München.

Lynch, Kevin (1984) *Good City Form*, MIT, Cambridge, MA.

McDonough, William and Braungart, Michael (2002) *Cradle to Cradle: Remaking The Way We Make Things*, Jonathan Cape, London.

Miller, Donald (ed.) (1995) *The Lewis Mumford Reader*, University of Georgia Press, Athens.

Mumford, Louis (1966) *The City in History*, Pelican Books, London.

Nicholson-Lord, David (1987) *The Greening of the Cities*, Routledge, Kegan Paul, London.

Oekom e.V. (2011) *Post-Oil City: Die Stadt von Morgen,* Oekom Verlag, München.

Packard, Vance (1960) *The Waste Makers*, Pelican, London.

Ponting, Clive (1991) *A Green History of the World*, Penguin, London.

Ravetz, Joe (2000) *City Region 2020: A Case Study on Greater Manchester*, Earthscan, London.

Register, Richard (2002) *Ecocities: Building Cities in Balance with Nature*, Beverly Hills Books, Berkeley.

Rifkin, Jeremy (1985) *Entropy – A New World View*, Paladin Books, London.

Rogers, Richard (1997) *Cities for a Small Planet*, Faber & Faber, London.

Rudlin, David and Falk, Nicholas (1999) *Building the 21st Century Home: The Sustainable Urban Neighbourhood*, Architectural Press, Oxford.

Sassen, Saskia (2000) *Cities in a World Economy,* Pine Forge Press, Thousand Oaks, CA.

Sassen, Saskia (2001) Cities in the Global Economy, in Paddison, Ronan (ed.), *Handbook of Urban Studies*, Sage Publications, Thousand Oaks, CA.

Satterthwaite, David (ed.) (1999) *The Earthscan Reader in Sustainable Cities*, Earthscan, London.

Schaffer, Frank (1970) *The New Town Story*, Granada Publishing, London.

Scheer, Hermann (2002) *The Solar Economy: Renewable Energy for a Sustainable Global Future*, Earthscan, London.

Sit, Victor (ed.) (1988) *Chinese Cities: The Growth of the Metropolis Since 1949*, Oxford University Press, Oxford.

Steel, Carolyn (2009) *Hungry City: How Food Shapes Our Lives*, Vintage Books, London.

Thünen, Johann Heinrich von (1960) *The Isolated State*, Loyola University Press, Chicago.

UNCHS (2003) *Water and Sanitation in the World's Cities, Local Action for Global Goals*, Earthscan Publications, London.

UNDP (1996) *Urban Agriculture: Food, Jobs and Sustainable Cities*, UN, New York.

UN Habitat (1996) *An Urbanising World: Global Report on Human Settlements*, Oxford University Press, Oxford.

UN Habitat (1997) *The Istanbul Declaration and The Habitat Agenda*, UNCHS, Nairobi.

UN Habitat (2003) *World Urbanization Prospects: The 2003 Revision*, UN, New York.

Vance, James (1990) *The Continuing City: Urban Morphology in Western Civilization*, Johns Hopkins Memorial Press, Baltimore.

Wackernagel, Mathis and Rees, William (1996) *Our Ecological Footprint,* New Society Publishers, Gabriola Island.

Weber, Max (1958) *The City*, The Free Press, Collier MacMillans Publishers, New York.

Weizsäcker, E., Hargroves, K., Smith, M., Desha, C. and Stasinopoulos, P. (2009) *Factor Five: Transforming The Global Economy Through 80% Improvements In Resource Productivity*, Earthscan, London.

Wohl, Anthony (1977) *The Eternal Slum: Housing and Social Policy in Victorian London*, Edward Arnold and McGill-Queens University Press, Montreal.

Worldwatch Institute (2002) *Vital Signs*, WW Norton, New York.

WWF (2012) *Living Planet Report*, wwf.panda.org/about_our_earth/all_publications/living_planet_report/2012_lpr/.

WWF (2012) *Urban Solutions For A Living Planet*, WWF Stockholm.

WWF (2012) *Reinventing The City*, WWF Stockholm.

Yeang, Ken (1996) *The Skyscraper Bioclimatically Considered*, Wiley-Academy, London.

Yi-Zhong, Cai and Zanghen, Zhang (2000) Shanghai: Trends Towards Specialised And Capital-Intensive Urban Agriculture, in Bakker, N., Dubbeling, M., Guendel, S., Sabel Koschella, U. and de Zeeuw, H., eds, *Growing Cities, Growing Food, Urban Agriculture on the Policy Agenda*, RUAF.

Index

Locators in *italic* refer to figures/diagrams

Abu Dhabi, Arabian Gulf 56, 57, *155*, 154–5
ACARP (Accra Compost and Recycling Plant), Ghana 151
Accra, Ghana, case study 150–1
acidification, oceans 180–2
Addis Ababa, Arabian Gulf 62, 107
Adelaide, Australia 86, 134–9, *136*, *137*, *139*
affluence 5; and urban sprawl 30
Africa *53*; hydroelectric dams 61–2; pollution 54, 55, 56; urban agriculture 116; urban growth 52–4, 62
agriculture. *see* agropolis; urban agriculture
agropolis *16*; allotments 19–20; garden city projects 20–3, *22*; traditional land use practices 15–8, *17*, *19*
air pollution: entropy 69; and urban growth *55*, 55–6
airplane invention, Wright brothers 40
allotments 19–20, 171
Amazon rainforests *10*, 35, *50*
Ancient Rome 82, 83
anthropocene 4
Arabian Gulf: food supplies 61–2; urban growth 56–61, *58*, *59*; water use 59–60, *61*
architecture, energy efficiency 71–3, 142
Asia: megacities 41; traditional land use practices 18; urban growth 62
Aswan Dam, Egypt 106–7
Atlanta, USA *30*, 31
Australia 86, 102, 134–9, *136*, *137*, *139*

Bangladesh 63, 78, 128–30, *129*
Barcelona, Spain *30*, 31, *32*, *90*
Bazalgette, Joseph 84
Beckton Sewage Works, London *83*
Beddington Zero Energy Development project, London 152–3
Beijing, China 115, *175*, 175–6
Berlin, Germany 35, 84–6, *85*
Bertalanffy, Ludwig von 90
Bickleigh Down Eco Village, UK 153, *153*
'Billion Trees Campaign' UNEP 118
biodiversity: cities 10, 91; loss 36
biogas 101, 129
biological carbon capture and storage. *see* bio-sequestration
biological resources 82–4, *83*, 84–6, *85*
bio-sequestration 118, 177–82, *179*
Bolivar treatment plant, Adelaide 135
Booz Allen, Hamilton 98–9
Braungart, Michael 88, *89*
Brazil 99–100
Broadacre City utopian vision *22*, 22–3
brown field sites, Ruhr Region 145, 146
buildings, energy efficiency 71–3, 142

cadmium, soil pollution 49
Californian coast, USA, seagrass meadows 181–2
capital, financial: Africa 51; Catskills watershed 184–5; conservation of natural 89–92, *90*; petropolis 41–2
car transport 39, *39*, 40; avoiding 141; energy efficiency *73*, 73. *see also* petropolis
carbon dioxide. *see* greenhouse gas emissions
carbon neutral city, Copenhagen, Denmark 140, 141, 142
carbon sequestration 117–9. *see also* bio-sequestration
case studies 134; Accra 150–1; Adelaide 134–9, *136*, *137*, *139*; bio-sequestration 177–82, *179*; Copenhagen 139–45, *140*, *141*; Crossrail *158*, 158–9, *159*; desertification 190–1; ecocities 153–6, *155*; eco-districts 151–3, *152*; ecovillages *153*, 153; Kalundborg 156–7, *157*; Oakland 149–50; renewable energy *164*, 164, 165–7, *167*; Ruhr Region 145–9, *146*; Seville *164*, 164; Singapore 159–61, *160*; urban agriculture 167–76, *169*, *172*, *173*, *175*, *176*; water supply 182–90, *185*, *187*
Castells, Manuel 120
Catskills watershed, New York, USA 182–5, *185*
Chicago, USA 172–3, *173*
China 42, 51; closed-loop systems 115, *116*; desertification 190; Dongtan Eco-City project 154–5; energy consumption *48*; energy use 74; Loess Plateau watershed project 186–90, *187*; Pudong *46*, 47; resource use 5; solar energy *101*, 101–2; urban agriculture *19*, 114–5, *115*, 174–6, *175*; urban growth *46*, 46–50; waste recycling 79
chlorination of water supply 184
cholera 54, 82, 84
Chongming Island, China 154–5
circular systems: bio-sequestration 178; ecocities 153; ecopolis 96; ecosystems as 8, 36; Kalundborg 156–7, *157*; urban agriculture 115, *116*; urban metabolism 80–1, *81*; waste management 149–50; water management 159–61, *160*

cities as attraction for humans 5; as living organisms 3; regenerative urban development 11–13; resource use 2, 4–8, *5*; systems theory 7–9; as technical systems 3; urban ecology 9–10. *see also* agropolis; ecopolis; petropolis; urban/urbanisation
Clean Energy Cashback 103. *see also* feed-in tariffs
Climate Alliance of European Cities 122
climate change 27, 36, 56; Adelaide 135; Arabian Gulf 58; and carbon sequestration 118–9; and energy use 71; and entropy 69; and extreme weather events 63–4; and fossil fuels 62; Ruhr Region 148
ClimateExpo-NRW, Ruhr 2022 148
closed-loop systems, China 115, *116*. *see also* circular systems
coal 27–9; open cast mining 61. *see also* fossil fuels
coastal cities 62–3
coastal wetlands, Essex, UK *158*, 158–6, *159*
combined heat-and-power 139–40, *140*
Commoner, Barry 8–9
community involvement (participatory budgeting) 109–10
community ownership, wind energy installations 104
commuters, London, UK 32–3
composting organic waste 86, 91, 113, 170, 178; Adelaide 134, 135, *137*, 137, 139; Oakland 149–50
concentrated solar power (CSP), Seville, Spain *164*, 164
conservation of natural capital 89–92, *90*
conservation tillage 178
Constanza, Robert 89
consumerism 8, 48
contamination, brown field sites 145. *see also* pollution
cooling/ventilation systems 5, *160*; Arabian Gulf 57; Copenhagen 142; Masdar City plan *155*, 155–6; Singapore 161
Copenhagen , Denmark 101, 104, 139–45, *140*, *141*
Cradle to Cradle methodology 88–9, *89*
'Creating a Sustainable Adelaide' report: (Girardet) 136
Crossrail, London, UK *158*, 158–9, *159*
CSP (concentrated solar power), Seville, Spain *164*, 164
Cuba, urban agriculture 168–70, *169*
cycle routes, Copenhagen *140*, *141*, 141–2

Daly, Herman 89
dams, hydropower 61–2, 106–8, *108*
decoupling concept 77, 88–9, *89*
deforestation 35–6. *see also* Amazon rainforests; reforestation
Denmark 102; feed-in tariffs 125; Kalundborg case study 156–7, *157*; wind energy 104
desalination of drinking water 60
Desertec project 106
desertification case studies 190–1
developed countries 11; urban agriculture 170–4, *172*, *173*, *175*, *176*. *see also specific countries by name*
developing countries, urban growth 5–6. *see also specific countries by name*
diamonds, ecological rucksack 37
Dinkelsb¸hl, Germany 17
district heating, Copenhagen, Denmark 142
Dodman, David 5
Dongtan Eco-City project, Chongming Island, China 154–5
downcycling 78–9
Downton, Paul 97
drought: Adelaide 135; Horn of Africa 56
Dubai, United Arab Emirates 56, 57, *59*
Dunster, Bill 153

ecocities 97, 153–6, *155*. *see also* ecopolis
eco-districts, case studies 151–3, *152*
eco-feedback technology 99, *102*
ecological densification 113
ecological footprints 2, 6, 10, *10*, 29, 31, *134*; Arabian Gulf 59; ecopolis 96; food supplies 110–12; London 32, *33*, 34–5, 110; petropolis *35*, 35–7, *37*
ecological retrofits 11, 97, 99, 101, 142, 148, 151, 167
ecological rucksacks 36–7, *37*
ecology: laws of 8–9; urban 9–10
economic growth 98; decoupling from resource use 77
ecopolis *96*, 96–7; carbon sequestration 117–9; case studies 166; circular systems 80; eco-feedback technology 99, *101*; financing mechanisms 119–20, *121*; food supplies 110–3, *111*; global city networks 121, 122–3; information revolution 120–2; infrastructure investments 98–9, 119; policy frameworks 123–5; privatisation 108–10; regenerative development 97–8; renewable energy systems 100–6, *101*, *102*, *103*, *104*, *105*; urban agriculture 113–6, *115*; urban regeneration initiatives 99–100; village living *125*, 125–30, *127*, *129*
ecosystems 7, 8, 12, 36; forests 177; ocean 36; regenerating 13, 186–90, *187*; services 91, 177

ecovillages 126–30, *127*; Bickleigh Down *153*, 153; Findhorn Foundation 127, *127*; Grameen Shakti organisation 128–30, *129*; Ralegan Siddhi 128
efficiency, energy. *see* energy efficiency
'Efficiency in Buildings Research Project' (World Business Council for Sustainable Development) 72
electric vehicles (EVs) 73, 143–4
electronic wastes 79, *80*
Ellen MacArthur Foundation 88–9
Emscher Landscape Park, Ruhr Region, Germany 145–7, 148
Enclosure Acts (1776, 1842 and 1875), UK 28
energy consumption/use *5*; China *48*; Europe *70*, 70; India 51; internet 75; petropolis 41–2; rebound effects 75–6; 2000 Watt Society 73–4; urban metabolism *70*, 71–6, *72*, *73*
energy efficiency 71; buildings 71–3, 142; Copenhagen 139, 142; rebound effect 75–6; transport systems *73*
energy slaves 70, *70*
energy storage systems 105–6
entropy: general systems theory 90–1; internet 75; resource use 77–8, 79; urban metabolism 69–70
Essex, UK, coastal wetlands *158*, 158–9
Europe: energy use 76, 80; petropolis 39–40, *40*; privatisation 109; sewage treatment 86; urban agriculture 114
EVs (electric vehicles) 73, 143–4
externalities of urban systems 11, 36, 37, 63

farming: organic 178; vertical *176*
Farmlandgrab website 61
feed-in tariffs (FITs) 102–3, *105*; Adelaide 138; Germany 152, 166; policy frameworks 125
fertilisers: artificial 6, 18, 49, *50*, 69, 84, 97; organic *83*, 87, 91
financial systems: ecopolis 119–20, *121*; globalisation 119–20. *see also* capital
Findhorn Foundation, Scotland *127*, 127
fires, forest *10*
fish: farming *157*, 157; nurseries 182
FITs. *see* feed-in tariffs
Food and Agriculture Organisation (FAO): Forest Resources Assessment 177; Global Carbon Gap Map 179
food miles 114
food supplies: Arabian Gulf 60–1; ecopolis 110–13, *111*
food waste 112
footprints. *see* ecological footprints; urban footprints
forests, bio-sequestration 177–9. *see also* deforestation; reforestation
fossil fuel use 4, 5, *5*, *26*, 26–8; Arabian Gulf 57, 59; coal 27–9; ecopolis 96; human impacts 62–4; oil 52–4, *53*. *see also* petropolis
Future Forest, South Korea 190–1
future visions/scenarios 86–8

garden city projects 20–3, *22*
general systems theory. *see* systems theory
Georgescu-Roegen, Nicholas 89–90
geothermal energy 101
Germany: energy storage systems 105–6; feed-in tariffs 102, 125; Industrial Revolution 39–40; privatisation 109; renewable energy regions 165–7, *167*; Ruhr Region 145–9, *146*; Solarsiedlung *152*, 152; wind energy 104
Ghana 150–1
Gibe III Dam 107
Girardet, Herbert 156, 136
Global Carbon Gap Map 179
global city networks 121, 122–3
Global Ecovillages Network 126–7
global network society, information revolution 120–1
globalisation 11, 45, 47–8, 53; financial systems 119–20
governance, Ruhr Region, Germany 148. *see also* policy frameworks
Grameen Shakti (GS) organisation, Bangladesh 128–30, *129*
Grand Coulee Dam on the Columbia River: United States 106
Grand Ethiopian Renaissance Dam 107
Great Inga Dam, Congo 107
great stink, River Thames, UK 82
green business/job opportunities 96, 139, 141
green urban economies 12
greenbelts 30
greenhouse gas emissions: Africa 56; Arabian Gulf 57, 59; Australia 139; internet 75. *see also* climate change
growth. *see* economic growth; urban growth

Hahn, Eckhart 97
Haiyan, Typhoon 63–4
Havana, Cuba 168–70, *169*
hazardous materials, China 48–9. *see also* pollution
health and well-being 19–20; Africa 54; air pollution *55*, 55–6; Arabian Gulf 59; Industrial Revolution 28; water pollution 54, 82, 84
heavy metal pollution 110

hinterland of cities. *see* ecological footprints
historical perspectives: ancient Rome 82, 83; evolution of human settlements 12; garden city projects 20–2; traditional land use practices 15–8, *17*, *19*. *see also* agropolis; Industrial Revolution
Hong Kong 41, 58, 120
Hoover Dam, Colorado River, USA 106
Howard, Ebenezer 20–1
Hughes, Brent 182
human impacts 4; fossil fuel use 62–4
hydroponic vegetable cultivation 171, 172, 174
hydropower 61–2, 106–8, *108*

IBA. *see* International Building Exhibition, Emscher Park
imports, London 39–40. *see also* ecological footprints
India 42, 50–2; Ralegan Siddhi 128; resource use 5; rural–urban migration *125*; waste recycling 79
industrial ecology *157*
Industrial Revolution 18, 19, 26, 27–9, 28, *28*; Germany 39–40; Ruhr Region 145; United States 39–9
information revolution 120–2
infrastructure, urban 3, 30, 77; Africa 54; China 47; ecopolis 119; Europe 31, 32; India 51; investment 98–9
insulation materials *72*
integrated energy systems, Copenhagen, Denmark 144
Integrated Water Resource Management Programme (IWRM), Singapore 159–61, *160*
Intergovernmental Panel on Climate Change (IPCC) 27, 71
internal combustion engine 40. *see also* car transport
International Building Exhibition, Emscher Park (IBA), Ruhr Region 145–7, 148
International Council for Local Environment Initiative (ICLEI) 139
International Resource Panel, UNEP 76
International Union for the Conservation of Nature 118
internet *122*, 123; energy use 75
irrigation: Arabian Gulf 60–1, *61*; wastewater 86

Japan, urban agriculture 176
Jasper Power project, South Africa 164
Jeddah, Saudi Arabia 56, 57, *58*
Jeffries composting facility, Adelaide, Australia *137*
Jenkins, Robin 18
Jevons Paradox 75–6

Kalundborg, Denmark 156–7, *157*
King, F. H. 18, 21
Kirklees Warm Zone, UK 76–7
Kropotkin, Peter 21
Kuwait 57, 59

Lagos, Nigeria 52–3, *53*, 63
Lake Chad, Africa 56
Lal, Dr. Rattan 117
land grab 61
land management, Catskills watershed, USA 184
landfill *78*; Denmark 144; USA 149–50
Latin America: privatisation 109; urban growth 52–4; waste 6
laws of ecology 8–9
Liebig, Justus 82–4, 85
limits to growth 36; Arabian Gulf 61; energy use 71, 73–4; planetary boundaries 123
Living Machine, Findhorn Foundation *127*
Living Planet Report (WWF) 35, 117
local food supplies 19–23. *see also* urban agriculture
local government level policy frameworks 124
Lochiel Park Solar Village, Adelaide, Australia *136*, 139
Loess Plateau watershed project, China 186–90, *187*
London, UK 32–5, *33*, 41; allotments 171; Beddington Zero Energy Development project 152–3; ecological footprints 32, *33*, 34–5, 110; international influence 120; sea level rises 63; sewage 82–4, *83*; wind energy 105
long-term perspectives 98
Lovelock, James 91
Lutz, R¸diger 97

MacArthur Foundation 88–6
Manila watershed, Phillipines 185–6
manure 178. *see also* composting organic waste
Mao, Chairman 46, 47
Marinka watershed, Phillipines 185–62
market economy, China 47. *see also* neoliberalism
Masdar City plan, Abu Dhabi, Arabian Gulf *155*, 155–6
material flow analysis 77
McDonough, Bill 88, *89*
megacities 41
metabolism of cities. *see* urban metabolism
middle class, urban 41, 47, 49
Middelgrunden wind farm, Copenhagen,

Denmark 143
Migge, Leberecht 21
Millennium Ecosystem Assessment, UNEP 177
mining. *see* open cast mining
mobilisation, cities as 40. *see also* petropolis
Mongolia, desertification 190
mulches, soil 178
Mumford, Lewis 26
Mursi tribe, Africa 61–2

national government level, policy frameworks 124
nature reserve, Wallasea Island, Essex, UK *158*, 158–9, *159*
Nazeing, Essex, UK 171
neoliberalism 11, 41–2
new towns, Britain 21
New York, USA 35, 38, 41, 58; Catskills watershed 182–5, *185*; Central Park 20; international influence 120; sea level rises 63; urban agriculture 170, 171–3, *172*
night soil 115, *116*, 174
Nile River, Aswan Dam 106–7
nimbyism (not in my backyard) 104
nitrogen fertiliser 87
non-government organisations (NGOs) 9, 92, 100, 118, 123, 183, 186, 190; Findhorn Foundation 127
non-renewable capital 89
non-renewable resources: ecological rucksacks 36; fossil fuel use 63; water use 61
Norway, hydropower 106
nuclear power 107–8

Oakland, USA 149–50
oceans: carbon sequestration 180–2; ecosystems 36; Pacific Trash Vortex 78; sea level rise 27, 63
oil 52–4, *53*. *see also* fossil fuels
Olmsted, Frederick Law 20
Omo River, Ethiopia 61–2
open cast mining: coal 62; lignite 40
organic: farming 178; fertilisers *87*, 87–8; vegetable box schemes, UK 171; waste recycling. *see* composting

Pacific Trash Vortex 78
Palestine, solar energy 101
palm oil plantations 35–6
paper, recycling 73
paradigm shifts 31, 62
participatory budgeting 103–4
pasture management 166
Peabody Trust 147
pearl industry, Arabian Gulf 51
pedestrian street systems, Copenhagen, Denmark 134, *134*
petropolis 25–7, *26*; car transport 39, *39*, 40; ecological footprints/rucksacks 32–37, *33*, *35*, 110; energy use/capital 41–2; Europe 39–40, *40*; fossil fuels *26*, 26–7, 27–8; Industrial Revolution 27–9, 28; London 32–5, *33*; as outmoded model 96; transport systems 40; United States 38–6; urban growth/sprawl 29–31, *30*, *32*
Philippines: Typhoon Haiyan 69–70; Manila watersheds 185–6
phosphorus fertilisers, organic *87*, 87–8
pig-iron smelter, Industrial Revolution *28*
pipelines *68*
Pittsburgh, USA 38, 42
planetary boundaries 123. *see also* limits to growth
planning. *see* urban planning
The Plant, Chicago 172–3, *173*
Plant a Pledge initiative 118
plastics waste 78–9, *79*
policy frameworks: ecopolis 123–5; forestation 177; regenerative development 98; renewable energy systems 102; Ruhr Region, Germany 148; urban regeneration 11
Polli Phone scheme, Grameen Shakti organisation 129
pollution: Africa 54; air *55*, 55–6; brown field sites 145; China 48–9; Denmark 142; fertilisers 6, 49, 84; heavy metals 116; open cast coal mining 62; sewage treatment 180, 181; waste 79
population growth, urban. *see* urban growth
Porto Alegre, Brazil 109–10
Portugal, traditional land use practices 18
poverty 6; Africa 53, 54; China 188; India 51
power stations: carbon sequestration 124; circular systems 156–7, *157*; fossil fuel 26, 49, 51, 55, 56, 62, 69, 70; solar energy 102, *103*, *164*, 164; Three Gorges Dam, China 107
privatisation 108–10
public participation: infrastructure investments 99; Porto Alegre, Brazil 109–10; urban regeneration 11
public transport 5; Barcelona *30*; Copenhagen *140*, 141–2; energy efficiency *73*; India 51
Pudong, China *46*, 47

Qatar 56–7, 59

rainforests *10*, 35, *50*

Ralegan Siddhi, India 128
Rann, Mike 135–6
rebound effects, energy efficiency 75–6
reconnection to countryside, ecopolis 90
recycling 78–9; Adelaide 135, 139; Copenhagen *140*, 144–5; Oakland 149–50; sewage 84–6, *85*, 86–8, *87*; waste hierarchy 149
reed beds, sewage treatment 85
reforestation 91; Adelaide 139; bio-sequestration 177–9; China 188; South Korea 188–9
regenerating ecosystems 7; China 186–90, *187*
'Regenerative Cities' (World Future Council) 26
regenerative energy resources 12
regenerative urban development 11–3, 97–8, *134*. *see also* ecopolis
regional government level, policy frameworks 124
Register, Richard 97
renewable capital 89
renewable energy regions, Germany 165–7, *167*
renewable energy systems *5*, 11, 100–6; Adelaide *136*, 138; Copenhagen 140, *140*; cost reductions *102*; ecovillages 129; large-scale projects 106–8, *108*; solar energy *101*, *103*; wind energy *104*, *105*
resource use 2, 4–7, *5*; conservation of natural capital 89–92, *90*; ecological footprints *134*; and economic growth rate 77; entropy 83–4, 85; urban metabolism 82–5, *84*, *85*, *86*
restoration ecology 11
retrofits, ecological 11, 97, 99, 100, 142, 148, 152, 167
Rieselfelder sewage systems, Germany 84–6, *85*
Rio de Janeiro, Brazil 6, *7*
Ruhr region, Germany 39–40, 145–50, *146,148*
rural living, resource use 5–6. *see also* villages
rural–urban migration *125*, 126; China 46, 47
Russia: large-scale dams 106; urban agriculture 115

Sassen, Saskia 121
Schmidt-Bleek, Friedrich 37
Schrebergärten 19
seagrass meadows 63, 119, 181–2, 182
sea level rise 27, 63
sea otters 181–2
second law of thermodynamics 69–70, 77–8, 90–1. *see also* entropy
self-sufficiency, traditional land use practices 18
Seoul, South Korea 190–1
services, ecosystem 91, 177
sewage: night soil 115, *116*, 174; pollution 6, *7*, 180, 181; recycling 96–8, *87*; Rieselfelder systems 84–6, *85*; urban metabolism 82–4, *83*. *see also* wastewater
Shanghai, China *56*, 47; international influence 120; sea level rises 63; urban agriculture 114, *115*, 174–5
Shanghai Industrial Investment Corporation (SIIC) 154
Singapore 41, 58; air pollution *55*; case study 159–61, *160*; international influence 120
slaves, energy 70, *70*
Small Holdings and Allotments Act (1908) 19–20
smart supergrids 106, 144
soil: erosion 187, 190; maintenance 112, 178; pollution 49
solar energy 90–1, *101*, 101–3; Adelaide 138; Masdar City plan *155*, 155–6; Solarsiedlung 152; Spain *164*, 164; Taiwan *103*
solar home systems (SHS), Grameen Shakti 129
Solarsiedlung, Germany 152, *152*
South Africa: Jasper Power project 164; urban agriculture 116
South Korea, Future Forest 190–1
Soviet Russia, large-scale dams 106
soybean production *10*, 35, *50*, 50, 111
Spain, concentrated solar power *164*, 164
steel industry: ecological rucksacks 37; Industrial Revolution *28*, 29; Ruhr Region 145; United States 38
storage, renewable energy 105–6
Summers, Larry 54, 55
superorganisms, cities as 3
sustainable development (SD) 4; Arabian Gulf 59; China 49; moving beyond 97–8
Switzerland: energy use 73–4; Schreberg%orten 19; urban sprawl 31
symbiosis, Kalundborg 156–7
synergistic infrastructure developments 99
systems theory 90–1; cities 7–9, 91–2; food supplies 112

Taiwan, solar energy *103*
tar sand mining 62
technical systems: cities as 3; sewage treatment 86–7; urban regeneration 11
Thailand, waste recycling 79
Thames, River, UK: sewage 82–84, *83*; wind

energy 105
Theoretische Biologie (Bertalanffy) 90
Theri Dam, India 107
'Thinker in Residence', Adelaide 135–6
Thorhaug, Anita 181–2
Three Gorges Dam, China 107, *108*
Tokyo 41, 120
traditional land use practices, agropolis 15–18, *17*, *19*
transport systems: Africa 53; Arabian Gulf 59; Denmark *141*, 141–2; energy efficiency 73, *73*; fossil fuels *26*
tree planting. *see* reforestation
2000 Watt Society 73–4
Typhoon Haiyan 63–4

United Kingdom: new towns 21; urban agriculture 171; villages 126; wind energy *104*, 104–5
United Nations Food and Agriculture Organisation (FAO): Forest Resources Assessment 177; Global Carbon Gap Map 179
United Nations Environment Programme (UNEP) International Resource Panel 78; Millennium Ecosystem Assessment 177
United States 20; energy use 74; fossil fuel extraction 62; garden city projects *22*, 22–3; petropolis 38–9; solar energy 164; urban agriculture 170–3, *172*, *173*
urban agriculture 167–76, *169*, *172*, *173*, *175*, *174*; Adelaide *139*, 139; ecopolis 113–16, *115*; Ruhr Region 148; traditional land use practices 17, *19*. *see also* agropolis
urban design 8, 135. *see also* cities
urban ecology 9–10
urban footprints 49; London 32, *33*; New York 38; and urban sprawl 31
urban growth *3*, 4–6, 9; Africa 52–4, *53*, 62; and air pollution *55*, 55–6; Arabian Gulf 54–5, *58*, *59*; Asia 62; China *46*, 46–50; India 50–2; Industrial Revolution 28; Latin America 52–4, *53*; petropolis 29–31, *30*, *32*
urban metabolism 8, *68*, 68–9; circular systems 80–1, *81*; conservation of natural capital 89–92, *90*; decoupling 88–9, *89*; energy use *70*, 71–76, *72*, *73*; entropy 69–70; new visions 86–8; resource use 76–7, *78*, *79*, *80*; sewage 82–84, *83*, 84–6, *85*; 2000 Watt Society 73–4
urban middle class 41, 47, 49
urban planning 8; Arabian Gulf 58; Germany 21; integrated 8; sustainable development 36, 153
urban regeneration 11; ecopolis 99–100. *see also* regenerative urban development
urban sprawl 329–31, *30*, *32*, 71, 96
urbanisation 2–4, *3*
utopian vision, Broadacre City *22*, 22–3

vegetable box schemes 171
ventilation systems. *see* cooling/ventilation
vertical farming *176*
villages, ecopolis *125*, 125–130, *127*, *129*
Virginia, Australia *137*, 138; pipeline project 135
visions, future 86–8
Vögele, Jürgen 188
von Thünen, Johann Heinrich 16

Wallasea Island nature reserve, UK *158*, 158–9, *159*
waste management: Africa 53, 54, 150–1; China 154; Denmark 140, 144–5, 156–7, *157*; food 112; Germany 147; hierarchy 149; landfill *78*; Latin America 6; plastics 78–9, *79*; urban metabolism 79, *80*, 81–86, *83*, *85*; USA 149–150. *see also* composting organic waste; recycling
waste water processing: Adelaide 135, 139; irrigation 86; Singapore 159–1, *160*; urban agriculture 116. *see also* sewage
water management 10, 188–96, *191*, *193*: Adelaide 141; Arabian Gulf 59–62, *61*; circular systems 159–62, *160*; new visions 87; New York 182–85, *185*
Watt, James 27
Welwyn Garden City, Hertfordshire, UK 21
wetland area nature reserve, UK *158*, 158–9, *159*
wind energy *105*; Adelaide 138; Copenhagen 143; ecopolis 101; feed-in tariffs 102; UK 104–5
World Business Council for Sustainable Development (WBCSD) 71–2
World Future Council 124
Wright, Frank Lloyd 22–3
Worldwide Fund for Nature (WWF) Living Planet Reports 35, 117

Xiaoshuichi Dam, China 107

Yangtze River: dams 107; Dongtan Eco-City project, Chongming Island 154–5
Yunus, Muhammad 130

zero carbon policies: Abu Dhabi 155; Bickleigh Down Eco Village 153
zero-waste strategies: Adelaide 139; Oakland 149–50
zoning policies 29